Christopher Wilkins saw active service in Aden, the Radfan and Oman. He attended the School of Military Intelligence and read for the Bar before joining the *Sunday Times*. He subsequently built up a successful business and was a member of the Scottish Economic Council for ten years. He lives in London and the Scottish Borders.

'This book, to which readers will repeatedly return, serves to remind us of the importance of looking south of the Pyrenees, as well as to the English possessions in France, if we wish to obtain a full understanding of important aspects of chivalric behaviour in the late Middle Ages.' – **Professor David Hook, Research Fellow in the Faculty of Medieval and Modern Languages, University of Oxford**

'This is an entertaining biography that provides a fresh view of Richard III's *coup d'état* and Henry Tudor's subsequent success. ... The author's original research into the foreign adventures of Sir Edward contributes to our understanding of the period, and his keen sense of military and political events and personalities brings vivid life and colour to the narrative.' – **Sir John Chilcot, GCB, Advisory Council of the Institute of Historical Research (and Chairman of the Iraq Inquiry)**

1. The knight. The upper woodcut is from Chaucer's *Canterbury Tales* (1484) and shows the knight in full parade order; the lower is from his *Game and playe of Chesse* (1498 edition) and shows the knight riding out to war.

THE LAST
KNIGHT ERRANT

SIR EDWARD WOODVILLE AND THE
AGE OF CHIVALRY

Christopher Wilkins

I.B. TAURIS
LONDON · NEW YORK

New paperback edition published in 2016 by
I.B.Tauris & Co. Ltd
London • New York
www.ibtauris.com

First published in hardback in 2010 by I.B.Tauris & Co. Ltd

ISBN: 978 1 78453 486 8
eISBN: 978 0 85772 959 0

A full CIP record for this book is available from the British Library
A full CIP record is available from the Library of Congress

Library of Congress Catalog Card Number: available

Typeset in Perpetua by A. & D. Worthington, Newmarket, Suffolk
Printed and bound by CPI Group (UK) Ltd, Croydon, CR0 4YY

MIX
Paper from
responsible sources
FSC
www.fsc.org   FSC® C013604

CONTENTS

ILLUSTRATIONS

NOTE ON ILLUSTRATIONS

Illustrations have been selected to provide a contemporary depiction of the activities of the period.

(1) The woodcuts are from E. Hodnett, *English Woodcuts 1480–1535* (Oxford University Press, 1935), and Caudall, *Wood Engraving* (London, 1895). The Spanish woodcuts are from J.P.R. Lyell, *Early Book Illustration in Spain* (1926). The Flemish carrack was reproduced from R. and R.C. Anderson, *The Sailing Ship* (1926).

(2) *Mittelalterliches Hausbuch. Bilderhandschrift des 15 Jahrhunderts*, ed A. Essenwein ('Medieval House Book. 15th-Century Illustrated Manuscript') (Frankfurt: Heinrich Keller, 1887). The book is a facsimile of an original fifteenth-century text with engravings (by 'JP') of 19 illustrations and 28 drawings. The first edition was published in Leipzig in 1866 and a second in Paris in 1885. The engravings show a range of lively and graphic illustrations of military and social scenes. The majority probably date from the 1470s or 1480s and are the work of one draughtsman; however, some are the work of a sixteenth-century hand and the technical drawings (not reproduced here) are probably by a third; some show cannon of a type illustrated by Dürer in a 1518 engraving. Only a part of one engraving has been previously reproduced in the UK: plate 24 of *The Battle of Towton* by A.W. Boardman.

The illustrations were presumably selected from the collection of Melchior Goldast (1570s–1635), 'an industrious but uncritical collector of documents relating to the medieval history of Germany'. He may have had some drawings improved.

I am grateful to Professor Jonathan Osmond and Professor Ralph Griffith for giving me their views on aspects of authenticity and to James Holloway (Director of the National Portrait Gallery of Scotland) for his opinion on the engravings.

(3) *Pageant of the Birth, Life and Death of Richard Beauchamp, Earl of Warwick, K.G. 1389–1439* (British Museum, facsimile, published 1914) (hereafter referred to as *The Beauchamp Pageant*). There are interesting illustrations in the *Pageant*. Beauchamp was the father-in-law of Warwick the Kingmaker. The *Pageant* consists of 53 fine line drawings depicting the chief events of Earl Richard's life. The artist is an unknown Englishman who was commissioned, it has been assumed, by the Countess Anne, Earl Richard's daughter and the Kingmaker's widow, who died in 1493. While the *Pageant* is supposed to depict the Earl's life and times, it was drawn between 1485 and 1490 and actually depicts the costume and armour of that period.

(4) H. Talhoffer, *Fechtbuch aus dem Jahre 1467* (Talhoffer's Martial Arts Manual [literally 'fight-book'] from the Year 1467) (ed Gustav Hergsell, Prague, 1887). A manual of close-quarter combat with some 260 drawings illustrating techniques of fighting with most weapons. The six drawings reproduced are for the poleaxe practice (see p 31). The three on the left show: (i) the combatants poised to thrust and strike; (ii) the man on the left deflects the thrust and is set to hook his opponent behind the knee; (iii) having parried a blow to the legs the man on the right hooks his opponent's neck to pull him to the ground. The three on the right show: (iv) combatants with their axes locked in a bind; (v) from the bind the man on the right traps his opponent behind the arm and pushes; (vi) the right-hand man breaks the bind and uses his butt to jab his opponent in the stomach.

(5) G.A. A'Beckett, *The Comic History of England*, illustrated by John Leech. Wood engraving, 295 (London: Bradbury, Agnew, 1879).

PRINCIPAL CHARACTERS

T he following is a select list of people, by family and group, who are important to the story, which runs from the 1460s to 1488. Of the 22 Englishmen listed, 15 suffered violent deaths and seven died peacefully.

THE WOODVILLES (OR WIDVILLE, WYDEVILLE, WYDEVIL, VEDEVILL ETC)

Edward Woodville, knight. He was born in 1458 or 1459, appointed Knight of the Garter in 1488 and killed later that year at the battle of St Aubin du Cormier.

Richard Woodville, Edward's father, was knighted in 1426. He was a captain under the Duke of Bedford in France and then married the Duke's young widow. He continued as a soldier and champion tournament fighter and was said to be the handsomest man in England. He was a minister of the king, made baron in 1448, Knight of the Garter in 1450 and 1st Earl Rivers or Ryvers in 1466. He was executed, without trial, by the Earl of Warwick in 1469.

Jacquetta, Edward's mother, beautiful and lively, daughter of Pierre de Luxembourg who was Count of St Pol and Brienne and keeper of the Somme towns. She first married John, Duke of Bedford and younger brother of King Henry V, who died 1435. In 1436 she was appointed a 'Lady of the Garter' and secretly married Sir Richard Woodville. Her eldest brother, Count Louis, certainly disapproved but her next brother, Jacques, brought the Burgundian delegation to her daughter's wedding to King Edward. (In the 1470s Count Louis endeavoured to divide his loyalties between France and Burgundy, failed and lost his head.) She died in 1472.

Elizabeth, the Woodville's eldest daughter and Edward's sister, was probably born in 1437. She inherited her parents' good looks and was first married to Sir John Grey, by whom she had two sons. Sir John was killed and she then married King Edward IV in 1464, by whom she had ten children, Edward Woodville's nieces and nephews. These included the two little princes, Edward and Richard, who were murdered in the Tower of London. She was crowned queen in 1465, appointed a 'Lady of the Garter' in 1477 and much enjoyed her position, but after her king died in 1483, she had a bleak time and died in 1492.

Elizabeth (of York), Elizabeth Woodville's eldest daughter and Edward's niece, was born in 1465. She was betrothed to Charles the Dauphin of France from 1475 to 1483. In 1486 she became Henry (Tudor) VII's queen. She was mother of several children, amongst whom were Henry, later Henry VIII, and Margaret, later Queen of Scotland. The latter is an ancestress of the present British royal family, having married King James IV of Scotland, and so was grandmother to Mary, Queen of Scots, whose son became King James VI of Scotland and I of England. Elizabeth of York was noted as kind and beautiful and died in 1503.

Anthony, Earl Rivers and Baron Scales, Edward's eldest brother, was born around 1442. He became Lord Scales through his first wife, whom he married in 1460, and then the second Earl Rivers when his father was killed in 1469. He was Champion of England (in tournament fighting), elegant, intellectual and one of the most powerful noblemen in the land. Governor of the Prince of Wales, soldier and diplomat, he was also Caxton's patron: the first book printed in England was *The Dictes and Sayings of the Philosophers*, translated and commissioned by Anthony. He was executed without trial in 1483 on the orders of Duke Richard of Gloucester.

There were three other elder brothers: John, who was killed 1469, Lionel, who was a bishop, and Richard, the last Earl Rivers, who died in bed. There were at least six other sisters, Jacquetta, Margaret, Anne, Mary, Catherine and Eleanor, all of whom married well. Catherine was closest in age to Edward and appears several times in the story; her first marriage was to the Duke of Buckingham.

Thomas and Richard Grey, the children of Elizabeth and her first husband, Sir John Grey, a Lancastrian who was killed at the second battle of St Albans in

1461. These were Edward's nephews, though they were similar in age to him. Thomas married the greatest heiress of the time, became Marquis of Dorset but was reckoned a weak man. They were both drinking companions of the King. Richard was executed without trial in 1483.

THE HOUSE OF YORK

Edward of March and then of York became King Edward IV in 1461. He was born in 1442 and married Elizabeth Woodville, Edward's sister, in 1464. He was the eldest son of Duke Richard of York and won the throne in battle at the age of 19, was 6ft 4ins tall, a formidable fighter and an excellent general. He was an efficient king who laid the financial and administrative foundations on which the Tudors built. He was also charming, lazy, 'licentious in the extreme' and loved women. He overindulged, became fat and died in 1483.

George, Duke of Clarence, born 1449, King Edward's middle brother, was seriously unreliable but possessed great charm. He was executed for treachery in 1478 (probably) by being drowned in a butt of malmsey – the method of execution was apparently his choice.

Richard, Duke of Gloucester, born 1452, King Edward's youngest brother, was an able soldier and administrator who was loyal to his brother during his life. After King Edward's death he became 'Protector' to his nephews, then took the crown as King Richard III and was killed at Bosworth in 1485.

Both George and Richard married daughters of the Earl of Warwick.

THE HOUSE OF LANCASTER

King Henry VI, born in 1421 and inherited the throne in 1422. Head of the House of Lancaster, he was the well meaning but slightly simple son of King Henry V and Katherine (of France, born 1401). He married Margaret (of Anjou), who was tough and determined to keep the throne. His son Edward, Prince of Wales, was killed at Tewkesbury and he was murdered in the Tower in 1471.

Margaret Beaufort, born in 1441, was an heiress descended from Duke John of Lancaster (John of Gaunt), Edward III's third son, through his eldest bastard son, John Beaufort. She married Edmund Tudor, Earl of Richmond, in

1455 and when he died she married Henry Stafford, second son of the Duke of Buckingham, then afterwards Lord Stanley. She was the mother of:

Henry Tudor, Earl of Richmond, the grandson of Owen Tudor from his clandestine marriage to Katherine, Henry V's widow and daughter of the unstable King Charles VI of France; Henry's father was Edmund Tudor (1430?–56). He was first cousin once removed of both King Louis of France and Duke Francis of Brittany, but his claim to the English throne was through his mother. He was born in 1457, took the throne in 1485 and died in 1509.

English Noblemen

Richard Neville, Earl of Warwick, usually referred to as the 'Kingmaker', was a charismatic man who was an immensely rich and powerful magnate. Born in 1428, he was killed at the battle of Barnet in 1471.

William, Lord Hastings, ultra-loyal follower of King Edward who rewarded him very generously. He was probably born in 1430 and was executed in 1483.

Lord Thomas de Scales, hard man of the French wars and father of Elizabeth de Scales, first wife of Anthony Woodville. He was probably born in 1399 and was killed in 1460.

Henry (Harry), Duke of Buckingham, descended from Thomas of Woodstock, Edward III's youngest son. He was married to Catherine Woodville. He was probably born in 1454 and was executed in 1483.

John Tiptoft, Earl of Worcester, brilliant and a ruthless servant of the king. He was a friend of Anthony Woodville and Caxton, who reported that he 'flowered in virtue and cunning'. He was probably born in 1427 and was executed in 1470.

Jasper Tudor, Earl of Pembroke, born 1431(?), was totally loyal to his half-brother King Henry VI, then guardian to his nephew, Henry Tudor. He married Catherine Woodville, Buckingham's widow, and died in bed in 1495.

John de Vere, Earl of Oxford, a die-hard Lancastrian and able soldier. Born in 1443, he spent 20 years in exile or prison but died in his bed in 1515.

Thomas, Lord Stanley, politically astute magnate with power base in the north-west, probably born in 1435 and died in 1504. In 1483 he married Margaret Beaufort.

EUROPEAN RULERS

King Louis XI of France was born in 1423, succeeded in 1461 and initially had a difficult time but later established his absolute authority by clever political manoeuvring and manipulation. He died in August 1483.

Duke Francis of Brittany, a generous man with intermittent mental problems. He was a first cousin of Henry VI of England, Henry Tudor and Louis XI of France. He succeeded to the dukedom in 1458 and died in 1488.

Duke Charles of Burgundy, called 'Le Téméraire', i.e. 'The Bold' or 'The Rash' (he was given this nickname in the nineteenth century; some of his contemporaries called him 'Le Travaillant'). He was the richest prince of his time, born in 1433, and Count of Charleroi until he succeeded his father in 1467. He was killed at Nancy in January 1477.

Duchess Mary, his daughter, who married Maximilian of Austria. She died from a fall from her horse in 1482.

Archduke Maximilian, born in 1459, son of the Habsburg emperor, Frederick III of Austria. He was one of the most successful princes of the period who made his fortune by his marriage. In 1486 he was elected King of the Romans, succeeded as Emperor in 1493 and died in 1519.

Anne de Beaujeu, born around 1462, became Regent of France on the death of her father, Louis XI, in 1483, whose grasp of politics she inherited. She died in 1522.

King Charles VIII, the young King of France, brother of Anne and second cousin of Henry Tudor. He was born in 1468, succeeded in 1483 and died in 1498.

King Ferdinand (1452–1516) and **Queen Isabella the Catholic** (1451–1504), monarchs of, respectively, Aragon and Castile.

King João (John) II of Portugal, reigned 1481–95.

SOME OTHER IMPORTANT PEOPLE

Antoine, 'the Bastard of Burgundy' (1421–1504), half-brother to Duke Charles of Burgundy, a key member of the Burgundian establishment, soldier and a knight of 'great renown'.

William Caxton (1422–91), merchant, diplomat, translator and publisher. He introduced the printing press to England in 1477; Anthony Woodville was his first patron.

Andrew Dymmock, lawyer and confidential man of business to Anthony Woodville.

Robert Poyntz, friend and supporter of Anthony Woodville, his lieutenant at Carisbrooke Castle and married to his (natural) daughter, Margaret. He lived at Iron Acton, close to the Severn.

Louis de Bretelles, Gascon knight, soldier and occasional diplomat in English service, a friend and supporter of Anthony Woodville.

Dominic Mancini, an Italian cleric who spent from the end of 1482 to July 1483 in London in the suite of the French ambassador. He reported to the Archbishop of Vienne on English affairs.

Isabel and Anne Neville, daughters of the Earl of Warwick. Isabel married the Duke of Clarence and died in 1476. Anne was first married to Edward, the Lancastrian Prince of Wales, and after his death in 1471 to Richard, Duke of York, later Richard III. She had one son by Richard, Edward of Middleham, who died in April 1484. She died in March 1485.

ACKNOWLEDGEMENTS

A number of distinguished historians have written on the period and I have been fortunate in being able to use their work. They are, principally, S.B. Chrimes, R.A. Griffiths, M.A. Hicks, R. Horrox, J.R. Lander, A.J. Pollard, C.D. Ross and J.S.C. Bridges. Some earlier books and manuscripts have been of particular interest: *The Crowland Chronicle*, *The History of Richard III* by Thomas More, Mancini's account of the usurpation of Richard III, Bacon's *History of the Reign of Henry VII*, the Harleian Manuscript, together with parts of Hall, Commines, Vergil, Molinet, Bernáldez and Hakluyt's voyages. In addition I have used *L'expédition d'Edouard Wydeville en Bretagne* by de Beauchesne and Prescott's *The History of the Reign of Ferdinand and Isabella*. The other books I have used are listed in the bibliography.

I am grateful for the help of a number of people and organizations, in particular Professor David Hook for Spanish translation and generous help with Hispanic matters; Andrew Shaw for Latin translation; Michael Reynolds for advice and for French translation; Professor Ralph Griffiths for his kindness in reading my manuscript; and Malcolm Rifkind, Adrian Sykes and George Wadia for their advice. I would also like to thank my editor, David Worthington, for his painstaking work, Peter Wilkins for his help with the illustrations, the National Archives at Kew, the Bodleian Library, the Morbihan Archives Départementales and particularly the London Library, but most of all the help and support of an adored wife.

INTRODUCTION

The late fifteenth century was a time of brilliance, excitement, chaos, mystery and, of course, brutality. In this arena was a family who rose from obscurity to great power and then vanished, all within 30 years. They were the Woodvilles or Wydvilles. The family made an important contribution to history but are now partly forgotten and much besmirched.

This book is mainly about the youngest, who signed himself 'Sir Edward Wydevile kynghte'. I discovered him almost by accident. Early one spring my wife and I were in Spain admiring the Moorish palaces, fortifications and garden structures in Granada and Cordoba; the almond blossom was just out and there was a sense of sophistication about the places, which was in stark contrast to the grim architecture of the succeeding Catholic monarchs. Fascinated we moved on to look at some of the smaller Moorish citadels.

We inspected Loja, Illora and finished up at Moclin, where the ruined castle is perched high on a rocky pinnacle. It controls the only pass through precipitous mountains and dominates the approach from the north, then the frontier with Christian Spain. From the ramparts you can see miles down the approaching road, which winds up the valley towards you and then passes 500 dizzy feet below the castle's western towers. On the southern side are the remnants of the medieval town and below its ramparts is the present village. Beyond is Granada itself, just visible, although much of it is hidden by one last foothill. In the distance beyond is the gleaming white Sierra Nevada.

This stronghold might seem impregnable but the Moors lost it in 1486, and so it was from these ramparts that Ferdinand and Isabella first saw Granada. We leaned on the parapet and imagined the Spanish monarchs with their courtiers and captains looking hungrily at the final prize, the great citadel in the distance. I wondered idly if an Englishman had been there with them.

We went on to visit Santa Fe, a village six miles south-west of Granada, in the *vega* or plain below the citadel. Originally built as the Christian siege camp and laid out in the disciplined format of all military camps, it was here, after the fall of Granada, that Christopher Columbus finally received royal approval for his voyage of discovery on 17 April 1492. I wondered if the Englishman had been there, watching the Spanish war machine, talking to Columbus and reporting back to King Henry VII?

A year later in a second-hand bookshop and quite by chance, I picked up a book called *The Art of War in Spain*.[1] It fell open at a page that told me that a young Englishman, whom the chroniclers called the 'Conde de Escalas', had fought for Spain in the 'War of the Reconquista'. The young nobleman, 'related to the blood royal of England', had arrived with '300 splendid house-hold troops all armed in the English way with longbow and battle-axe'. He was at the siege of Moclin and had particularly distinguished himself at the fall of Loja, a critical event in the campaign. Why was he there? What was he doing? What was happening? This book is the result of my investigation into the late fifteenth century, an investigation that has opened a box of delights.

Viewed from the fat of this century, it is hard to have a feeling for those times. While many of our ideals and instincts are similar to those of our fifteenth-century ancestors, there are some clear differences. They believed in an all-powerful God and lived in a near feudal society where the nobil-ity and knightage subscribed to rules of the Code of Chivalry. The 'Ordene de Chevalerie' declared there were four principal commandments to which a newly made knight must be bound for his life. He must not consent to any false judgement. He must not be party to treason, which included killing his lord or sleeping with his lord's wife. He must honour all women and be ready to aid them to the limit of his power. He must hear a mass every day and fast, whenever possible, every Friday.

Tales of romance, high ideals and derring-do, such as Malory's *Le Morte d'Arthur*, were the taste of the day and they transmuted into chivalric orders such as 'The Garter' or 'Le Toison d'Or' (the Golden Fleece of Burgundy). Knights errant embodying both the spirit of adventure and the religious quest became an important part of the poetic consciousness of society, while real life was supported by that unblinking faith which provided our ancestors with certainty and remarkable courage.[2] However, new ideas were circulating and times were about to change.

The Conde de Escalas of Spain turned out to be Sir Edward Woodville of England, sometimes known as Lord Scales and a knight whose family, it seems, was one of the most unpopular in English history. King Richard III called them 'insolent, vicious and of inordinate avarice'. Warwick the King-maker damned them as social climbers; others have described them as greedy, selfish and without public spirit.

Nevertheless they played an important part in fifteenth-century England

and there is little evidence to show they were in fact any worse than their contemporaries; indeed some of them were rather better. Edward's sister, Elizabeth, was King Edward IV's beautiful queen and his brother was the erudite Anthony, Earl Rivers, who was, amongst other things, Caxton's first patron and a champion of tournaments. Edward himself was deeply involved in the great events of his day and became one of Henry VII's paladins before fighting his final battle.

The family has had a terrible press, but then none of them survived for long enough to worry. Skilful propaganda is no modern innovation and King Richard specialized in character assassination. He needed to damn the opposition, principally the Woodvilles, and he did that very effectively.

King Henry could have corrected matters but did not. In consequence Edward Woodville is ignored by Tudor historians. Polydore Vergil, Henry's appointed historian, makes only a passing reference to him in exile in Brittany, then nothing for five years, nothing about him at the battles of Bosworth or Stoke. Other sources have Edward doing important things during these five years but Vergil, the principal narrative authority for the period, is silent.[3]

However, Vergil does report a heated argument over aid for Brittany and Edward's outright disobedience. Twenty-two years after his death when Polydore was commissioned to write, Edward was simply not of interest. King Henry had either forgotten Edward's contribution or not forgiven his transgression. Was it just a lack of interest in Edward's contribution to his achievement of the throne, or did Edward's transgression still rankle, or were uncomfortable facts from the past just ignored? 'Twas ever thus!

The Woodvilles galloped through the closing years of the Middle Ages and into the dawn of the Renaissance and Modern History. Nowadays we can only glimpse this, making the story something of a scurry through the fog of the late fifteenth century, looking here and there for a friend.

Perhaps Edward was the last knight errant, for, in a sense, the Middle Ages died with him. But he was also one of those who ushered in the next period with its new ideas and dynamics. This was when England, France and Spain coalesced as nation states, politics was changing, the art of war was being re-written, voyages of exploration undertaken, the influence of Renaissance art was spreading out from Italy, books were printed and people were starting to think in new ways. Edward witnessed the demise of the Age of Chivalry and the dawn of modern Europe.

A work such as this book, which endeavours to capture the excitement and colour of the period, depends, in no small measure, on creating a feel for the period. Contemporary quotations help, and I have included them liberally.

However, there are vast areas of near obscurity, if not total darkness; these have teased me, taxed my narrative skills and led to occasional moments of delight in discovery. The illustrations, which are nearly all contemporary, seem to me to give a sense of the energy of the time and help the history.

There are several ways of spelling Edward's surname and while 'Woodville' is probably the least correct, it is the spelling that most of us recognize and so I have used it.

CHAPTER ONE[1]

A SPANISH VENTURE

In the spring of 1486 Edward Woodville arrived in Cordoba with 'a beautiful train of household troops, three hundred in number, armed after the fashion of their land with longbow and battle-axe.'[2] Sir Edward had come to fight in the War of the Reconquista.

The war had been a testing ground for young warriors ever since 'Pelayo', traditionally a Visigoth nobleman, won the legendary battle of Covadonga sometime between AD 718 and 722. That victory was the first check to Muslim expansion in Spain and so marks the start of the Reconquista.

Over the next 300 years or so, Moorish Spain flourished and grew into the glory of the Cordoban Caliphate, but then it dissolved into a series of petty states that were no more than 'cats puffed up to look like lions'. By the second half of the eleventh century the Christians were already picking off these 'Taifa' kingdoms, Toledo being captured in 1085.

There was a crucial Christian victory in 1212 at Las Navas de Tolsa, which was so complete that the emir retreated to Fez in North Africa.[3] This was followed by a series of Christian successes.[4] The fighting swayed back and forth but the Moors eventually became confined to the Kingdom of Granada, where the Nasrids ruled with moderate success until the fifteenth century.

Granada had a population of around 200,000 but was torn by tribal differences, economically weak and its treasury depleted by paying tribute to the kings of Castile. However, it survived because its enemies were divided and weak. But when Ferdinand of Aragon married Isabella of Castile in 1469 and they subsequently succeeded to their separate thrones, the threat to Moorish Granada gained teeth. The demise of the kingdom seemed probable, provided – of course – there was no major Muslim victory or any nasty upheaval in Christian Spain.

The War of the Reconquista began as a struggle for survival coupled with the natural inclination of mountain men to plunder the plains; it was later presented as a crusade. Now that its end seemed to be in sight, the campaign captured the imagination of Christian Europe and also offered prospects of pay

and loot for the less devout. Swiss mercenaries were recruited while volunteers from France, England and other parts of Europe flocked to Spain. It was
at this stage that Edward and his company arrived.

They had sailed with some merchants. The ships had called at Lisbon and
then sailed down the coast to Seville where Edward's arrival was reported
to King Ferdinand in a letter dated 1 March 1486. Edward and his troop
disembarked at Seville[5] which was at the mouth of the Guadalquivir. It had
been captured from the Moors in 1248, was one of Spain's important cities
and would be a good place to gather news of when and where the Christian
army was assembling. The answer was Cordoba, 85 miles upriver, where King
Ferdinand and Queen Isabella were due on 28 April.

By March the rains have stopped in the Guadalquivir valley where Cordoba
sits, the sun is bright, the orange trees heavy with fruit and, in the fifteenth
century, the hills were covered with ilex interspersed with almond and apple
blossom. Riding along those white tracks came Edward, all the way from
England, with his banner of the silver scallop and his 'beautiful train'.

Edward brought at least six chargers and also pack animals to carry trunks
of clothes, combat armour and other essentials. Marching behind, past the
rich valley farms with their fields of sugar cane, olive groves and grazing stock,
came the 300 men of the company, who probably marched to music from
the fife and drum. There would have been three captains and a few squires,
among whom were 'Edward Wyngfielde', 'Canteloupe' and Rupert (the
Queen's household accounts refer to 'Ruberte, Englishman, who came with
the Count of Escalas'), a couple of trumpeters, ten peti-captains,[6] 100 archers,
'all dexterous with the long bow and cloth yard arrow',[7] and 200 yeomen 'of
robust frame and prodigious strength, armed cap-a-pie'.

An infantry company with a pack-train and supply cart would cover around
20 miles a day. The soldiers marched wearing or carrying their steel helmets
and dressed in 'jacks', which were stuffed leather jerkins that 'withstood the
blows of arrows and swords', according to Mancini:

> Their bows and arrows are thicker and longer than those used by other
> nations, just as their bodies are stronger than other peoples for they seem to
> have hands and arms of iron. The range of their bows is no less than that of
> our arbalests [crossbows]; there hangs by the side of each a sword no less long
> than ours but heavy and thick as well.[8]

When they arrived in Cordoba they found it full of the bustle of campaign
preparation. It had been the capital of Moorish Spain at its most brilliant and
even today its architecture reflects the civilized tastes of the period. In the

2. Infantry companies on the march with officers, supply and
artillery wagons, trumpeter, fifer and drummer.

centre of the city is the great sprawling mosque where the cool gloom is filled
with serried ranks of marble columns supporting red and white chequered
double horseshoe arches. Roman outer walls still encircle an inner ring of
towering Moorish walls pierced by occasional horseshoe-headed gates decorated with Islamic patterns. At the west end is the Alcazar, the fortress palace
with high crenulated walls, where King Ferdinand and Queen Isabella held
court and where Edward was received.

He must have walked in the gardens – which still survive – amongst the
orange trees that line the pools, canal and terraces. The 28-year-old was a
popular recruit, 'Young, wealthy, high born and related to the blood royal
of England. He was much honoured by the King and Queen and found great
favour with the fair dames about the court,' wrote Washington Irving.

From here Edward wrote to King João (John) of Portugal apologizing for
having had no time to call on him on his way through Lisbon. The King replied
generously to the 'Magnificent and puissant Count, Kinsman and Friend',
accepting his excuses but expecting to see him on his return journey.[9] So it
seems that Edward had previously made friends with King João, presumably
when he had been there with his brother in 1472.

The current phase of the war had been running for around six years and
had been triggered by the Moorish King Abul Hacan, who refused to pay his
annual tribute to Spain. He proudly told the Spanish monarchs, 'The mints
of Granada coin no longer gold, but blades for scimitars and the heads of
lances.' Then to demonstrate his defiance he attacked and captured Zahara, a
supposedly impregnable frontier town, and took its citizens into slavery. The
outraged Spaniards demanded retaliation. A captain of *escaladores* (scalers of
fortifications) saw the opportunity for glory and plunder and approached Don
Rodrigo Ponce de León, Marquis of Cadiz, with the idea of a freelance operation against Alhama.

This citadel was deep in Moorish territory, an important commercial
centre with a tax-collection office as well as the best hot baths in the kingdom, which were particularly popular with the Moorish monarch and his
court. Don Rodrigo arrayed 8,000 men and marched for three days, reaching
Alhama undetected. They scaled the ramparts, took the surprised fortress and
restored the honour of Spain.[10] It was the start of a string of Spanish successes
that continued until 1482 when, over-confident, the Christian army was
caught in a devastating ambush outside Loja, a key border citadel.

The Moors gained the ascendancy but then the ruler of Granada, Abul
Hacan, enraged his principal wife by having an affair with a Greek girl. The
row escalated to tribal fighting and led to a division of the emirate between

the King and his eldest son, Boabdil. The split was hugely propitious for the Spanish and brought success against the feuding Moors. But Granada's defence arrangements were good: a chain of castles every five miles or so, along its northern and western frontiers and the military resources of North Africa in the background, although these came at a heavy price.

The Spanish strategy for the spring campaign of 1486 was to capture the citadels guarding the northern border of Granada. So on 14 May, the army set off across the Guadalquivir plain, into the low rolling hills and then up the valleys towards the spectacular Sierras. In the mountains the edges of the army were exposed to harrying attacks by light Moorish cavalry, but they lumbered on undeterred. Diego de Valera recounted:

> And the said knights departed together with the aforementioned people, and went to feed their horses at Peña de los Enamorados [Lover's Rock]. And thence they departed in the afternoon, and at day break they were outside Loja: whither there came an English knight, a very noble man, called Lord Scales, with eighty or a hundred fighting men.

Loja was originally a Roman military city. It is perched on a rocky outcrop that rises from the steep side of a valley; the river Genil curves round it like a moat and there is a single bridge crossing. The previous attempt to capture Loja had come to grief in the mountains. Now there was a new plan: the vanguard was to make a difficult climb and take the heights above the city, while the main army was to arrive on the opposite side of the river. Edward volunteered for the vanguard but the King said there would be 'no lack of perilous service' in the campaign and kept him back.

The vanguard were supposed to take up their position surreptitiously, so they started clambering up the rocky escarpment towards the high ground. Coincidentally the forward pickets of the main army arrived on the plain and broke ranks to make camp. It was then that the Moors sprang their ambush. They had been waiting for such a moment. Two divisions charged out of the city, one to roll the supposedly surprise attack back down the escarpment while the other attacked the disorganized men on the plain.

At this juncture it seems that King Ferdinand and Edward rode over a hill and saw the fighting on the plain below them. They sat on their horses watching the Moors driving the Christians off the plain.

> Many Moors came out on foot and on horseback to prevent the royal camp being established and fired arrows and gunshot from the fruit groves. The fighting involved the Moors, the Englishmen and some northern mountaineers, who had come with the Dukes of Infantado and Najera ... and are called Biscayners [Basques].[11]

Edward turned to the King and asked if he could fight in the 'English way'.
Given permission, he dismounted, ordered his trumpeter to blow the charge,
probably the same call that has echoed down the ages urging English soldiers
forward, then, with battle-axe in hand and his banner-man beside him, he
marched forward.[12] His men must have hurried to catch up and so formed a
wedge behind his banner. He charged straight for the Moorish weak point, the
single bridge to the city. In Prescott's translation, Bernáldez tells the story of
Edward asking:

> for leave to fight in the manner of his country and dismounting from his horse,
> and armed with sword and battle-axe he charged forward at the Moorish
> host before them all, with a small company of his men, armed like himself,
> slashing and hacking with brave and manly hearts, killing and dismounting
> the enemy right and left.

> He then dealt such terrible blows around him that even the hardy mountaineers
> of the North were filled with astonishment.

It must have been a terrific sight, the Englishmen charging forward,
perhaps led by a banner emblazoned with the silver scallop of Scales, weapons and armour gleaming in the sun. Their surcoats were probably uniform,
perhaps brilliant white, quartered by the scarlet cross of St George.[13]

There was vigorous action with arrows and gunfire:

> The Castilians, seeing his charge, rushed on to support it, following on the
> heels of the Englishman with such valour that the Moors turned tail and fled
> ... and the Christians mixed in with them, entered the outskirts of Loja
> outside the walls, which they never left or lost thereafter. The king then came
> in person to support his men.

They had fought their way across the flat farmland to the bridge. The river
is deep and fast flowing in May but they captured the bridge and broke through
the city gates. The inhabitants – women, children, goats, hens and all – must
have scattered squawking as the Englishmen rampaged across the lower town
which clusters on the lower slopes of the castle crag.

The fortress sits high above, 100 paces forward and 100ft (30 metres) up
to the base of the walls that then rise 20–30ft (6–9 metres). Edward, in his
role as the Conde de Escalas, led his men on, up scaling ladders while the
defenders bombarded them with rocks from above. The *escaladores*, the scalers of fortifications, were the English company and it was remarkable piece of
organization, or luck, to find ladders for scaling at the end of a spontaneous
rushing attack.

Edward took a rock in the face.[14] He was knocked cold but his men surged on. Fernando del Pulgar reported:

> And thus the combat lasted for around eight hours, during which, because some of the Christians were tiring and others seeing the danger of the fighting, fainted. The knights and captains, each where he was fighting, encouraged his men and by placing himself in the position of greatest danger, revived their spirits, making them set to and fight. Especially the Englishman, the Conde de Escalas with the bowmen and foot soldiers he brought, ventured into dangerous situations and places.

This is a good account of an English knight leading ordinary foot soldiers as a tactical officer. Traditionally infantry captains came from the ranks and infantry fought as a separate group without knightly officers in the ranks. If knights dismounted then they fought as a group of knights. In early or tribal armies, all ranks fought as a single unit, with the chief of the family or clan as the tactical officer, but not in civilized Europe, where status was of paramount importance. In the Middle Ages, knights and men-at-arms were grouped together to fight as a unit, either as heavy cavalry or very heavy infantry, certainly separate from common soldiers who were given their orders as a group. Indeed Alonso de Palencia – a contemporary – believed that Edward had 300 knights with him.[15] However, here Edward is leading ordinary infantrymen, while his archers are presumably providing covering shots, probably in the initial stages and certainly when the walls were being scaled.

It was the Swiss who first had knights fighting in the ranks as infantry officers and this proved very effective, Charles the Bold paid the price of underestimating them and the idea spread, but it was innovative and contrary to the perception of what was correct.[16] The arrival of officers to direct tactical infantry marks one of the step changes in warfare. Edward was at the forefront of military thinking, with no regard, in this instance, for traditional ways.

Both Bernáldez and Petrus Martyr, an Italian intellectual who was then 'exchanging Muses for Mars', reported the results:

> Many Moors were killed in this encounter and some Christians as well and the English lord was struck with a stone which broke his teeth and three or four of his men were slain.

> Unfortunately just as the suburbs were carried, the knight, as he was mounting a scaling ladder, received a blow from a stone which dashed out two of his front teeth and stretched him senseless on the ground.

> The Conde de Las Escalas was brought back senseless to his tent where his life was saved by the extraordinary skill of the surgeons, though it was found

3. Siege. Men-at-arms scaling a city; archers and artillery
bombard a castle supervised by a knight in a fur hat.

impossible to replace his broken teeth. He lay some time under medical supervision. When he had sufficiently recovered he received a visit from the King and Queen who complimented him on his prowess and testified their sympathy for his misfortune of the missing teeth. To which he replied:

'It is little to lose a few teeth in the service of him, who has given me all.' He added: 'Our Lord who reared this fabric, has only opened a window in order to discern the more readily what passes within.'

This witty response gave uncommon satisfaction to the sovereigns. The Queen, not long after, testified to her sense of the Earl's services by a magnificent largesse.

The largesse manifested itself as, 'twelve Andalusian horses, two beds with richly wrought hangings, coverings of cloth of gold and a quantity of fine linen together with sumptuous pavilions for himself and his suite'. It was unusual generosity from the blue-eyed Castilian monarch, who was known to be careful with her money. The inventory of the materials is in Appendix C; it totals 88,791 maravedis, over £47.[17]

Fernando del Pulgar tells a similar story of the King visiting Edward in his tent:

to console him for the wounds that he had received, especially for the two teeth that had been knocked from his mouth. And he told him he should be happy that his courage had lost him two teeth, which he could have lost through age or disease. And considering the place in which he had lost them, rather did they make him handsome, than deformed; and that rather did this loss increase his worth, than the wound constitute a loss for him.

The Count replied that he gave thanks to God and the glorious Virgin, to have been visited by the most powerful King in all Christendom, and that he accepted his gracious consolation for the teeth that he had lost. Although he did not consider it much to lose two teeth in the service of He who had given them all to him.

Getting hit on the head seems to have been a common hazard for brave men who scaled fortifications. Tirant Lo Blanc, the hero in a near-contemporary novel, suffers a similar misfortune when besieging a Moorish castle: 'Tirant dismounted and led the charge, but as he reached the wall, one of the stones thrown by the defenders struck his head. His men dragged him out of the ditch.' He was put to bed and grandees came to visit him: 'Tirant thanked them for their generous aid, but it was hard for him to speak because his head ached. The doctors poulticed it with broth from a sheep's head cooked in wine, and the next morning he felt much better.'[18]

History does not relate what poultice or medicine was administered to Edward, but he certainly mended. Not all the English were so lucky. De Valera reported that 20 were killed in the fighting at Loja, while Bernáldez puts the deaths at three or four. There were certainly some who were badly wounded.

Meanwhile the artillery had arrived, and six days after the capture of the suburbs the lombards[19] began a bombardment. 'A great stretch of the city's walls' was soon demolished. The defenders knew they were beaten and the following day they surrendered. The citadel was captured and with it came an unexpected prize, King Boabdil, the young Moorish monarch – his mother's boy – who shared the throne so uneasily with his father.

King Ferdinand, wise in politics (his statecraft was much admired by Machiavelli), magnanimously released Boabdil and sent him back to Granada so that the internal feuding could continue in that unfortunate emirate. The surrender terms for Loja allowed the inhabitants to leave 'with whatever they could carry of theirs ... and these Moors and Mooresses wept and wailed bitterly as they went'. Also at their request, the King provided the Marquis of Cadiz and an escort to ensure they reached Granada in safety. 'The date on which Loja was surrendered to the king was Monday 28th May of the said year of 1486. ... The king then moved his host and his artillery and went to lay siege to Illora.'[20]

A week later the army was camped outside Illora where there was bitter fighting. The citadel surrendered after four days and the entire population was again sent off to Granada. Two days later, on 11 June, Queen Isabella arrived at Illora. She was there to celebrate. There was a grand parade to greet her, with the Christian battalions drawn up in line along the valley below the captured city. The Queen, wearing a scarlet cloak and a broad-brimmed black hat over her auburn hair, passed down the ranks on a mule with a saddle blanket of gold-embroidered satin and a saddle of gilded silver. Fernando del Pulgar describes her as having 'blue-green eyes, a gracious mien, and a lovely, merry face; most dignified in her movements and countenance; a woman of great intelligence and great wisdom'.[21]

It was a proud Queen who rode before her troops with the sun glinting on her trappings. The army dipped their standards and shouted in acclamation. Andrés Bernáldez, the chaplain of the Archbishop of Seville, an eyewitness, wrote:

> The Queen was accompanied by her daughter the Infanta Isabella and a courtly train of damsels. ... The Infanta wore a skirt of fine velvet, over others of brocade, a scarlet mantilla in the Moorish fashion and a black hat trimmed

with gold embroidery. The King rode forward at the head of his nobles to receive her. He was dressed in a crimson doublet and breeches of yellow satin ... by his side, close girt, he wore a curved sword ... mounted on a noble war-horse of bright chestnut colour.

The King kissed his wife and ten-year-old daughter. Bernáldez took satisfaction in writing of Edward, the English nobleman, accompanying the King: 'Then there came up the English Count, after the King, to welcome the Queen and the Princess, very formally and in a striking manner, after everyone else.' He was 'armado en blanco a la guise [in full-bleached plate armour]' ... and 'on a chestnut horse with caparisons down to the ground', which were 'of azure silk with fringes of smooth white silk as wide as a hand's breadth, the whole caparison was covered with gold stars and lined in purple. He wore over his armour a French surcoat of smooth black brocade and a white French hat with extravagant plumes which were made in so novel a way that everyone was impressed. He carried on his left arm a small round shield decorated with gold bends. He had with him five caparisoned horses with his pages on them [who] were all dressed in brocade and silk and there came with him certain of his gentlemen, all very well arrayed.'

Edward was obviously recovered and quite well enough to undertake an entertaining display of horsemanship: 'And thus he came to make reverence and give welcome to the Queen and the Princess, and afterwards he made reverence to the King. He then paraded for a while amusing them with his horsemanship, prancing and pirouetting with all the grandees and all the people looking at him. He impressed them all. And their Highnesses took great pleasure from all this.' Perhaps that was when Edward knighted two of his men: 'Sir Edward Wyngfeilde made Knight in Granada by Sir Edward Woodvill warringe on the infidels', and also: 'Sir ... Cantelupe made knight in Granada with Sir Edward Wyngfielde'.[22]

After that the council of war reviewed the position. Matters looked good, so the army marched on to the next objective, Moclin, a citadel perched on an impossible crag.[23] From its ramparts, the garrison and townsfolk gazed on the Christian army winding up the distant valley towards them. It would seem to be moving at a snail's pace but there would be a grim inevitability about its progress, far, far below them.

First came the *vanguardia* with its flanking cavalry, next the mainguard, ten infantry battalions with cavalry wings guarding the flanks. (Martorell, writing 30 years earlier, says that battalions were divided into *centuries* and *decades*, i.e. companies of hundreds with sections of tens.) Then followed

6,000 pioneers, making the road for the heavy guns, ammunition and baggage wagons crawling along behind, pulled by their ox teams.[24] An army with oxen doing the heavy haulage travelled around eight miles a day but where they had to make the road through the mountains – when Pulgar was watching – they managed just nine miles in 12 days.

The 'flanking cavalry' were *genitors* or *jinetes*. After centuries of warfare against the Moors, the Spanish had developed light cavalry that were unique to the campaign. These *genitors* wore steel caps and a mail shirts, no other armour, and rode un-armoured horses; their weapons were javelins and swords. They were used for reconnaissance and patrolling, while in a pitched battle they were the 'skirmishers'; they swarmed around the enemy, threw javelins at them, picked off stragglers but avoided fighting with anything bigger or stronger than themselves.

Moorish cavalry was similar in weight and function, and as the Spanish army marched they would have been trying to pick away at it.[25] There would be an increasing amount of light cavalry skirmishing as the army marched deeper into Granada. The Spanish also had the traditional heavy cavalry of knights and men-at-arms, but these were kept for formal attack.

The Moors might have felt safe on their crag until they saw the siege cannons. These massive weapons were each four tons of iron, 12ft (3.66 metres) long and designed to fire stone balls. Newer, heavier cannon could throw iron balls up to 2,000 yards (1,830 metres) at the rate of one per hour.

The guns were set up at *punto de blanco*, or point-blank range, i.e. within a few hundred yards on a hill to the south.[26] Stone or marble cannonballs around 14ins (36cm) in diameter and weighing 170lbs (77kg) were fired at the walls, which were breached. But the breaches were rebuilt and then re-breached and so forth for two nights and a day until, suddenly by lucky chance, a ball of wildfire – a ball of inflammable ingredients mixed with gunpowder which 'scattered long trains of light in their passage through the air'– flashed through a window and into the magazine. There was a tremendous and stunning explosion that hurled the men on the battlements into the air and flattened the surrounding buildings.

The battered Moors were in profound shock. They had never dreamed of such devastation and immediately surrendered. So from the walls of Moclin the triumphant Christians could at last see all the rich plain about Granada and the snow-capped Sierra Nevada beyond. It must have seemed, after eight centuries of war, that victory was within their grasp. There was a clamour for a bold new plan: ignore the outlying citadels and head straight for Granada.

The council of war resisted the pressure to rush headlong to Granada. It was getting hot and the season was nearly over. They decided on just one more success and besieged Montefrio. It capitulated and the army marched back to Cordoba.

Also fighting in this campaign was the young Gonzalo de Cordova, who later became the 'Great Captain' in command of the Spanish in the Italian wars of the 1490s. He established the well-officered, well-disciplined Spanish infantry divisions, the 'Tercos', which were to dominate land warfare for the next 200 years. His experience came from these frontier wars where he was at the capture of Illora and led the scaling party at Montefrio. He and Edward would certainly have known each other.

The King and Queen – and presumably Edward – arrived back at Cordoba on 29 June and remained there until 17 July. This was when the monarchs could catch up with their administrative work, a role undertaken with their courts revolving around them. The court was formal and pious, but also buzzing with activity. The Inquisition had just been properly established in Spain but the Spanish ethnic cleansing of the sixteenth century was not yet a developed policy, so the atmosphere was relatively tolerant. The court was expansive and attracted all sorts of hopefuls and adventurers. One such was Christophoro Colon de Terra Rubra, a Genoese master mariner now known to history as Christopher Columbus. He was promoting his big project: to reach the Indies going west instead of east, which meant confirming that the world was round.

He arrived at the Spanish court in January 1485 and pestered and pushed for an audience with the Queen, but got nowhere. Sixteen months later he was still trying when Edward rode into Cordoba with his 'three hundred splendid household troops'. The court and camp must have hummed with talk of the Conde de Escalas, friend of the new English king, of the blood royal of England and who had captained ships of war.

Here was a worthwhile target for a threadbare explorer-aspirant. For the two weeks that Edward waited for the campaign to start, killing time in a foreign city, he would be easy to approach and perhaps prepared to hear a story. He could look at Columbus's map, would understand about going straight to the objective and appreciate the courage of the scheme. If he did hear and like Columbus's plan, then he could offer access to King Henry of England.

But it was some time around then that Columbus finally got his meeting with the Spanish monarchs.[27] We do not know which day Columbus had his audience. It may have been before the army marched and, if so, Edward could have been there, listening. The Queen considered Columbus's proposal of going backwards to China and passed the project on to her confessor, Father

Hernando de Talavera, who doubled as her chief of staff. He decided, in time-honoured fashion, that an expert committee should be appointed to investigate the proposal in detail.

Edward set off for home in July.[28] He left at least one wounded officer, Rupert, behind in the Queen's care and we also know that four of his soldiers had been taken prisoner by the Moors (of whom more in Chapter 10). As all of Edward's recorded battles had been successful, presumably the four had been captured by Moorish light cavalry harassing the army on the march, or when straying from camp.

What is interesting is that one of the four was Petrus Alamanç of Bruges and the other three were his relations. It means that they were professional or mercenary soldiers and would expect to be paid three months in advance for an expedition such as this, so we may wonder how many of Edward's company were mercenaries. However many it was, all would want to be paid, so the expedition would have cost some £700 in wages alone. Did Edward pay them himself as a contribution to the crusade or was he an early military enterpriser providing a company of foot soldiers to the Spanish crown on a commercial contract? Given the period and the fact that professional soldiers needed to be paid, the latter is certainly possible, if not probable.

Edward rode back to Portugal, which, undistracted by war, had been pushing on with her discoveries. That summer Diego Cão (Cam) arrived back from as far south as Walvis Bay; he had also sailed up the Congo looking for the mythical Christian king Prester John. The King was about to commission Bartholomew Diaz to sail even further south, de Aeiro was setting off to explore Benin, and João do Estreito had been awarded a concession for 'the discovery of the islands and continents of the West Atlantic'. The Portuguese seem to have known there was an undiscovered continent in the west but were being single-minded in their eastward push to India.

Battered and toothless from his crusading, Edward arrived in Lisbon for his visit to King João. He was particularly honoured at one banquet, 'when washing hands after the meal, the King would not take the water sitting down but rose from the table'.[29] (The significance of this may not be clear to us but it impressed everyone present.)

Around the court, the city and the quays Edward and his men would have heard and smelled the excitement of explorations. Perhaps he met Christopher Columbus's brother, Bartholomew, who would visit London 18 months later and was then in Lisbon. Maybe Edward saw West African gold dust from El Mina (the mine) and felt England was missing out on the discoveries.

Sir Edward Brampton had taken refuge in Portugal after King Richard's defeat the year before. Would he have avoided Edward? After all, their last encounter had been an armed engagement in the Solent when they were enemies. But Brampton was keen to gain King Henry's favour (and was pardoned two years later). Bad blood was probably put behind them while Edward enjoyed the entertainments laid on for him by King João: bull fights, cane fights, plays, feasts and pageants. Edward and his men sailed for England some time around August 1486. He had certainly liked what he had seen in Lisbon, for as soon as he was home he proposed that one of his younger royal nieces should marry King João's cousin and heir.

On the whole, it had been a fortunate expedition, Edward had fought the Moors,[30] learned and seen much, perhaps fulfilled a vow. But who was he, this Conde de Escalas, friend of the new English King, of the Portuguese King, of Ferdinand and Isabella and of the blood royal of England?

He signed himself 'Sir Edward Wydeville knight' and he was not the Conde de Escalas or the Earl of Scales. His elder brother had been Earl Rivers and Baron Scales. There is no record of Edward claiming to be anything other than a knight, although the Spaniards did write about him as the Conde de Escalas. He had grown up under his brother's wing and his brother used the silver scallop as his badge. It may be that he continued to use it as his fighting badge, for it had been a celebrated Woodville emblem for 20 years. Of course, the Spaniards were keen to emphasize the importance of all who joined them, and 'Conde' might have been a courtesy title, while the name 'Escalas' might be regarded as particularly appropriate as Edward had scaled the walls of Loja and that made him an *escaladore*.

Whatever the reason, he was a Woodville, one of that family that had risen so rapidly to become so powerful under King Edward IV. Their meteoric rise had started in 1464 when Edward's elder sister caught the King's eye.

CHAPTER TWO

PASSION

Edward was the youngest son of Sir Richard Woodville and his wife, Jacquetta of Luxembourg. Fortune had favoured the family in the spring of 1464 when King Edward IV visited their manor of Grafton in Northamptonshire.[1] Tradition has the young King cantering through the park when he suddenly saw their eldest daughter, Elizabeth, and was smitten. Legend has him planting an oak tree at the spot where he first saw her, later called the Queen's Oak; it had a 25ft girth and was still just alive in the 1940s.

Matters of foreign policy may have been the reason for the King's visit, as Elizabeth's mother had powerful relations at the Burgundian court. There is a less convincing view that King Edward came accidentally to the house after hunting but, whatever the reason, it is clear that the 22-year-old monarch had heard about the beautiful girl.

She was a penniless widow with two small children who had recently asked Lord Hastings, one of the King's cronies, for his help in a court case against her avaricious mother-in-law. Hastings had taken full advantage of the situation and contracted to use his influence on her behalf.[2] He also told the King about her. It sounded a good opportunity and so the young King, a great womanizer and 'licentious in the extreme', came to see for himself. Elizabeth was certainly beautiful and predictably took the opportunity of appealing 'that she might be restored unto such small lands as her late husband had given her in jointure'. She must have been quite enchanting:

> The King was moved to love her by reason of her beautiful person and elegant manner. But neither his fits nor his threats could prevail against her jealously guarded virtue. When Edward held a dagger to her throat in an attempt to make her submit to his passion, she held still and showed no sign of fear, preferring rather to die than live unchastely with the King. This incident only fanned the flames of Edward's desire. He judged her worthy to be a queen whose virtue could withstand the approaches of even a royal lover.

So reported Dominic Mancini, an Italian cleric visiting England in 1483, who was providing political intelligence for his master in France.

Apart from his lack of success with Elizabeth, the King had other pressing problems: rebellion in the north and an empty exchequer. Reacting to the emergency, he postponed the opening of parliament, sold royal jewels, borrowed money, sent his artillery on and, summoning troops to meet him at Leicester, rode out from London on 28 April 1464.

At Stony Stratford he paused, told the court he was going hunting and rode the four miles over to Grafton. There he married Elizabeth on 1 May 1464 at a service in the little chantry at Grafton which was held in the presence of her mother, four or five others 'and a young man who helped the priest to sing'. Afterwards King Edward took his new wife straight to bed. When he eventually reappeared at his court he told them he was exhausted from 'hunting' and went to his official bed.[3]

He went hunting for the next two days and then rode off to run his war. It was the first time an English king had married for love or lust[4] and it remained secret until four months later when the matter of finding a 'befitting bride' for the King was raised at a meeting of the Great Council. 'Perchance our choice may not be to the liking of everyone present,' replied the King, adding, 'nevertheless we will do as it likes us.'[5] He then declared that he had married Elizabeth Woodville. The Council was horrified. Not only did they regard it as the loss of a strategic opportunity but also as most unsuitable.

The King may have argued that it was better to have an English bride than a foreign one; that her mother was sister to the Count de St Pol, descended from great men such as Simon de Montfort and had been wedded to the much admired Duke of Bedford; or that the heroic Black Prince had married a divorcee with five children. It would not have made any difference. The Council knew that Elizabeth had neither land nor money, was five years older than the King and that her father's family were not even proper nobles. They were promoted gentry who had risen with little more than courage, ability and good looks. Rather more importantly it meant giving up the opportunity of a useful diplomatic marriage. Nevertheless this marriage was to shape Edward Woodville's life.

The last 30 years had been an exciting time for nobles and knights, with wars in France and then war at home. Edward's father, Sir Richard Woodville, had been a captain in the French wars under the great Duke of Bedford and then, in the campaign following the Duke's death in 1435, he had fallen in love with Jacquetta of Luxembourg, the Duke's young widow. She was 20 years old, 'handsome and lively', recently appointed a 'Lady of the Order of the Garter' and a rare good match for a mere professional soldier. Her marriage to Bedford had been diplomatic, so she was available for love and came with an inheritance of one-third of his English income of £4,000 a year, together with the share of his huge estates in France.

Sir Richard moved fast and married the young Duchess before anyone thought to stop them, although she was later fined 1,000 marks (about £666) for failing to procure royal consent.[6] The 15-year-old King Henry VI was understanding and pardoned them after six months, but Jacquetta's smart relations in Burgundy were horrified at the misalliance. It mattered little to them that Sir Richard was regarded as the handsomest man in England, or that he was an accomplished knight and a brave captain who made a career fighting the French and whose special interest was taking part in tournaments.[7] However, it was as an able military commander that he was recognized in England and raised to the peerage in 1448 as Baron Rivers,[8] 'for his valour, integrity and great services' in the French wars. He was later elevated to the Order of the Garter and appointed to the Privy Council.

At the time, England was sinking into chaos. King Henry was mentally unstable (inherited through his mother from King Charles VI of France) and many people regarded his powerful Queen, Margaret, as a frightful woman from Anjou, particularly after 1457 when one of her French friends amused himself by burning Sandwich.[9] English possessions in France had fallen like ninepins and there was no general of Bedford's standing or calibre to stop the collapse. The French had recently discovered how to use cannon against castles and the brothers Bureau established a great train of artillery with which they blasted the English out of their castles in Normandy and Guienne.

The 63-year-old Talbot[10] tried to re-establish English supremacy but was killed at the battle of Castillon in 1453. He had 2,500 men and decided to attack a French army of 10,000 that was dug into a defensive position with cannon. Bordeaux fell to the French soon after (as Constantinople was falling to the Turks). The hard men in the front line were fighting a losing, unpaid war while covetous noblemen and sycophants ruled at court.

Debts were mounting, administration was falling apart and there was no money in the Treasury. There was an imaginative offer to use alchemy to make money, which William Hatclyf, the King's secretary, was appointed 'to investigate touching the means proposed to the king, whereby within a few years, his debts may be paid in good money of gold and silver'. Unfortunately it came to nothing and the country plunged further into debt.[11]

In one of the King's mad spells Richard, Duke of York, whose blood claim to the throne was arguably stronger than Henry's, had been appointed

Protector (1454) and then, while suspicion, sedition and skirmishing engaged the great men of the land, Richard thought he would take advantage of the King's madness. He tried to usurp the throne and so triggered the 'Wars of the Roses', or 'the Cousins' War' as it was then known.

Edward Woodville was born some time around then and the Cousins' War was to last intermittently for his lifetime. His father, Sir Richard, now Lord Rivers, was one of those summoned to the Great Council of 1458 which attempted a reconciliation between the rival factions. It proved impossible. A campaign ensued,[12] which culminated in the Duke of York withdrawing to Ireland with his son, Edward, Earl of March, who then moved on to Calais, where their cousin and ally, the Earl of Warwick, controlled its garrison of around 2,000 men.

For the King, Lord Rivers was sent to assemble an expeditionary force at Sandwich, and his 18-year-old son, Anthony, Edward's eldest brother, went with him. However, the Yorkist Earls, March and Warwick, took the initiative and on the night of 15 January 1460 sent a raiding party across the Channel. The Woodvilles, both father and son, were surprised in their beds and carried off to Calais as prisoners.

The Earl of Warwick clearly had a sense of theatre, for the Woodvilles were brought at night 'before the Lords with eight score torches' and bitterly 'berated' for their 'upstart insolence'. It was the recent attainder which really rankled; the Yorkists had been, in absentia, convicted of treason by the King's Council, of which Rivers was a member. Not only was the mighty Earl furious at the attainder but was also deeply insulted at being found guilty of piracy by a royal investigator. To rub salt in the wound, that investigator had been Lord Rivers.[13]

In the huge Gothic hall at Calais in the flickering torch light, Warwick contemptuously reminded Rivers that he had been 'made by marriage and also made a Lord' and 'it was not his part to have such language of Lords'.[14] History does not relate whether the Woodvilles stood in silence or answered back; they might well have made some pithy remarks about Yorkists getting above their station and Warwick's title coming from his wife.

Somehow the Woodvilles escaped from Calais and were back in England when, on 26 June, the Earls of March and Warwick returned in vengeance with 2,000 men. The King and court retreated north, leaving Thomas, Lord Scales, 'a man of violent passion' who also happened to be Edward of March's godfather, in command of the Tower and keeping an eye on Yorkist-leaning Londoners.

4. Men-at-arms ride
out and two knights
compete with lances.

Scales had fought in every campaign against the French[15] and was a firm establishment man with no sympathy for Yorkists, or for Londoners, all of whom he regarded as treacherous. They were besieging him! Believing the rebels would be speedily dealt with and with relief imminent, he unwisely bombarded the City. 'They that were within the Tower cast wild fire [medieval napalm] into the city and shot in small guns, and burned and hurt men and women and children in the street. And they of London laid great bombards [cannons] on the further side of the Thames against the Tower and crashed the walls in divers places.'[16]

But Scales had miscalculated. The King did not come to the rescue because the royal army had been soundly defeated at Northampton, rations had run out and he was obliged to surrender on 19 July. The Yorkist earls let the choleric baron slip away upriver towards sanctuary but his luck ran out when he was recognized by the boatmen. They killed him and left his body – covered in stab wounds – in the churchyard of St Mary Overy.

His heiress was his only surviving child, Elizabeth, whom Anthony Wood-ville married six days after the killing (her mother and Anthony's mother were friends). There had been a son, Thomas, but he was killed in single combat at the age of 15, so Elizabeth inherited wide estates and Middleton, a grand moated manor near King's Lynn.[17] Today's visitor can still see the gatehouse, a four-storeyed symmetrical tower topped with corner turrets, rising proudly from the still waters of the moat.

The fighting went on, with battles at Wakefield, Mortimer's Cross and, again, at St Albans.[18] Duke Richard of York had been killed early in the increas-ingly bitter campaign that culminated in the dreadful dawn-to-dusk battle of Towton on Palm Sunday (29 March 1461). The Lancastrians were drawn up in a good defensive position but on a very exposed ridge facing south and looking straight into a blizzard. Anthony was in the vanguard with his father who was commanding 6,000 Welshmen.

The battle started with an archery exchange in which the Yorkists had the advantage of a strong wind. The Lancastrians were forced to advance from their position; Jean de Warin described Rivers and Somerset initiating a two-battle (or division) attack on the Yorkist line. They advanced steadily, cheer-ing and shouting 'King Henry'. The armies clashed together. It seems Rivers's 'battle' won through and, thinking they were part of a successful advance, chased the Yorkists they had been fighting for several miles. In the blizzard no one could really see what was happening and those who remained battered away at each other. The Lancastrians were doing well until the arrival of fresh Yorkist troops, which turned the tables. Retreat turned into rout and then grim slaughter.

In this, the biggest and bloodiest battle of the Wars of the Roses, the build up of hatred seems to have negated the conventional rules of war. Each army probably started around 25,000 strong, rather than the more usual 5,000 to 10,000, but casualties were recorded by the heralds as 28,000 slain, 'a number unheard of in our realm for almost a thousand years', commented the Bishop of Salisbury. The Milanese ambassador reported a split of 8,000 Yorkists to 20,000 Lancastrians. Whatever the true figure, the casualties were certainly awful.[19]

Anthony, 'recently made Lord Scales', was reported dead. But both he and his father had in fact miraculously survived both the bitter fighting and the subsequent mopping-up operations, probably because they were still chasing Yorkists when disaster hit the Lancastrians.

Edward of March, commanding the Yorkists in place of his dead father, had issued orders: 'Kill the nobles, leave the commoners'.[20] This was not conventional. Throughout the Middle Ages you took prisoners and made good money on the ransom, so while death might be accidental it would not be by intent. However, in this civil war each side regarded themselves as legitimate and the other as illegitimate. The opposition would one day be attainted and therefore would have no property rights from which ransom could be paid. They might as well be killed and, anyway, dead rebels will not rebel again.

The battle of Towton established Edward of March as king. He was very handsome and tall and led his army on foot, from the front, 'where with great violence he beat and bare down afore him all that stood in his way'. His skeleton has been measured and he was found to be 6ft 4ins (192cm) tall.

He immediately embarked on a campaign for hearts and minds. Well aware of the importance of public opinion, he was the first king properly to issue proclamations in English rather than Latin.[21] His proclamation of March 1461 is seminal in the development of England's rulers engaging the public; it heralded a control of news that gave him and his successors the capacity to present events in a particular light. He also ran a reconciliation programme for Lancastrian notables, with men such as Rivers, who was military rather than political, being a prime target.

So it is hardly surprising that four months after the battle both the Woodvilles, Lord Rivers and Anthony, were released from the Tower and pardoned. A little later the ambassador of the Duke of Milan was reporting: 'Lords adherent to King Henry are all quitting him, ... one of the chief of them ... Lord de Rivers with one of his sons, men of great valour, come to tender obedience [to King Edward]. I held several conversations with this Lord Rivers about King Henry's cause and he assured me that it was lost irredeemably.'[22]

In December King Edward confirmed the continuation of Jacquetta's dowry, the restoration of Rivers's land in Calais and his position as 'chief rider'[23] of a forest in Northamptonshire. Just one year after Towton Edward appointed Lord Rivers to his Council and confirmed Anthony in his wife's title as Lord Scales, with silver scallops on a red (gules) background as a part of his coat of arms and his badge. The Woodvilles were now Yorkist. As Talleyrand remarked, 'treason is a matter of date'.

Re-established in the ruling hierarchy, Lord Rivers and the beautiful Jacquetta were based at the family home at Grafton. Their eldest daughter,

Elizabeth, had been one of the ladies of the bedchamber to the Lancastrian Queen Margaret and married to a Sir John Grey. But the unfortunate girl was widowed when Sir John was killed at St Albans in 1461 and now had mother-in-law problems. The mother-in-law had recently remarried and was determined to hold onto all the Grey property,[24] so Elizabeth was left penniless and obliged to return home to Grafton with her two small children.

The other Woodville siblings were Anthony (Lord Scales), Jacquetta (the younger), who was already married to Lord Strange of Knockin, and four younger brothers, John, Lionel, Richard and Edward. There were at least five more unmarried sisters: Margaret, Anne, Mary, Catherine and Eleanor. This was the family the King might possibly have found on his visit to Grafton and the first time Edward, then perhaps six years old, would have met him.

King Edward had married Elizabeth on 1 May 1464. The ceremony had been conducted in secret but five months later all England knew and talked of little else. Apparently everyone but the Woodvilles and their relations regarded the marriage as highly irresponsible, particularly the Earl of Warwick, who had spent much of the last few months negotiating an engagement for the King to a niece of the French King. The King of Castile (Henry IV, 'the Impotent') had also just offered Isabella, his half-sister and heir, as a bride, but the real cause of Warwick's anger was Edward's total disregard of his advice. Warwick had believed he was the power behind – and not that far behind – the throne.

A wit told King Louis XI of France that there were 'Two kings of England, M. de Warwick and another whose name escapes me'.[25] This other king, Edward, unconcerned by Warwick's displeasure, arranged a magnificent coronation for his new queen at Westminster Abbey on 26 May 1465. There was a strong Burgundian delegation led by one of Elizabeth's uncles, Jacques de Luxembourg and, for added ceremony, 40 Knights of the Bath were created to escort the new Queen to the Abbey. Included were Elizabeth's next two brothers, Richard and John; amongst the others were Duke Harry of Buckingham and his younger brother who was then eight or nine years old.

An enormous municipal effort had been made in the City where, amongst other things, 45 loads of sand were shovelled on to London Bridge at a cost of four pence per load. There was spectacular pageantry and sumptuous feasting in Westminster Hall, followed by a grand tournament the next day where Lord Stanley won the prize, a ruby set in a ring.[26]

The date of Edward Woodville's birth is unknown. He was obviously too young to be knighted at his sister's coronation, and another sister, Catherine, was born in 1457, so he was probably born after that, in 1458 or perhaps 1459.[27] Nothing is known of his youth but being noble and related to the blood royal of England his education would follow the established pattern. It was generally believed that the best possible way of bringing up a child was to thrust him or her out of the family to learn the ways of the world. This practice amazed a Venetian diplomat: 'The want of affection in the English is strongly manifested towards their children. For after keeping them at home till they arrive at the age of seven, or nine years at the utmost, they put them out ... for everyone, however rich he be, sends away his children into the houses of others.' (It is easy to see where the English public school system started.)

Young Edward would have been sent away to a royal or noble household to be instructed in 'polite learning', which meant reading and writing in English and Latin. They were standard for nobles, gentry and the merchant classes. In addition there were 'manly exercises' and the art of pleasing elders and betters.

Both the King and Queen had their own training establishments. The King's Ordinances make careful provision for the training of his six or seven pages. These boys were known as his 'henchmen' because they rode on either side of the haunch of their sovereign in ceremonial parades; they were looked after by the Master of Henchmen.[28] Instruction also came from a range of manuals, and later Caxton produced his *Book of Curtesye*, all with good advice for small boys (then and now): don't slump, fidget, stick your finger in your nose, put your hands in your hose to scratch, etc. And: 'Pick not your nose, nor that it be dropping with no pearls clear. ... And always beware of thy hinder part from guns blasting.'

The Queen's establishment was attended by the young Duke of Buckingham and his brother for two years. She received £300 a year for looking after them and employed a schoolmaster, John Giles, at £2 a year for their tuition.

It was in the 1460s with his family flourishing at the centre of power that young Edward started to grow up. The King found the Woodvilles useful as he developed his own form of government; initially he used them as part of the counterbalance to the power and arrogance of the established nobility, but later also for their own abilities. Edward was to be educated and brought up to be a member of this ruling elite, a group that was to have its pleasures and its problems, with no half measures.

CHAPTER THREE

POLITICS

E dward Woodville's eldest brother, Anthony, was the archetypal hero
and something of a polymath. He was one of the Champions of England
(a top tournament fighter), a poet and scholar, busy with land management as well as being an able administrator and military commander.[1] There
is strong circumstantial evidence that he and Edward were very close over the
next ten years or so and, in all probability, Edward served first as his page and
then as his squire.

Anthony's abilities had been recognized when the King confirmed him in
his wife's title as Lord Scales, two years *before* his sister's marriage to the King.
But after his sister's coronation he was given a more central role in serving
King Edward.

It started with moves in a diplomatic game, brilliantly recorded: 'One
April morning in 1465 Lord Scales was holding converse with the Queen,
kneeling before her with his bonnet sitting on the floor beside him. Suddenly,
the ladies of the court surrounded him; one of them tied around his shapely
thigh a collar of gold and pearls and dropped in his bonnet a little roll of
parchment bound with gold thread.'[2] It was a petition asking Anthony to challenge Antoine 'le grand bâtard', the Bastard of Burgundy, 'a Knight of great
renown', to a two-day joust. Anthony was enthusiastic and so a herald rode
off to deliver his challenge. The Bastard, who had recently returned from a
crusade against the Moors, also liked the idea.[3] But, duty before pleasure, the
joust was for the future, as the Bastard was presently occupied, first in the war
of the Public Weal (against France) and then in the destruction of Dinant. So
it was a further two years before four Burgundian ships dressed with fluttering
pennants brought the Bastard and his party, 400 of them, across the Channel
and up the Thames to London. They stayed at the Bishop of Salisbury's palace
in Fleet Street which was 'richly apparelled with arras and hanged with beds
of cloth of gold'.

Tournaments were spectacular events designed to provide popular entertainment and a focus of national interest, as well as having a political purpose.

5. The start of a joust. The combatant gets final instructions.

England had enjoyed six years of Edward's rule, the finances were back in order and it was time to show off. There had been a tournament at Eltham in April, four against four, where the King and Anthony had fought on the same side.[4] But this one was going to be *the* spectacular, to take place at Smithfield where the lists, an area 90 yards (82 metres) long and 80 yards (73 metres) wide, had been carefully prepared and smoothed out with gravel. There were two grandstands, one for the king and court, the other for the mayor and citizens. They had cost a lavish £90 to construct.

On Thursday 11 June 1467 the stands were full and the crowds agog. Olivier de la Marche, who was with the Bastard, particularly approved the royal stand and reported it to be 'very spacious and made in such a manner that there was an ascent by steps to the upper part where the King sat. He was clothed in purple, having the Garter on his thigh and a thick staff in his hand; and truly he seemed a person well worthy to be King for he was a tall handsome Prince, Kingly in manner. An earl held the Sword of State before him, a little on one side and around his throne were grouped twenty or twenty five councillors all with white hair.'

Below the King, sitting in massed ranks, were nobles, knights and squires. The Archers of the Crown were on parade and heralds, the Kings of Arms in full regalia complete with their crowns, were at each corner. The Earl of Worcester, as Constable of England, was the Master of Ceremony and the previous May he had issued new rules for jousts and tourneys, so everyone was clear about how affairs should be conducted.

The first to ride into the lists were the Duke of Clarence and the Earl of Arundel, each carrying a helmet for the Champion. Other lords carrying his battle-axe, lances and sword followed them, together with his nine horses, ridden by pages, all in flamboyant trappings. Anthony rode in alone; his horse had trappings 'of white cloth of gold, with a cross of Saint George of crimson velvet, bordered with a fringe of gold half a foot long'. He did reverence to his king before going to his blue satin pavilion to arm. The Bastard, wearing the ducal arms, and his entourage made an equally impressive entrance.[5]

Eventually the two champions, encased in *alwite* – gleaming bleached – plate armour[6] and mounted on their chargers, were ready at opposite ends of the lists, the horses no doubt snorting and stamping and the crowd expectant. When the trumpets sounded, the contestants loosed their reins and spurred their chargers forward. Their shields up and lances couched, they thundered towards each other ... and missed completely. Giving up their lances and heaviest armour, they drew their swords and charged again. This time they crashed together. The Bastard's horse gashed its nostril on Scales's saddle;

the 'pain was so bad that the horse reared up and fell over backwards'. The Burgundian was extracted from under his unconscious horse and Anthony was obliged to prove he had not resorted to dirty tricks. The King offered the discomforted Burgundian another mount.[7] 'It is no season,' said the Bastard and muttered to his friend, Olivier de la Marche, 'Doubt not, he has fought a beast today, tomorrow he shall fight a man.'

The next day they resumed the tournament and set to with their battle-axes. These were poleaxes or 'head' axes, beautifully balanced weapons, some 4ft 6in (140cm) long with a head which combined a steel spike on the length for thrusting, an axe blade on one side and a hammer head on the other, used either for striking or tripping.[8] The contest would have had the rhythm of a heavyweight boxing match, ducking and weaving with the added excitement of the wallop and thrust of top-class quarterstaff work or bayonet fighting.

Anthony, confident and flamboyant, did not bother to lower his visor and the spectators loved it. The contest was furious and became so violent that the King thought it should be stopped for fear of serious injury so shouted, 'Whoa!' and threw his staff down between them. Yet the combatants continued to exchange 'two or three great strokes' before breaking off their fight.[9] Eventually the heated warriors were persuaded to take each other by the hand and promise 'to love together as brothers in arms'.

'The Lord Scales had the worship of the field',[10] but there was great debate over who had done best. The English believed Anthony was starting to hurt the Bastard, while the Burgundians took the opposite view. 'Ask of them that felt the strokes, they can tell you best,' suggests one contemporary scribe, while Fabyan reported that Anthony had 'the point of his axe in the visor of the Bastard's helmet and so by force was likely to have born him down'. Young Edward was then about nine years old and must have felt immensely proud of his elder brother.

The *Excerpta Historica* reports: 'As for the King and Queen, they had caused a supper to be prepared on the second day of the tournament in the Grocers' Hall; and thither came the ladies sixty or four score, of such noble houses that the least was the daughter of a Baron. And the supper was plentiful; and Mons. [Monsieur] The Bastard and his people feasted greatly and honourably.'[11]

There were other combatants who followed after the stars: the next pair who fought on foot on the Saturday and mounted on Sunday were Louis de Bretelles for Anthony and Jean de Chassa for the Bastard (de Chassa switched allegiance from Burgundy to France in 1470 and two years later was the Grand Senechal of Provence who arranged for the building of the towers at St Tropez).

6. Weapon training: the poleaxe. Six illustrations of close-quarter
combat from Talhoffer's *Fechtbuch* of 1467.

King Edward had almost certainly engineered the original challenge and now used the occasion for informal talks on an alliance with Burgundy, one of England's traditional allies. There had been a freeze in relations because her ruler, Duke Philip, the Bastard's father, had Lancastrian blood on his mother's side and disapproved of the Yorkist regime.

Meanwhile the social whirl went on, 'and Mons. The Bastard prayed the ladies to dine on the next Sunday, and especially the Queen and her sisters: and he made great preparation'. But the celebrations were cut short. The Bastard was urgently recalled to Burgundy because his father, Duke Philip 'the Good', had died on 15 June 1467. Some of the ladies may well have been disappointed, as Antoine loved women, rather like his father who had 24 documented mistresses. Indeed, the following year at the chapter of the Golden Fleece, the Bastard was admonished for 'fornication and adultery', despite his 'valour, prowess and prudence and several other good habits and virtues'.

Three months later Anthony sailed to Burgundy at the head of an embassy to arrange the marriage of the King's sister, Margaret, to the new Duke of Burgundy, Charles, the Bastard's half-brother. The embassy, perhaps with Edward as his brother's page, was also tasked with organizing a trade treaty together with a new anti-French alliance between Burgundy, England and the Dukedom of Brittany. The anti-French alliance proved easy to arrange but the dowry, which was eventually agreed at 200,000 gold crowns (£41,666-13s-4d), had to be paid in instalments, and trade agreements took a difficult three months to negotiate. This was probably made harder because apparently Duke Charles did not wish for the marriage, or so reported Philippe de Commines, then a Burgundian advisor.

Eventually it was time for the wedding. Vows were exchanged in the town hall at Damme, a little port just downstream from Bruges, on 3 July 1468; the wedding mass was celebrated and then the party moved on to Bruges. It was a brilliant, courtly and extraordinarily lavish affair that lasted for nine days, with jousts, plays and dinners. The high Gothic crown Margaret brought with her and wore is now kept in Aachen Cathedral. It is a dainty crown of plain polished gold, decorated with a simple jewelled lozenge pattern, bands of pearls and eight huge jewels, above which are eight high spikes, each topped with a five-sided flower. It belongs in a fairy tale.

The Tournament of the Golden Tree was the most elaborate spectacle ever staged by any of the Dukes of Burgundy, and this was the joust that accompanied the wedding celebrations. Anthony broke 11 lances against Adolf of Cleves, a highly regarded fighter (who actually broke 17 and so was declared the winner). The Bastard had decided not to compete against Anthony because they were *frères d'armes*, having fought against each other in the lists, and so he had nominated Adolf to guard the *pas*.

Unfortunately, while the Bastard was watching the event, a horse kicked him and broke his thigh. He did not allow this to spoil the day and insisted the jousts went on. They did, and the final prize was awarded to John Woodville, an elder brother of Edward's, although Olivier de la Marche says that his youth and good looks were the reason. The reports of the banquets show them to have been gargantuan and amazing: one had 30 courses and another had the dishes served in 30 little ships, each of which was a 7ft (213cm) model of a three-masted carrack, floating on a silver lake. And so it went on.[12]

William Caxton was the headman of the English colony in Bruges who formally welcomed Margaret. It is clear from Caxton's own account that he later advised her on a number of matters and they also discussed politics and trade (she was an active dabbler in the cloth trade). More importantly she commissioned him to undertake the translation of the *Recuyell of the Histories of Troy*. There is an engraving that shows Caxton presenting a book to her.[13]

That autumn the new alliance was to be put to the test when Brittany and France started skirmishing along their border. King Edward appointed Anthony, now aged 26, to be 'Captain of the King's armed power proceeding to sea and elsewhere for the resistance of the King's enemies'. The commission was for five knights, 55 men-at-arms, 24 shipmasters, 1,076 sailors and 2,945 archers for three months.[14] Anthony probably took his brother, Edward, as his page, who would then have been ten or 11. This would be logical and the start of the naval experience that would have him commanding the fleet 15 years later.

Faced with an allied front King Louis ostensibly came to terms with Duke Francis of Brittany, but this did not deter Anthony, who took his fleet to sea in October. He cruised the Channel in appalling weather and recaptured Jersey, which had been in French hands for the last six years. Anthony and his fleet were back at the Isle of Wight a month later. But it was unsatisfactory for King Edward: all he had for about £18,000 of expenditure was the reconquest of Jersey, while Duke Charles of Burgundy had proved a most unsatisfactory ally; he had made a private settlement with King Louis (the Treaty of Péronne, October 1468) by which he had undertaken not to aid the English if they invaded France.

Meanwhile Edward's sister, Queen Elizabeth, was very active around the court. She had been given lands worth 4,000 marks a year.[15] and was now busy arranging suitable marriages for her family. Four of her sisters were married to the richest available nobles,[16] while Thomas, her eldest son by her first husband, had married the King's niece, the only child and heiress of the Lancastrian and recently attainted Duke of Exeter. Her second brother, 20-year-old John, had married Warwick's aunt, the immensely rich Dowager Duchess of Norfolk. Some people disapproved, as she was 65 and had already survived three husbands (and would outlive John). Presumably she liked them young.[17]

All in all, it meant that the King had effectively arranged for his wife's family to be raised to a suitable status without funding it himself. These activities irritated much of the establishment, who disliked being upstaged, to say nothing of the upstart Woodvilles having the best available heirs and heiresses. In the fifteenth century marriage was a business aimed at finding suitably rich spouses while love was reserved for dreamy ideals, courtly or adulterous affairs. But apart from marriages, the family gained little direct financial benefit from their royal connection, particularly when compared to noblemen such as the Lords Hastings and Herbert or Warwick's family, the Nevilles, all of whom received far more than the Woodvilles in titles, lands, offices and money.

However, the Woodvilles did make the best use of their easy access to the King and so became powerful lobbyists. Influence was hugely important, and while Warwick, 'the over mighty subject', resented the family and their increasing importance, his real problem was his own declining influence.

Apart from finding his in-laws useful, it seems the King also liked them and certainly supported them. For instance, when he sent the Earl of Worcester to govern Ireland in September 1467, it was King Edward who encouraged Worcester to sell two of his key appointments to them, that of Constable of England to Lord Rivers and Constable of Porchester to Anthony. To coincide with this purchase Anthony was granted the Captaincies of the Isle of Wight and Carisbrooke Castle, the latter acquired from a follower of Warwick, the ownership (effectively private equity) in these positions being exchanged for four of the manors from Jacquetta's Bedford inheritance. In these arrangements the King merely renounced the rights of the crown and confirmed the new appointments.

But such moves fuelled the establishment's antipathy towards the Woodvilles, as Mancini surmised, 'mostly because of ... jealousy which arises between those who are equal by birth when there has been a change in their station'. To rub salt into the wound, Lord Rivers was elevated to an earldom and made Treasurer of England. As the court jester joked, 'The Ryvers are so high he could scarce escape them.'[18]

This was the court where Edward Woodville grew up, his family working closely together with his sister right at the centre and the old nobility watching for mistakes. Unfortunately the Queen did make enemies and irritated a number of people. She was certainly manipulative and sometimes unwise, but has been unfairly blamed for a number of events. For instance, she is said to have brought about the death of the Earl of Desmond because he had disparaged her. There is no evidence to show that she had anything to do with his execution. It was simply a matter of Irish politics.

Lord Worcester had been appointed Lieutenant of Ireland in place of Lord Desmond. His job was to sort out the mess of the day. On his arrival in Ireland, he gathered information, made his inquiries, worked out his plan and then held a parliament at Drogheda where Desmond was attainted for, 'Fosterage and alliance with the Irish [enemy], giving the Irish horses, harness [armour] and arms and supporting them against the faithful subjects of the King', i.e. encouraging and arming the rebels.[19]

Desmond was found guilty and sentenced to death. Worcester may have been a ruthless, cunning man but his integrity is unquestioned, and in ordering Desmond's execution he would be certain that he was improving the security of the realm. The Queen's involvement is most unlikely. She could certainly arrange patronage and access but her influence on actual government was no more than marginal at most.

Real government of the country was by the King, with his Council to help and advise.[20] The King's objective was to 'maintain the peace both outward and inward', or so wrote Sir John Fortescue, the leading political theorist of the day. The Council was the inner circle of the powerful men of the land, the great and the good, the forum where the King tested his ideas and gathered a consensus for his plans, which could be tricky when there were 'over-mighty' members such as Warwick.

King Edward's solution was to use the Woodvilles and other friends as a counterbalance, which made Warwick very aware of his declining influence. He issued his own proclamation criticizing the King for 'his estrangement of the great lords of his blood'. The King ignored him, and Earl Rivers as Lord Treasurer remained a powerful member of the King's executive team, which had its hands full trying to keep abreast of Lancastrian plots.

Just such a plot was uncovered in 1468 when 18 people were arrested, among them Sir Thomas Cook, a considerable City merchant living in conspicuous luxury. At the time, Lord Rivers was the Lord Treasurer and so responsible for taking surety and collecting fines. He was certainly so vigorous in the pursuit of his duties that it has led to the affair being used by some historians as proof of the Woodvilles' cupidity.

Unrest continued, with a disgruntled Warwick persuading Duke George of Clarence, the King's brother and heir presumptive, to join him in sedition. The result of their machinations was a rebellion that broke out in June 1469 while King Edward was on a pilgrimage to Our Lady of Walsingham in Norfolk (an important shrine since a vision in 1061; it also claimed to have a phial of the Virgin's milk). The King was dangerously far from his power base and so rode north, recruiting while his companions – including several Woodvilles and presumably young Edward – galloped off to gather aid.

Anthony went to raise men from nearby Middleton, his home outside King's Lynn, while Lord Rivers and his second son, John, were dispatched to the marches of Wales, strong Yorkist territory. There had been marching, counter-marching, skirmishes and battles that ended in a royal disaster. The King could only order his little group of followers to split up and run for cover.

Warwick was a ruthless and arrogant adversary. He executed men as he felt inclined and without the slightest regard for the laws of either God or the land. Lord Pembroke and his brother, Sir Richard Herbert, were caught, taken to Northampton and beheaded. Lord Devon was captured and executed. Lord Rivers and John Woodville were caught beyond the Severn, taken to Warwick and Clarence at Coventry and then executed. John, with his drooping moustache, may lie in the church at Grafton with the other Woodville tombs.[21]

The King was caught at Olney on his way to London. Appearing to accept defeat, he was put under house arrest at Warwick Castle. But the Earl soon found it difficult to control the country without a cooperative head of state. Law and order broke down, there was rioting and powerful men took or tried to take what they wanted. The Duke of Norfolk laid siege to the Pastons at Caistor Castle; the Duke of Clarence organized an attack on Anthony's house at Middleton; Berkeleys fought Talbots in Gloucestershire and Stanleys fought Harringtons in Lancashire. There was rebellion in the north and fear of rebellion in Wales.

To stop the chaos Warwick needed formal royal authority, and it was this that gave the King his chance. Assenting to a number of measures, he then sent for his Council and announced he was going to London. Warwick, nonplussed, let him go, and so by force of personality the King was back in power by late October. The Milanese ambassador at the French court was amazed:

> From England we never hear one thing like another, but always more different than day is from night. The last intelligence received thence by the king here is that the Earl of Warwick had gone north to take possession of the castles and estates of those lords whom he had caused to be beheaded. The King of England was with him, going freely to amuse himself by hunting wherever he

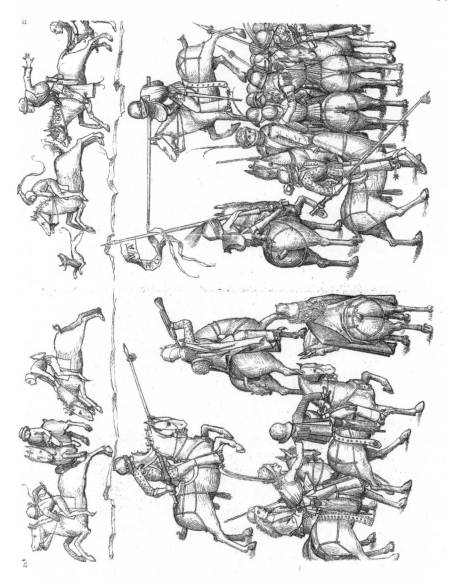

7. Lance practice with a horse race above. Two men-at-arms prepare for
a practice joust with a trumpeter while a horse race happens above. Note the
fashion of the top of the thigh boots turned down at the knee.

chose. One day, being in the country, he took the road towards London, and
entered that city, where he was very gladly and cordially received, as it seems
that the king is much beloved by the men of that city, while the earl is hated.[22]

Anthony became the head of the family as the second Earl Rivers and
was also made Hereditary Constable of England, although he immediately
resigned that position to Duke Richard of Gloucester, the King's youngest
brother. Already a Knight of the Garter, a large landowner, Captain of the
Isle of Wight, Constable of both Carisbrooke and Porchester Castles, Anthony
was an important figure with particular responsibility for a crucial part of the
coast.

Young Edward Woodville would then have been about 12, which was the
age when noble boys moved from paging to squiring, when they learned to
wear their armour and to ride cleanly and surely.

> At fourteen they hunt the deer; and catch on hardiness ...
> At sixteen year to war and to wage, to joust and ride, and castles to assail.[23]

Some started even younger, such as Anthony's late brother-in-law, Thomas
Scales the younger, who was killed in single combat at the age of 15.

The evidence that makes Edward squire to Anthony is circumstantial:
Edward was squire to someone and his brother is the obvious candidate. It
seems that they were together on expeditions to Brittany and Portugal when
Edward was of squiring age; also Anthony's later patronage and the will he
wrote the night before he was executed (1483) demonstrate how close the
relationship was. Edward's squiring started around 1470 in a period of unpre-
dictable politics, vividly described in the Paston letters as 'a queasy world'.

Although for the ordinary person England seems to have been a much better
place to live than France, Sir John Fortescue, the earliest English constitutional lawyer, was in exile with Queen Margaret in the 1460s and wrote for
the instruction of the young Prince Edward (of Lancaster):

> You remember, most admirable prince, you have seen how rich in fruits are
> the villages and towns of the Kingdom of France, whilst you were travelling
> there, but so burdened by the men-at-arms and their horses of the king that
> you could be entertained in scarcely any but the great towns. There you
> learned from the inhabitants that those men ... pay absolutely nothing for the
> expenses ... and what is worse they compelled the inhabitants ... to supply
> them ... with wines, meats etc ... if any declined to do so, they were quickly
> compelled by cudgelling. Moreover the king does not suffer anyone to eat salt
> unless he buys it from the king himself at a price fixed by his pleasure. ...
> Furthermore all the inhabitants give to the king a fourth part of all wines. ...

In addition each village maintains at least two archers ... equipped to serve the king in his wars etc ... in England, no one billets himself in another's house ... in public hostelries where he will pay in full. ... Nor does anyone take with impunity the goods of another ... nor is anyone hindered from providing himself with salt or any goods what ever. ... The king may take necessaries at reasonable price. ... Because by those laws he cannot despoil any of his subjects. ... Nor does the king ... impose tallages, subsidies or any other burdens whatever on his subjects, nor change their laws, nor make new ones, without concession or assent of his whole real expressed in his parliament.' [24]

No wonder the Lancastrians were keen to return. It is hardly surprising that plotting and revolution continued. Warwick had been forgiven for his earlier revolt, but despite this he again intrigued and fostered rebellion. This time 'the king prevailed', so Warwick and Clarence were obliged to turn tail in mid-April. 'They fled West to the coast, boarded ships there and went towards Southampton, where they were expecting one of Warwick's great ships called the Trinity. However, Anthony, Lord Scales was sent there on the King's order; he fought with the Duke and the Earl and captured their ships with many men on them. So the Duke and the Earl were forced to flee to France.' [25]

Anthony, now Earl Rivers, and Edward must have taken great pleasure in chasing Warwick round Southampton Water and capturing 20 of his followers. The Earl of Worcester, who had been recalled from Ireland, was sent to deal with the prisoners. He tried and convicted them, had them executed and had their heads and trunks impaled on stakes and displayed at Southampton for three weeks as an example to others. It did not endear him to the locals, but Lord Worcester was not a man to court popularity; indeed he was indifferent to public opinion. He was an intellectual, a collector of books and manuscripts, translator of Cicero, Caesar and a novel by Buonaccorso. He had been a successful general, admiral and Treasurer of England, spent three years studying in Italy – 1458–61, which was a sensible time to be away – and visited Jerusalem, all before he was 30. Caxton tells us that 'he flowered in virtue and cunning'. He was also a friend of Anthony's who is credited with having Caxton eulogize him ten years later. [26]

With the crisis far from over and the ringleaders still on the loose, the King proclaimed that whoever captured them would have a reward of land to value of £100 annually or £1,000 in ready money. Warwick, however, had no intention of being caught. As he passed through Wiltshire his men came upon Anthony Woodville and a Lord Audley, who they captured and sent on to Warder Castle for execution. Fortunately a Dorset man came in the night 'with a good company of hardy fellows ... [and] found means to deliver these two lords from captivity'.[27] It sounds a very lucky escape.

Meanwhile Warwick had reached France and was joined by his cousin, the Bastard of Fauconberg, who had deserted from the English fleet with several ships. He had captured a number of Burgundian ships, been chased by what was left of the English navy and finally anchored in the Seine in May.

At this stage Anthony, already in charge of the Isle of Wight and Porchester, was appointed governor general of Calais with the commission to organize naval operations in the Channel. He arranged a blockade against the French ports and patrolled aggressively over the next few months. Sailing into the Seine he fought Warwick's fleet, inflicting casualties and capturing prizes (for return to the Burgundians). The tub-like little ships will have been driven crab-wise by gales roaring up the Channel, buffeted by waves, and the men-at-arms would have to be very sure footed to board a rolling and pitching enemy ship, particularly wearing 50lbs (20kg) of armour.[28] To run an operation of this sort required considerable organizational ability and an efficient staff, and young Edward probably served in an aide-de-camp role to Anthony – more useful naval experience.

Sea battles were the business of the very brave, for they usually ended in either victory or death. Even if you avoided being killed by the enemy, the open sea was a dangerous place for a man in armour. Froissart described an earlier engagement which gives a sense of the action. A big enemy ship under full sail was bearing down on the English ship which decided to *joust*. They crashed together and the English ship would have been crushed but for its sturdy construction. They rebounded from the collision but the castles on the mastheads had became entwined. The enemy's mast shattered, throwing the soldiers from its top castle into the sea. Then the English ship was leaking very badly so they threw hooks and chains, grappled the big enemy ship and fought their way on board where there was ferocious hand-to-hand combat. The English captured the enemy ship and threw its defenders into the sea.[29] Martorell in *Tirant Lo Blanc* gives a another vivid description: 'Both ships heaved boiling pitch at each other and fought without pause until there were so many lances, shields and quarrels floating in the sea that the corpses could not sink.'

While these sea battles raged, Warwick was in Paris with the arch intriguer King Louis, who was delighted to destabilize Edward by orchestrating reconciliation between Warwick and the exiled Lancastrian Queen Margaret. On 9 September 1470 a storm broke the English blockade, enabling Warwick with an invading army to sail for England. Queen Margaret and her son, Prince

Edward, who was now engaged to Warwick's daughter, were shortly to follow. The Lancastrian Earls of Pembroke and Oxford were allied with the previously staunch Yorkist Warwick; it was going to be an uneasy relationship.

There had been sporadic rebellion in the north, and King Edward was there when his enemies landed in the West Country. They declared Henry VI to be King – again. Popular sympathy seems to have veered towards the silver-tongued Warwick and the Lancastrians. The Lords Shrewsbury and Stanley declared for King Henry and there were outbreaks of violence in Kent. King Edward set out from York but detoured to meet Warwick's brother. The latter, previously loyal, had secretly changed sides, assembled troops and made a night march to surprise and capture the King. Luckily a sergeant of the Royal Minstrels discovered the plan and warned the King, who with a few followers including Gloucester, Hastings and Anthony Woodville (and so probably young Edward) galloped away to the east coast.

On the north shore of The Wash they found small boats and escaped to sea, rode out a storm during the night and reached King's Lynn on Sunday 30 September 1470.[30] Anthony's home at Middleton is close to Lynn and it seems likely they stayed there until the Tuesday when they were able to arrange fishing boats to sail for Burgundy. King Edward later told Philippe de Commines that he had been quartered in 'a building that could only be entered by a bridge'. This sounds like Middleton.

The excitement was not over, for Easterling ships[31] sighted them and crammed on sail in pursuit. The tide was out, so the little flotilla was chased on to the beaches of Alkmaar in North Holland. The Easterlings beached beside them and were ready to board when Louis de Gruthuyse, the Burgundian governor, fortunately appeared, just in time to warn the Easterlings away.

For three months the evacuees lay low in The Hague. From England came word that Warwick had wheeled the feeble-minded King Henry, in his old blue coat, out of retirement in the Tower.[32] However, there were two pieces of good news. Edward's queen, Elizabeth (Anthony's and Edward's sister), had given birth to a son while in sanctuary and there was already friction between Warwick and the Lancastrians. But sadly the brilliant Earl of Worcester had been caught and condemned. The Earl was impassive as he was taken through violent crowds to his execution. On the scaffold an Italian friar reproached him for his past cruelty, to which he replied coldly, 'I have governed my actions for the good of the State.' Then he turned to the executioner and asked him to use three strokes to do his work, 'in honour of the Trinity'. It was later commented: 'Then did the axe at one blow cut off more learning than was left in the heads of all the surviving nobility.'[33] His tomb is by the high altar in Ely

Cathedral, where he lies between two wives, his face strong and bony.

Over in France, King Louis was enjoying the novelty of having England on his side with his new ally, Warwick, in power and so felt able to renew his war on Burgundy. Duke Charles of Burgundy, later nicknamed Le Téméraire ('The Bold One' or perhaps 'The Rash One'), was alarmed by the turn of events and gave up his supposed neutrality in the English power game.[34] In practice Duke Charles had not been neutral: Milanese intelligence noted that he had written to England offering to hand over King Edward but he changed position and 'almost by compulsion helped King Edward'. Anyway now he lent money – the equivalent of about £4,000 English – to King Edward. It was enough to fund a small force and so invasion planning started.

Royal messengers went out to potential allies and providers, Burgundian and Easterling ships were hired, Flemish gunners recruited and munitions bought. Anthony Woodville and William Hastings had responsibility for commissioning the fleet and equipping the invasion force, and anyone who was part of that team – as young Edward probably was – would have been very busy. Gathering together such a force on a restricted budget is time consuming and difficult work. At one point Anthony was in Bruges, the financial capital of northern Europe, bargaining for more ships and was probably helped by William Caxton, then governor of the English merchants there.[35] By March 1471 the invasion army was ready. It consisted of 900 Englishmen and 300 Flemings, armed with 'handguns'. They sailed from Flushing in four carracks and 14 little ships. Anthony was captain of *La Calanta*, a Spanish carrack hired from an English merchant and carrying 200 soldiers.

The fleet sailed to the Norfolk coast and a scouting party was put ashore at Cromer. They discovered Lancastrian forces in control, so the King decided his chances would be better in Yorkshire, where he would not be expected as he had no links with the county and it was Warwick's traditional territory. It was a daring plan and must have seemed over-bold when a March storm scattered the ships that night. In the grey dawn of the following day lone ships landed where they could. Anthony was 14 miles from the King, but either by good luck or good planning they all met up at Ravenspur on the Humber and then marched towards York.

However, the city closed its gates and the King had to use his charm to persuade its citizens that he had only come to take up his dukedom of York. You can just see the councillors listening to his plea with scepticism – they knew what he was after and were very uneasy. Nevertheless, after discussion, they allowed him and a few others in, although the army had to camp outside.

This unpropitious start was not improved when the army marched south and word came of two armies between them and London. They dodged one at Tadcaster and slipped into Nottingham to gather recruits. There they heard news of other enemy armies converging on them. It made the invasion seem a forlorn hope and its chances were not rated high by observers.

'It is a difficult matter to go out by the door and then try to enter by the window. They think he will leave his skin there,' commented the Milanese ambassador in France. But the King was a far better strategist then his opponents. He marched east. This was a feint that fooled the Earl of Oxford, whose prompt retreat gave Edward the chance to double back and go straight for the Earl of Warwick, who was coming south to meet the others. Warwick, deciding on discretion rather than valour, shut himself up safely inside Coventry to wait for Oxford or Clarence, King Edward's brother, to join him.

George, Duke of Clarence was marching north with 4,000 men. The King's little army turned to meet him and at Banbury the two armies came face to face. But the brothers, instead of fighting, threw their arms around each other and King Edward achieved both reconciliation and reinforcements.

This reconciliation was critical to Edward's success. It was public, dramatic and had been carefully arranged by an unnamed lady who, nine months previously, had landed at Calais where the governor was a trusted lieutenant of Warwick. He was told she had come to comfort the poor Duchess of Clarence who had given birth to a stillborn son on the voyage from England. The governor was suspicious and sent for her. Under interrogation she confessed to being on a secret mission for the King, who was eager to make peace with Warwick. She had documents to prove her story and, as emissary for the King, she was empowered to offer all sorts of attractive concessions. The governor was convinced and sent her on to Paris where Warwick was plotting. However, instead of going to Paris, she rode through hostile France and found Clarence in Normandy. Philippe de Commines says she was young, one of the Duchess's ladies and 'neither light headed nor frivolous'. He was very impressed by her adroitness.

Her mission was not to comfort the Duchess or to offer concessions to Warwick; it was to persuade Clarence to return to his family allegiance. She convinced him of his brother's goodwill and was able to persuade him that all would be forgiven if he deserted Warwick, his father-in-law. Clarence, who was not enjoying life in exile and felt neglected by Warwick, sent her back with a promise that he would show his allegiance at a propitious moment. This turned out to be nine months later outside Banbury.[36] No more is known about the unnamed lady negotiator, but Edward loved women and admired bravery so, no doubt, she was well rewarded.

After acquiring his brother's army, King Edward made the unexpected move of marching south to London. The city was surprised and uneasy, and the Lord Mayor took to his bed and refused to exercise his authority. But there were others who made the King welcome. Commines points out that many of the merchants were keen to have their biggest debtor back and in power. He also says 'the influence of many ladies of rank and the wives of rich citizens, formerly very good friends of his, won over their husbands and relatives'.

Left to their own devices, Warwick and the Lancastrians joined together and marched south, tempted by Edward's move. Just north of Barnet they occupied an east-to-west ridge and sent out scouts. King Edward and his army had spent just 48 hours in London before they marched north. They threw Warwick's scouts out of Barnet and continued straight through. It was pitch dark but somehow the King's officers formed the army into battle lines that were much closer to Warwick than he realized. Warwick, knowing they were out there somewhere, ordered a night-long artillery bombardment but this sailed over the top of Edward's men, who were ordered to keep quiet.

Easter morning (13 April 1471) dawned thick with mist and between 4 and 5 o'clock King Edward, 'committed his cause and quarrel to Almighty God, advanced banners, did blow trumpets and set upon them first with shot and then, and soon, they joined and came to hand strokes'.[37]

Knowing what really happened is long lost in the fog of history. Probably the cannons stopped firing because no one could see anything. Then there was a pause while both sides were lined up. The trumpets blew and the armies charged into the fog, completely unaware that the two formations were not centred on each other. The lines crashed together and the Yorkist right then found they overlapped enough to turn their enemy's flank, which sent an urgent message to Warwick who dispatched part of the reserve to help. On the Yorkist left, where Hastings commanded, the Lancastrian Oxford had overlapped and swung into the Yorkist flank, forcing them to break and run. Oxford's men went off in hot pursuit, some reaching Barnet where they began plundering.

Eventually Oxford managed to gather some 500 horsemen together and sent word to Warwick that he was returning to attack the enemy's rear. After two hours of hard fighting the battle seemed to be going Warwick's way. The weight of more men was telling in the centre, his right had won and his left was holding. But the whole battle line had swung from east–west to north–south.

Oxford and his men rode up through the fog unaware that the battle lines had slewed 90 degrees. The Lancastrian right – at the south of their line – saw Oxford's badge, a star with rays, mistook it for the 'Sun of York' and loosed a flight of arrows at the horsemen who, fearing the worst, then charged the archers. There were cries of treason that unbalanced the Lancastrian line. King Edward, fighting in the centre, saw the hesitation, seized the moment and led a charge with all he had. It broke the enemy line which turned to flight.[38]

Warwick was discovered by a couple of Yorkist foot soldiers lumbering off the battlefield to look for his horse. Seeing a lonely, tired man weighed down with valuable armour,[39] hardly able to see through his visor, they knocked him over, probably with an axe blow to the un-armoured backs of his legs and then prized open his visor. A dagger driven into his eye delivered death and then his rich armour was stripped off.[40] Edward Hall wrote an epitaph: 'But death did one thing that life could not do, for by death he had rest, peace, quietness and tranquillity, which his life [he] ever abhorred and could not suffer or abide.'

Barnet was the first battle in which the 19-year-old Duke Richard of Gloucester fought. He is said to have distinguished himself commanding the Yorkist right. Anthony Woodville is recorded as having 'fought with great valour' and been wounded.[41] Edward Woodville, at 12 years old, might just have been there, but if he was then he should have been 'in attendance' i.e. with the baggage train.

The next threat was from the west where King Henry's queen, the 'She-Wolf of France', was beating the Lancastrian drum. Her invasion, delayed by the weather and lethargy, landed two days after the defeat at Barnet, but despite this she was assured that the Lancastrians still had an excellent opportunity. West Countrymen flocked to her standard and she marched north to join Earl Jasper of Pembroke's Welsh army. King Edward moved quickly to confront the enemy, leaving Anthony at the Tower of London to recover from his wound and guard the royal back.

On Wednesday 24 April, as the King marched west, a proclamation was sent throughout the land promising death and forfeiture to anyone succouring 'Margaret, calling herself Queen, which is a Frenchwoman born'. The King's objective was to fight her army before it recruited any more dissidents or joined up with the Welshmen. The objective of the Queen and her advisors was to avoid him until they could join up with the Welshmen. The Lancastrians dodged, but King Edward eventually caught them on 4 May by the Severn crossing at Tewkesbury.[42]

The day was 'right an hot' and the King's army had marched or ridden the last 35 miles in 12 hours while the Lancastrians had covered 24 miles in 16 hours, all of them in full fighting order. A complete set of field armour then weighed around 50lbs (23kg), a short mail coat 20lbs (9kg) and a helmet around 5lbs (2kg).

It was a bitter, bloody fight. The Lancastrian right wing tried a surprise attack that might have worked if it had been supported by the centre, but it was not and the wing was routed. The Duke of Somerset, its commander, who struggled back to his own side, was so angry with his commander-in-chief that he went and 'cleaved' him on his helmet. It was a resounding victory for King Edward. Even the Lancastrian heir, the 17-year-old Prince of Wales, had been killed in the battle and other loose ends were dealt with expeditiously, the King's men executing such die-hard Lancastrians notables as they found. Indeed, they found and dealt with some who had made their way to sanctuary at the Abbey and the unfortunate Queen Margaret was picked up the following day.

Meanwhile London was under attack from Warwick's half-brother, the Bastard of Fauconberg. His fleet had brought over part of the Calais garrison, and the men of Kent, always prone to rebellion, marched. His cannon bombarded the City and his men attacked over London Bridge and at Bishopsgate. They burned the houses on the bridge between the outer gate and the drawbridge but they got no further.

Anthony and his men-at-arms, perhaps 400 of them, sallied out from the Tower postern and attacked the rebels from behind. The rebels were unbalanced and this gave the Londoners the opportunity to open the gates and charge out. Some rebels were trapped on the bridge and killed, others escaped. There was a running fight along Southwark High Street but then the rebels turned and fled across the open fields towards Poplar. At Blackheath the Bastard rallied his forces but then, learning of the approach of King Edward and his victorious army, withdrew to his ships, leaving the Mayor of Canterbury and the men of Kent to their fate.

The King entered his capital in triumph with his two brothers, followed by three dukes, six earls, 16 barons, 'a host of horsemen' and his trophy, the captured Queen Margaret in her carriage. She was later sold to King Louis for £10,000.

The mayor and 11 aldermen were knighted to celebrate their doughty defence of the city but, during the euphoria of the victory night, the unfortunate King Henry died in the Tower while Duke Richard of Gloucester was in close attendance. There is some uncertainty about how Henry came to die. Thomas More believed Richard killed him 'with his own hands'. Fabyan says he was 'sticked with a dagger' by Richard himself, and Warkworth reports that he 'was put to death between 11 and 12 o'clock when Duke Richard of Gloucester was at the Tower'.

There was further tidying up to be done. As the Lancastrian sympathizer Fabyan noted, 'such as were rich were hanged by the purse and the other that were needy were hanged by the neck'. In reality far more were pardoned than punished. For instance, Sir John Fortescue, who had been captured at Tewkesbury, was, to many people's surprise, pardoned and wrote a recantation of his Lancastrian views that was particularly useful for King Edward's public-relations campaign.

'The Recoverie of England' was a setback for the French, and when the Milanese ambassador commiserated with King Louis, he was told with a sigh, 'I am busy with new schemes, it is impossible to fight against fortune.'

For the rest of King Edward's reign England remained peaceful. After all, who would challenge such a king, who was unbeaten in battle? According to Charles Oman, 'he was not only a good tactician, a hard fighter, and a genial leader of men, much loved by his troops, but he was one of the first mediaeval generals who showed a complete appreciation of the value of time in war. His marches were even more remarkable than his battles.' [43]

The only pretender was young Henry Tudor but his claim was so obscure that no one took it seriously and, anyway, he and his uncle Jasper were being chased westward into furthest Wales. The one remaining problem was the Calais garrison which, despite having been in open revolt, had sent its submission to the King in expectation of an easy pardon.

Anthony Woodville, as Captain of Calais, should have gone to deal with the truculent soldiers, but surprisingly declared he would 'to be at a day upon the Saracens'. Presumably this was the result of a vow made when the future looked bleak. He was a man who took his faith very seriously and if he had come to an agreement with God then he was going to honour it. Nevertheless it was still only a private crusade and the King was furious. He could not understand it;[44] what if the Portuguese were planning another expedition against Tangier? It mattered little to him that Tangier had been their goal ever since they had started their conquest of the Moroccan Atlantic ports[45] — he had a country to run.

King Edward remained unimpressed by the importance of the vow or the opportunity, and refused to give Anthony permission to go. He reassigned the Captaincy of Calais to Hastings on 17 July (this may just have been a re-arrangement of duties as Calais needed a resident captain) but Anthony seems not to have been included in the new round of royal rewards. However, he remained determined, arguing that the fighting was over in England. John Paston wrote home reporting, 'The King is not best pleased with him ... he [Anthony] desires to depart ... the King has said ... whenever he has most to do then Lord Scales will soon ask leave to depart ... it is most because of cowardice.' 'Cowardice', however, is rather unfair and bad tempered in the light of Anthony's form, particularly as he had been noted as fighting 'with great valour' at Barnet and beating rebels around London.

In August the Portuguese sailed for Morocco. After a ferocious and bloody attack they captured one key stronghold that so dispirited the Moors that Tangier itself fell shortly after. They returned home in great glory.[46] In early September the row between the King and Anthony seems to have been settled: 'Lord Rivers has licence to go to Portugale now within this seven night.' It was not until October, however, that the 'safe conduct for the King's kinsman ... who is going to fight the infidels' was issued, and there were further delays until at last John Paston reported, 'Men say Lord Rivers shipped on Christmas Eve to Portugal; I am not certain.'

Young Edward almost certainly sailed with his brother, although by the time they arrived it was too late for the honours of Tangier and the Portuguese African campaign. There was no Moor fighting in Spain, as King Henry IV, 'the Impotent' of Castile, lived up to his name and did nothing. Perhaps Anthony – and Edward – had a good holiday with a tournament or two for entertainment. Perhaps it was enough for Anthony to feel his vow was redeemed, but whatever they did it gave Edward the opportunity to make a friend of the future King João II who was to greet him so warmly 15 years later. Anyway, that year the Portuguese had good cause for celebration, for not only had they achieved their military goal in Morocco but had also discovered gold in West Africa.

Meanwhile the Speaker of the House of Commons praised the Queen for her 'womanly behaviour and great constancy' while her husband 'our most dread and liege lord the King Edward iiii', had been beyond the sea.[47] He also expressed 'the great joy and surety to this his land' for the birth of the prince; he noted the 'knightly demeninge' of Clarence and Gloucester and then 'the constant faith of my lords Rivers and Hastings'.[48] But what next for Edward Woodville now that he was reaching a useful age? The King was, of course, the fountain of patronage *and* his brother-in-law.

King Edward sounds a most engaging man. There is a delightful description of him taking a guest to the Queen's apartments. She was playing marbles with some of her ladies, others were dancing and some were playing skittles with ivory pins, his daughter Elizabeth among them.[49] The King, like any happy father, swept the little eight-year-old up in a dance. He was a big affable man who, reported Mancini, 'was so genial in his greeting that, when he saw a newcomer bewildered by his regal appearance and royal pomp, he would give him courage to speak by laying a kindly hand on his shoulder'.

He would certainly want to help his young brother-in-law who was now approaching the age when young noblemen were knighted and could become useful.

PRINCES AND PEERS

E dward Woodville was knighted some time in the first half of 1472. Knighthoods were often conferred on saints' days, and St George's Day (23 April) would be entirely appropriate. This was a seminal moment in Edward's life and, with his brother interested in matters spiritual, Edward would not be taking his vows lightly.

The ceremony would begin in the evening with a vigil, in church, with his arms beside him. It continued the next day with a bath of purification before he was dressed in full armour. Properly dressed, he would be conducted to church by two sponsors – perhaps one was Anthony – where he would hear high mass. After mass Edward knelt before his king who then dubbed him.[2] The words used by King Edward would be on the lines of, 'I now dub thee knight in the name of God and Saint George. Be faithful, bold and fortunate.' His sword would be belted round his waist and his new gold spurs, that only knights were entitled to wear, strapped to his heels. This strapping was often done by some noble lady who wished the knight well, in this case it might have been by his sister, the Queen.

The main commandments to which Edward would bind himself, in the name of God and the saints, were not to accept false judgement or be party to any form of treason; to honour all women and be ready to aid them to the limit of his power; to hear a mass every day and fast on Fridays (when possible). These were serious commitments undertaken by a young man who believed in the Trinity, also in Salvation and Hell. In addition there may have been further particular vows and undertakings. King Edward was good at display and inspiring allegiance, and this was an event for both of those; it also pleased some of those he wanted to please, such as the Woodvilles, and cost nothing. Such ceremonies were useful but he needed to replenish his treasure chest.

The King had considerable charm and that certainly helped when it came to his financial arrangements. *The Great Chronicle* reports that one rich Suffolk widow raised her tax contribution from £10 to £20 in return for a kiss from the King. Another account describes a widow who offered twice as much 'for thy lovely face' than he was expecting, so he kissed her in gratitude. She was so delighted that she doubled again the contribution. He needed all the money he could raise and it was not usually that easy. The coffers had been empty when he took the throne and he used a variety of devices to increase the royal revenues.[3] He also kept expenditure down by avoiding where he could the expense of war.

However, in March 1472 there was a plea from Duke Francis of Brittany for help against the French who had been conspiring. King Louis was threatening to invade and had persuaded King James III of Scotland to take 6,000 men to seize part of Brittany. But King Edward, rather than commit his realm, gave permission (on 20 June 1472) for his kinsman: 'Anthony Wydville, Earl of Rivers may take 1,000 men at arms and archers to Brittany and other parts beyond the seas at his own expense with captains appointed by him to go where he pleases.'[4]

Perhaps this was by way of pecuniary punishment for the trip to Portugal; the cost of contracting the men would have been around £2,500 to £3,000, plus rations and ship hire, but he would probably recover the costs from Duke Francis. Anyway the task would have appealed to Anthony, who was recently back from his disappointing 'day upon the Saracens'.

He raised his troop under the banner of the silver scallop of Scales and sailed to Brittany accompanied by 'Sir Edward Wydville'. This is the first time we hear formally of Edward who, knighted before the expedition sailed, would then be around 14, the age when young noblemen went to war.[5]

When the French invaded, the Bretons and their English allies were ready for them, and after a number of skirmishes the French were forced to withdraw in August. The Scots had not come, as King James had been unable to finance the expedition and neither did his Estates approve of their king gallivanting off abroad. King Edward had been watching closely and presumably had forgiven Anthony for his idiosyncratic behaviour, because he now commissioned him to negotiate the terms under which England would help Brittany. It was an interesting time for Edward to be watching and listening to his brother.

The diplomatic efforts culminated in the Treaty of Châteaugiron (September 1472) which was underpinned by the arrival of 2,000 archers from King Edward. This gave Duke Francis an edge when he negotiated a peace treaty with France in October and, a month later, John Paston was writing from London with the news that Lord Rivers was expected back shortly but had lost many soldiers through *fflyxe* or dysentery. While they were campaigning, the brothers' mother died; she left Edward a manor in Northamptonshire, which he later sold for £200, plus an annuity of £50.[6]

In Brittany Anthony had been given the additional task of getting 'possession of therls of Pembroke and Richmond' who had fled there from Wales after Tewkesbury. King Edward wanted both Tudors, Earl Jasper of Pembroke and Earl Henry of Richmond, under lock and key in England, as Lancastrians on the loose were dangerous. But Duke Francis had given his word for their safety and could not be persuaded to hand them over.

Nevertheless, after much haggling and prevarication, by the following summer England, Burgundy and Brittany had reached agreement on a battle plan against France under which England was to mount an invasion before July the following year. This meant the rest of the summer was free for private activities and so it is hardly surprising that Anthony took himself off on a pilgrimage to Spain and – given 'Sir Edward Wydville's' later interest in Spain – he was most probably accompanied by his brother.

They sailed from Southampton for the Jubilee and Pardon at Santiago de Compostela, the shrine of St James the Greater. Anthony wrote, 'I shipped from Southampton in the month of July the said year, and so sailed from thence till I came into the Spanish sea, there lacking sight of all lands, the wind being good and the weather fair, then for recreation and a passing of time I had delight and asked to read some good history.'

One of his fellow pilgrims was 'Lowys de Bretaylles' or Louis de Bretelles, a Gascon knight who had been in English service since the 1450s.[7] He gave Anthony a French manuscript to while away the time on the voyage. It was titled *Dits Moraulx* and was a compendium of information on a range of philosophers and heroes: Plato, Diogenes, Hippocrates, Alexander the Great and so on. Anthony much appreciated the gift, commenting that it was 'a book that he trusted I should like it right well'. The work has an interesting history, first compiled in a comparable form by an Arab philosopher in Damascus around AD 1053, then translated into Spanish in the thirteenth century, then into Latin and, in the late fourteenth century, into French.

The Cathedral of Santiago was described as 'immense, with four round and two square towers' where there are 'innumerable relics of St James, the most interesting were the sickle with which he was beheaded and his famous banner, already falling into sore decay'. It is 'of a red colour, and on it is painted his image, seated on a white horse and clad in garments of white. On the horse and on the head dress of the rider are to be seen painted shells or scales.'[8] So there was Anthony's scallop of Scales in pride of place at Santiago. No wonder he kept it as his badge even after he became Earl Rivers.

On their return to England appointments were heaped on Anthony: Chief Butler of England[9] and the Receivership of Cornwall – the latter having only recently been surrendered by Lord Hastings. In November Anthony was awarded the greatest honour with his appointment as 'Governor and ruler of the King's first begotten son that he may be virtuously, cunningly and knightly brought up'.[10]

This was a public statement of the King's belief in his brother-in-law's integrity and ability; Anthony was responsible for the prince's education. He thought about his new role: 'After the King's grace command me to give my mine attendance upon my lord the Prince ... when I had leisure I looked upon the said book (*Dits Moraulx*) and at the last concluded in myself to translate it into the English tongue.' His title was *The Dictes and Sayings of the Philosophers*. There was some editing; for instance he omitted Socrates's rather rude observations about women, writing, 'and the said Socrates had many seyings ayenst women which is not translated'.

It is clear that Anthony was an exceptional man and he must have been a wonderful elder brother. Thomas More declared Anthony to be 'a right honourable man, as valiant of hand as politic [prudent] in council', while Philippe de Commines, a senior civil servant, first in Burgundy and then in France, who knew him both socially and professionally, wrote that Anthony was 'un tres gentil chevalier' (a very gentle knight).[11]

Meanwhile the first steps were being taken towards the proposed war. It is fascinating to see how the diplomatic manoeuvring developed various alliances, then moved towards the invasion. However, there seems to have been a secret agenda – King Edward was concocting a plan to extricate England from the war, if necessary.

Anthony was directly involved with some of the diplomacy. The main work began with English embassies going to Naples, Urbino, Hungary and the German emperor, Frederick III. The trade war with the Hanseatic League was brought to a close and Scotland was seduced with promises of gold. At home the justice of the war was propounded and Edward needed money from parliament and recruits.

In the Middle Ages a war had to be a *just* war. Thomas Aquinas had mulled over the matter of a 'just war' in the thirteenth century and, in England, its proof was virtually a legal necessity for requisitioning men and money. War was approved after a public policy had been paraded by the king; the policy had to show a recognizable injustice and be supported by parliament. Of course, the right of spoil rested on the theory that if the king's war was just then the enemy was unjust and so had no rights to property, which was then available to the just.

King James of Scotland had offered to wage war against the English if King

Louis would pay him 60,000 crowns a year (about £12,000), or so the Milanese ambassador reported. King Louis would only offer a conditional 10,000 crowns but would try to arrange a marriage for the Scots heir whom he recommended for one of the Duke of Milan's daughters. The Duke was unimpressed; he did not think it was suitable for his daughter, commenting that Scotland was 'in finibus orbis' (at the ends of the earth). King James was hurt. He needed funds and, having a clear idea of his own importance, offered a treaty to King Edward who was keen to secure his northern frontier and so betrothed his daughter, Cecilia, to the Scots heir.[12]

On the Continent the diplomatic manoeuvring continued apace. King Louis of France and Duke Charles of Burgundy were both up to their tricks, Louis vicariously and Charles boldly. Alsace had revolted and murdered their Burgundian governor, so Duke Charles decided he would deal with the confederacy of German states, starting with the Electorate of Cologne. He assembled 20,000 men, including 6,000 English mercenary archers, and marched to the city of Neuss. It seems he had expected to walk straight in, but the city had other ideas and he was obliged to settle down for a siege.

The German emperor Frederick III and his electors felt this was an unwarranted incursion into their territory so turned up with an army, which was the best King Louis had hoped for. But the Germans sniffed, skirmished and then wondered about going home, as despite repeated promises, Louis had sent no army to join them. Instead of troops, he had sent an envoy to discuss the dismemberment of Burgundy.

The Emperor had listened and sent the envoy back with a convoluted story about a bear and two debtors. But the answer was clear: the Germans were not going to hang about or do the work, they were going home. So that part of the French plan came apart. However, King Louis was having more success with the Swiss. They were happy to take up arms against Burgundy, provided they were properly paid.

Meanwhile embassies from Burgundy, Brittany and England discussed the detail of the anti-French alliance and plans were made. King Edward agreed to invade France while Duke Charles undertook to provide 6,000 men for the campaign. Edward needed more money in his war chest, and his cash-raising arrangements fascinated a Milanese merchant in London who wrote in March 1475:

> he [King Edward] has been very active in the last four months and has discovered an excellent device to raise money. He has plucked out the feathers of his magpies without making them cry out. This autumn the king went into the country, from place to place, and took information of how much

each place could pay. He sent for them all, one by one, and told them that he wished to cross to conquer France and deluded them with other words. Finally, he has so contrived that he obtained money from everyone who has more than £40. Everyone seemed to give willingly.

I have frequently seen our neighbours here summoned before the King; when they went they looked as if they were going to the gallows. When they returned they were joyful, saying they had spoken to the King and the King had spoken to them so benignly that they did not regret the money they had paid.

From what I hear people say, the King's method was to give anyone who went before him a welcome as if he had known him always. After some time the King asked him what he could pay of his free will towards this expedition. If the man offered something proper the king had his notary ready who took down the name and amount. If the king thought otherwise he said: 'Such a one who is poorer than you has paid so much; you who are richer can easily pay more' and thus by fair words the King brought him up to the mark. In this way they say he has extracted a very large amount of money.[13]

On the diplomatic front, King Edward was having trouble with his main ally. Duke Charles of Burgundy had agreed to the plan but now prevaricated, as he was bogged down with his siege. His plan was to get the English to do the fighting and then join in for his share of the spoils. But at least England's back was safe – Scotland was now friendly with the promised marriage and payments of gold.

Anthony was sent to Neuss to persuade the Duke to abandon the siege and stick to the agreement. But Duke Charles was intent on destroying the city and calculated that Edward had gone too far to pull back. He was correct, for the English would sail for France with no more support than his vague promises.[14]

King Edward was assembling an army of some 1,100 men-at-arms and 10,000 archers. This was a strong turn out, with five dukes, five earls, 12 barons, 14 bannerets and 28 knights all bringing lances and archers. There was a 'headquarters' which included artillerymen, heralds, scurries, sergeants-at-arms, surgeons and clerks.[15] In addition to the men, there were munitions: cannons, gunpowder, shot, bows, arrows and all sorts of war materials, even an engine of war for digging trenches that took 50 horses to pull. It must have been colossal but we know no more about it.

The five-year-old Prince Edward of Wales was brought to London, knighted and appointed Guardian of the Realm in the King's absence. His mother was appointed custodian and granted £2,200 to maintain his establishment. This allowed Anthony, the Prince's governor, to join the campaign: his retinue is

8. The imperial army in camp. The emperor (presumably Frederick III, 1415–93) is under his standard. Tents, wagons and artillery carts are drawn up in concentric circles. Soldiers are busy with various activities, including patrolling and gambling.

recorded in the muster roll beside the Scales crest of the scallop shell: 'Therll of Ryvers, 2 knights, 40 lances, 200 archers'.[16]

We know that one of the knights was Louis de Bretelles;[17] the other was almost certainly Edward. The lances would have totalled over 100 horsemen; it meant that his contribution was 300 men or more, a substantial amount and well up to standard for an earl.

Before King Edward sailed he had sent a herald to King Louis with a formal letter of defiance but, interestingly, the herald also had a private word with King Louis about the possibility of coming to terms once there had been enough flag waving. The herald was well looked after and apparently advised King Louis that the men to talk to – at the appropriate time – about reaching an accommodation would be the Lords Howard and Stanley.

Just before the expedition sailed, on Whit Sunday, Edward Woodville and Richard Grey (the Queen's second son) were made Knights of the Bath, while her eldest son, Thomas, was created the Marquis of Dorset. The Bath ceremony was similar to that of becoming a knight, but grander and rather longer: a formal ceremony of sponsorship, bathing, prayer, vigil and then celebration. It finished with the new member being given a white silk scarf which he was to wear until he had performed a deed of prowess; it would then be removed by a noble lady.[18]

The Great Enterprise took three weeks to cross to Calais. They used 500 ships and barges, many of which were hired in the Low Countries by William Caxton, who was 'commissary and agent for the King of England'; the rate agreed was one month's hire paid in advance. The whole force arrived at Calais by 4 July, the date Duke Charles had promised to be there. Not only did the Duke keep them waiting for ten days, but then he arrived without troops and remarked, annoyingly, that with such a fine body of men King Edward could march through to Rome if he pleased. The English marched south alone.

They reached Peronne on the Somme on 6 August and a detachment was sent forward to take over St Quentin. The Count de St Pol, Constable of France (first cousin to Anthony and Edward through their mother), had promised King Edward and Duke Charles that the city would welcome the English but the detachment was met by unwelcoming cannon fire and came limping back empty handed.

According to Commines, the English were naive: 'King Edward and his people had little experience in dealing with French affairs; they practised a rather crude and simple form of statecraft. Hence it was that they were rather slow at seeing through the deceptions that are used here and elsewhere.'

The Count de St Pol had been endeavouring to divide his loyalty between

Burgundy and France but it all spun out of control. Commines says 'he constantly sought to keep both duke and king in a state of fear, using one against the other', with the result that neither trusted him. In this instance King Louis had smelled a rat and put serious pressure on St Pol to conduct the defence. Messengers were flying to and fro.

Duke Charles still provided the English with nothing but empty words. King Edward was angry and worried. He had been let down by Charles, particularly as the French were laying waste to the countryside behind them and summer was drawing to a close; there was a strong argument for strategic withdrawal.

Anthony was at Peronne with the King and the War Council when the contingency plan was implemented. But King Louis had to make the first move towards any negotiated settlement. Luckily the English had a prisoner from the French royal household and this gave the opportunity for finesse. Lords Howard and Stanley released the man and each gave him a gold crown, telling him to particularly recommend them to King Louis.

The signal was understood. Louis immediately sent a messenger to Edward saying France only wished for peace and all his hostile acts had been targeted at the selfish Duke of Burgundy. Also, said the messenger, King Louis quite understood that King Edward had a tricky position at home, but he was sure they could come to a sensible arrangement. The last thing King Louis wanted was war. He had crushed feudal anarchy and secured the imperilled unity of France but Duke Charles remained his rival and his problem. He needed to neutralize England and isolate Burgundy so his subtle mind had worked at the problem.

'He desired to know everything; he forgot nothing.' He rarely used the human touch, unless it suited him. Commines reports him saying, 'Speak to my people? I do not trouble myself with such affairs.' He also observed that King Louis 'dressed so badly that worse was impossible'. Apparently his standard dress was grey fustian, a shabby hat without diamond or pearl, only a lead badge and round his neck a rosary of large wooden beads. Neither does he seem to have been physically attractive: 'small and sharp eyes, a large nose, thin mouth and his cheeks and chin were a little flabby'.[19]

However, his intelligence gathering was exceptional and his chief intelligencer was Tristian L'Hermit. An English ambassador rated L'Hermit a formidable opponent and had warned the governor of Calais ten years earlier: 'the most diligent, brisk and keen spirited ... don't let him speak to anyone alone or have any opportunity of discovering the weakness of the forts. He will see and understand everything ... in truth he is a terrible man.'[20]

So King Louis was well served. He was also clear about his objectives and was a talented negotiator. King Edward and his advisors were rather different. Edward was not 'the cleverest man I have known at extracting himself from an adverse situation', as Commines remarked of Louis. Nevertheless King Edward was playing his hand rather well. He conferred with his Council and put a detailed financial proposal to King Louis with some useful political addenda. (Edward Woodville was far too junior to be involved with the convoluted negotiations but would have been building the relationship with his men that was to serve him so well eight years later.)

A deal was struck and the two kings met on a bridge over the Somme with their armies drawn up on opposite banks. 'In the meantime it fell a raining prodigiously which did considerable damage to the finery and furniture.' [21] All was friendship, with King Louis inviting King Edward to 'Come and visit me in Paris; we have ladies there who will entertain you right merrily – and you shall have for your confessor Cardinal Bourbon who knows how to lay light penances for pleasant sins,' or so Commines reported.

The Treaty of Picquigny was finalized to the satisfaction of both kings. There was a seven-year truce and free trade in France for English merchants. The Dauphin and Princess Elizabeth were engaged and there was much window dressing, but effectively France paid England to go home. There was a down payment of 75,000 gold crowns, followed by 50,000 crowns annually (one crown equalled about four shillings and three pence, so there were around five crowns to the pound).

The following day a public-relations campaign started to justify the treaty. Some Englishmen in Amiens were saying, 'the Holy Ghost has made the peace'. What was the evidence? Well, a white pigeon that had perched on King Edward's tent would not be frightened away. Louis de Bretelles, for one, was not convinced: he knew post-event rationalization when he met it and pointed out that the bird was wet from the rainstorm, the sun had then shone, so the pigeon, wanting to dry itself, chose the highest tent to perch on. Edward, as the other knight in the Rivers contingent, would have heard the cynicism of the older man and would have had a view as to what should or should not have been done.

However it looked, King Louis was content and arranged a celebration – four days of unlimited drink in Amiens for the English rank and file, who predictably misbehaved, and extra cash for the nobles. Duke Charles appeared shortly afterwards, discovered to his horror that Burgundy was excluded from the treaty and complained bitterly to King Edward. But the latter was unmoved, having neatly turned a deteriorating situation into success with no help from the perfidious Duke.

The Milanese ambassador reported, 'The King of England is very dissatis-fied with the Duke of Burgundy, although he calls him brother. It is because he [the Duke] did not receive him in his towns as promised and because he obtained no help from him of men or money.'

Neither would King Edward have forgotten that the Duke, just four years earlier, had offered to hand him over to the Lancastrians. Meanwhile Duke Charles tore his Garter to pieces with his teeth in fury and muttered that King Edward was a bastard; his father was an archer called Blaybourne and, anyway, he – Duke Charles – had a better claim to the throne of England.[22] It seems there was little love lost between them. Edward was also still in his debt, having only paid half of Duchess Margaret's dowry of 200,000 livres.

The Milanese also reported that King Edward did not want his brothers to precede him to England, 'as he feared some disturbance, especially as the Duke of Clarence had previously aspired to make himself king'. The ambassa-dor added, 'I gather some revolution [in England] would give secret satisfaction to the Duke here [in Burgundy].'[23]

The war had proved useful for King Edward. He had secured a double profit, 'from his subjects for the war and from his enemies for the peace'.[24] He had also anticipated some of the problems that might arise:

> He had brought with him ten or twelve men, big fat ones, some from London and some from other towns, who were leading figures of the English commons and who had done much to promote the invasion. King Edward had them quartered in handsome tents, but campaigning was not the sort of life they were used to and they quickly wearied of it; three days after they had landed at Calais they were worrying that there would be a battle. The king stimulated their doubts and fears and thus prompted them to look favourably upon the peace.[25]

Of course free trade with France dealt with any remaining misgivings the merchants might have had.

King Edward certainly regarded the Treaty of Picquigny as his master-stroke and shortly afterwards commissioned the building of St George's Chapel at Windsor Castle, where he had the treaty's conclusion carved on his miseri-cord. However, there was grumbling amongst the knights and young bloods who had expected to prove themselves in battle and improve themselves by plunder. Louis de Bretelles admitted privately to Philippe de Commines, who was a friend of his, that he thought the French were laughing at the English king. In de Bretelles's view the shame of the treaty outweighed the honour

King Edward had achieved by his nine victories, in all of which he – Louis de Bretelles – had fought.

This conversation was reported to King Louis who observed, 'He is a shrewd fellow, we must have a care of his tongue.' The next day he had de Bretelles to dinner and made 'very advantageous proposals if he would quit his master's service and live in France'. De Bretelles refused the offer but accepted 1,000 crowns (around £200) as a present and was asked to help promote good relations between the two kings.[26]

After the treaty, King Louis had some unfinished business. The Count de St Pol had oscillated between the two power blocks, irritating them both, and was now trying to ingratiate himself. 'It was then that Louis XI, taking pleasure in the Constable's discomfiture, gave him this reply with such a cruel double meaning: 'I have so much to deal with that I need a good head like yours.'[27] (Six months later King Louis caught St Pol and took his head.)

Once King Edward was safely back in England, Anthony's responsibilities became less onerous. He made a donation to Eton College that was so generous that a mass was said for him and his family every morning and the day, 30 October, was kept as an anniversary to remember him, which lasted for 60 years or more.

King Edward judged the time right for a spectacular parade and so arranged the reburial of his father and brother, Edmund, who had been killed at Wakefield in 1460. They were now brought in a splendid procession from Pontefract to Fotheringay where, on 29 July 1476, they were re-interned with two days of masses and ceremonies.

Now Anthony was free to embark on a pilgrimage to Italy. In practice it seems to have been more of a diplomatic mission. Whether young Sir Edward accompanied his brother is unknown but he may have; it looked an interesting trip. Since King Edward wished to develop good relations with the Duke of Milan, Anthony carried a personal introduction from the King who described him as 'one of his chief confidents and brother of his dear consort ... [who] will visit on his way to or from Rome'.

At this stage Milan was at its zenith and the huge recently completed Gothic cathedral dominated the city centre which the rulers were busy improving with the new architecture. The Duke, Galeazzo Maria Sforza, lived at the north end of the city in his rebuilt and recently decorated Castello Sforzesco, 'a massive pile impressive for its strength rather than its beauty ... the wealth of internal decoration turned it into the most sumptuous palace in Italy'. One of the principal rooms was the Sala degli Scarloni, so called from its decoration of zigzag stripes of mulberry and white; another was decorated with the

Duchess's favourite device of doves in the midst of flames.[28]

Anthony and the Duke would have discussed the hot news, the surprise defeat of the pride of Burgundy by Swiss peasants at Grandson on 2 March 1476. How serious did Sforza think this was for Duke Charles, who had even lost his baggage and much treasure? How would it affect European relations? What would happen to Savoy, which was then in the Burgundian sphere of influence and – importantly – might Sforza change his friends? If he was going to, then when might he? King Edward would want to know.

Milan was presently allied to Duke Charles but Sforza was mulling over a move towards King Louis, who did not trust him but would have liked him as a new ally. Just before the battle of Grandson, King Edward had picked up intelligence of the Burgundian plans and passed this on to Sforza; once the Swiss peasants were beaten the great Burgundian army would sweep on and take Milan.[29]

France also coveted Milan (and would get it 20 years later). One of the Counts Sforza observed, 'the security of states is like happiness in love; a happy miracle which it is necessary to create anew every day'. Convoluted diplomacy and good intelligence were the ingredients for the happy miracle of state security.

Anthony's next stop was in Naples where he visited shrines and, given the nature of his journey, would have talked to King Ferdinand who had a treaty of friendship with England. The King's son was leading a contingent in the Burgundian army and Ferdinand was uneasy about Duke Charles. He too was corresponding with King Louis. Whether it was that correspondence, Anthony's visit or both, the result was that the prince and his soldiers left Duke Charles's army two days before the next battle (Morat).

This was Renaissance Italy at its most exciting. Rome was a place of pilgrimage and rich with new buildings, paintings, sculpture and learning, all of which would have fascinated Anthony (and Edward). We know Anthony was interested in literature, and the Italians were then enjoying short stories, *novella*, which ranged from irreverent entertainment such as *Portantino's Pork* by Sabbadino delli Arenti to an early telling of Romeo and Juliet by Salernitano. Machiavelli's *Belphegor* was published in 1469.[30] Lord Worcester had already translated a novella by Buonaccorso into English as *The Declamacion of Noblesse*.

While he was in Rome Pope Sixtus invested Anthony with honours and they would have discussed the political issues around Duke Charles's ambitions.[31] Journeying north from there with two friends, they had their baggage plundered. Anthony lost 1,000 marks' (£660) worth of jewellery and plate. When he later heard it had been sold to some Venetians he went to Venice and pleaded with the Senate for restitution. They were swayed by his argument and his belongings were returned, the Venetians deciding to favour him out of 'deference for the King of England and his Lordship'.

The Pope was also looking after his new 'agent extraordinary'. He offered 300 ducats as a reward as well as threatening the thieves with excommunication, anathema, eternal malediction, confiscation of all property and loss of benefices. The Venetians made arrests and went after the 'whole truth' of the matter. Luckily for Anthony he was well in funds, as his sister, Queen Elizabeth, had sent him 4,000 ducats (£800) post haste by a 'gentleman of the royal household'.[32] (A courier from London to Venice took 25 to 30 days, so Anthony was short for two months. That was quicker than a 'letter of exchange', which would have taken around three months.[33])

They stayed on in Venice. The city was at the height of its power, dominating Mediterranean and eastern trade, while domestic activities ranged from building churches and palaces to turning out warships on a production line.[34] Giovanni Bellini and Carpaccio were painting there; Antonello da Messina had recently arrived and his work seems to epitomize the spirit of the time: 'the dawn of humanism and the conquest of reality that went with it'.[35] He had just finished the San Cassiano altar piece where he used 'the idea of unified figurative space, rather than a figurative panorama' and 'it became one of the most famous works of art in Venice'.[36] Anthony, perhaps with Edward, was there and so able to see this seminal work.

Philippe de Commines described the Grand Canal as 'the most beautiful street in the world'. Venice was – and is – a wonderful city with its palaces, churches, piazzas and, particularly, the Doge's Palace where Anthony would have again enjoyed discussions on international politics. The Venetians were allied to Burgundy, loved intrigue and loathed Milan.

If Anthony's tour had a foreign-policy objective, which seems probable, then on his way to Venice from Rome, he will have called at Urbino whose duke, Frederigo da Montefeltro, a celebrated *condottiere* (mercenary or 'contract' general), had been recently elected as a Knight of the Garter. Duke Frederigo was close to the Pope and a particular ally of King Edward, who regularly used him to exercise influence on England's behalf.[37]

Perhaps King Edward had sent Anthony on a covert mission to coordinate opposition to Duke Charles. The Treaty of Picquigny had been very lucrative and included a clause for mutual support, so it seems probable. The Milanese certainly thought King Edward was moving against Duke Charles, and King Louis wrote to the Swiss in July saying that he could bring the King of England over to help in the war against Burgundy.[38] A pilgrimage combined with a secret mission seem to fit the facts.

Did the 17-year-old Edward go too? Again it is probable. After all, Anthony had accompanied his father until he was 20. If Edward did then he too will have sensed the excitement of the Renaissance and listened to the policy discussions. Anthony turned for home and on his return journey reached the camp of Duke Charles of Burgundy at Morat (20 miles west of Berne) before dawn on 7 July 1476. The Milanese ambassador there reported, 'the Duke has made much of him' and he would stay for two or three days before returning to England.

He would have been curious to see how Duke Charles had weathered his defeat at Grandson and how he was progressing – against advice – in his renewed campaign against the Swiss. King Edward would need the report. What Anthony saw was a new and disciplined army with his old *frère d'armes*, Antoine 'the Great Bastard,' as Chief of Staff; gone was the post-Grandson chaos where ill-discipline had reigned. But when the Duke invited him to stay and join in the forthcoming battle, Anthony declined, saying 'he was sorry he could not stay'. He had to get home. Why should he fight in someone else's battle when he had little interest in the outcome? But his decision earned the Duke's sneer: 'If I was not laughing so much, I too would leave in fear.' [39]

However, Anthony – and perhaps Edward – avoided witnessing the Duke's awful defeat two weeks later. The Swiss infantry, well disciplined and armed with lethal 18ft (5.48-metre) pikes, surprised the Burgundians, and the Duke's smart new army was rolled up and put to flight with losses reckoned at some 25,000. It was the prelude to the Duke's death at the battle of Nancy in the snows of January 1477 where the Swiss commoners, who were consistently underestimated by Duke Charles, again out-manoeuvred and crushed him with an unexpected flanking attack. Le Téméraire could not believe it and died fighting to the last. His artillery train was captured and much of it is still displayed as trophies in Swiss town halls and museums.

Whether or not Edward was with his brother at the Burgundian camp, he would have heard all about it and discussed the whys and wherefores with his brother; it was a good lesson in deciding who and when to fight. The battle showed that Swiss infantry tactics had started a new kind of warfare and that, together with Duke Charles's interest in organization, was to change the way armies were recruited, organized and directed. The knight on his charger and the troop of feudal levies were suddenly out of date. The new requirement was for good artillery and tactical infantry, in addition to traditional cavalry. Whatever the shortcomings of Duke Charles may have been, he left an important legacy: his military ordinances on organization, formation, officers, tactics and practising were cutting-edge thinking and set a standard for others to follow.[40]

An important rediscovery for the Swiss was the tactical infantry officer, the man-at-arms class of officer who directed and fought in the ranks of the foot soldiers, the captain who told the petty officers what to do and led the foot soldiers when the going got tough. It was a new band of middle management for the infantry. However, while the Swiss were good at the tactical level, they were not so good on the strategic side, as they rarely had war leaders or generals at divisional level, which meant that they never really followed up and capitalized on their victories.

King Louis had been so impressed by the Swiss victory that he recruited Swiss *reislaufers* (petty officers) to come and train the French infantry that was to be reorganized on the Swiss model. He also annexed parts of Burgundy and persuaded several noblemen to change their allegiance – men such as Philippe de Crèvecoeur, a.k.a. Lord Cordes, who governed Picardy and had lands in both France and Burgundy.

Duke Charles's death changed the dynamics of European politics. The richest prince was dead, Burgundy was in chaos and the heiress was Mary, the Duke's only child and Margaret of York's stepdaughter. She now became the centre of diplomatic attention, not only the greatest heiress of the time, but also directly descended through her father's mother from John of Gaunt and thus with a perfectly good Lancastrian claim to the throne of England.

George, Duke of Clarence, whose wife had just died, had an eye for the chance. He fancied marrying the little Duchess, but the last thing King Edward needed was a competing claim for the English crown from his brother, who had a habit of treachery. He forbade the marriage. At this point, a suggestion arrived from King James of Scotland that Clarence should marry his sister, Margaret, while his brother, Duke Alexander of Albany, should marry the recently widowed Margaret of Burgundy. It was unsuitable and King Edward blocked both ideas.

Clarence seems to have been unstable and this treatment offended his sense of righteousness. He flew into a fury and planned retribution. He almost certainly involved himself in treasonable activities with King Louis, but he clearly overstepped the mark when he openly challenged his brother's authority in England. As a result he was immediately charged with 'heinous, unnatural and loathly' treason, which probably consisted of a plan to marry Mary of Burgundy, declare his brother illegitimate and then seize the throne with the help of Mary's claim, money and men.

The King put him on trial. He was found guilty, sentenced to death and probably met 'his end in a rondolet of Malmsey', a curious method of execution but apparently one of his own choosing. If this was his choice then, whatever his shortcomings, he clearly had a sense of style. A portrait of his daughter painted around 1530 shows her wearing a miniature cask of Malmsey on a bracelet.

The trial had started just two days after the spectacular marriage of the King's four-year-old (second) son, Richard, to Anne Mowbray, the richest heiress in England. There were jousts in which six champions challenged all-comers; Anthony Woodville, Edward Woodville, Thomas Dorset and Richard Grey were four of the six. They issued the challenge on 10 December 1477 for the tournament on 22 January 1478. Contestants would be dealt with in the order in which they wrote their names on the shield and there would be six courses with spears and 13 strokes with swords, all mounted.

Anthony, very much the flamboyant Champion, created a great stir when he appeared 'horsed and armed in the habit of a white hermit' with his pavilion 'walled and covered with black velvet' to resemble a hermitage. Edward was not far behind in his 'Osting Harness', with his horses dressed in crimson cloth of gold and his servants in blue and tawny velvet.

They all fought. Edward had the misfortune to have one of his horses hurt in a course, but he re-horsed and finished the six runs. Anthony and an opponent were fighting hard when the umpire called and dropped his batton to stop the fight. Anthony immediately stopped but his opponent unwisely took another swing 'so the Earl furiously returned upon him and so accomplished six strokes between them'.

The Woodvilles seem to have enjoyed themselves, as Anthony tipped the Kings of Arms and Heralds 20 marks. After all the spears were broken and blows exchanged it was time for the party, and they all went to the dance in the King's Great Chamber where the Princess of the Feast distributed the prizes.[41]

The King meanwhile was still mulling over Burgundian matters. He needed someone he could trust to marry the heiress and he was being pressed into action by his sister Margaret, the Duke's widow. Anthony Woodville seemed the best choice, as he could be trusted and his wife had died four years earlier,[42] although he did have 'a beloved mistress Gwentlian, only daughter of Sir William Stradling of Glamorganshire'.[43] That was irrelevant and this was politics, so King Edward sent Louis de Bretelles as his emissary to make the proposal. But the suit failed because, as Commines observed, 'Rivers was only a petty earl, and she the greatest heiress of her time.'

In any event the young Duchess had followed her father's choice and

9. The joust. Both knights have shattered their spears and the visor of the knight on the right has been broken. The herald stands in the middle. The king and his nobles are in their stands in a proper arena.

selected the hook-nosed Maximilian,[44] son of the Habsburg emperor Frederick III, whom she married in August despite his lack of funds. The Duke of Bavaria stood proxy for Maximilian and 'entered the nuptial bed clad in steel from head to foot and separated from the Princess by a naked sword'.

Also in that year William Caxton, the English merchant from Bruges in Burgundy who had been learning about printing, arrived in London with his new wooden printing press. He had letters of commendation from the Duchess Margaret and was looking for patronage. It was Anthony Woodville who provided it. He commissioned Caxton to print and publish his translation of *Dits Moraulx* as *The Dictes and Sayings of the Philosophers*.

Much to his amusement Caxton discovered that Anthony had omitted the aspersions of Socrates against women. How could this be? 'I suppose that some fair lady hath desired him to leave it out of his book, or he was amorous on some noble lady for whose love that he would not set it in his book.' In any case, Caxton observed, Socrates's strictures were hardly applicable to English women, for whatever 'condition women be in Greece, the women of this country be right good, wise, pleasant, humble, discreet, sober, chaste etc. etc ... and virtuous in all their works, *or at least should be so.*' (My emphasis; Caxton's wife, Maud, may well have had a word to say about this.)

It is inconceivable that Caxton would have dared to involve his patron in such a joke without first obtaining his full permission. In fact he translated the offending passage himself and included it at the end of his epilogue with the plea to his readers, 'if they find any fault to arrest it to Socrates and not to me' (the piece is rather an anticlimax).[45]

On 18 November 1477 the first book was printed in England. A manuscript in Lambeth Palace library shows Anthony, his face intelligent and amusing, giving the King a copy. In the preface he wrote that recent 'vicissitudes of fortune' had made a great impression on him and 'having been relieved by the goodness of God he was exhorted to dedicate his recovered life to His service'. Anthony also wrote that his translation of the manuscript was intended for the education of the young Prince of Wales, who is on the King's left in the illustration.

One of the popular books of the time was *The Wise and Holsom Proverbs* by Christine de Pisan, an early fifteenth-century (lady) intellectual. Anthony's mother had given him a copy which he had translated; this was published in February.[46] That was followed the next month by his version of the *Cordyale* where, in the printer's epilogue, Caxton writes of Anthony's devotion to works of piety and concludes: 'It seemeth that he conceiveth wel the mutabilite and the unstableness of this present lyf, and that he desireth, with a great zele and spirituel love, our goostlye help and perpetual salvacion and that we shal abhorre and uttely forsake the abominable and dampnable synnes.'[47]

Separately Caxton refers to other translations by Anthony and to his 'diverse Balades against the Seven deadly sins'. There is something rather mystical about his faith; it was clearly absolute and all encompassing and would have been a major influence on Edward. Anthony with his devotions and writing, together with the work of his several offices as well as politics, weapon exercising, hunting, entertainment and constant travelling around the country, would certainly have been kept busy. In all the travellings, his entourage of squires, pages, chaplains, clerks and assorted retainers would accompany him. Edward was probably there as well.

Anthony kept close to events in London through his lawyer and confidential man of affairs, one Andrew Dymmock, who also dealt with Anthony's business interests, ranging from the detail of legal agreements to the preferment of people. Both the management of his estates and building work on his houses were carefully supervised by Anthony in person. For instance, 'Daniell mastermason' was sent architectural instructions such as 'the turret may rise 14 feet from the lead', 'the stairs of my haght passé [dais] should be 6 foot' and 'you will leave a place over the entrance gate in the new wall, where you think it may best be seen, for an escutchon of the arms of Wodevile and Scalis with a Garter about them'.[48]

Anthony also built – or rebuilt – the chapel of Our Lady of Pewe at Westminster Abbey after it had been 'burnt to ashes by the negligence of a scholar'.[49] In addition to all this he was an agricultural improver, as reported by a bailiff to John Paston: 'My lord Rivers in his own person hath been at Hickling and his counsel learned ... it meanth my lord is set sore to approvement and husbandry.'

There is no doubt that Anthony was an intelligent nobleman with wide range of interests and highly regarded for his integrity. He was also head of his family, and, while we do not actually know what young Edward was doing, being squire and companion to his elder brother would be conventional.[50]

What was to happen next was – initially – predictable.

CHAPTER FIVE

THE GRADUATE

The full range of experience running from diplomacy to architecture, from campaigns on land to battles at sea, it would all come from squiring Anthony. Edward listened to powerful men discussing affairs of state, intelligent men discussing humanism and God. The erudite Anthony would have ensured his young brother was educated well enough to enjoy intellectual exercise and be able to hold his own in debate. He had strong religious convictions and so Edward would have assimilated at least some of those. Their clerical brother, Lionel, who became Chancellor of Oxford University in 1479 and Bishop of Salisbury three years later, may also have taken an interest in Edward's relationship with God.

He could speak and read French, which would be normal for the time, and there is the signature 'E Wydevyll', probably dating from 1482 or 1483, on the flyleaf of a collection of romances written in French. He probably read and spoke Latin as well. Apart from this, we know little of his learning or beliefs.

On the practical side, we know that he shared extreme discomfort with people ranging from the common archer to the King himself, but on occasions lived luxuriously. He learned to fight in structured tournaments and bitter mêlées. His father and brothers were great tournament fighters and champions. They had also made good money with spoil and ransom. Edward came from that stock and there would be pride in being the best in the field. But that also meant being a target; others would try to lay a Woodville low and it would have been very competitive. To understand such a man we need to have an idea about his training and the risks.

While Edward seems to have had a natural talent for combat it would still be essential for him to have daily exercise in armour, with a variety of weapons both on and off his horse. Gymnastic exercises were important; one of those required of boys was to ride at full tilt against a quintain (a horizontal bar pivoted in the centre with a wooden figure holding a small round shield or 'buckler' on one side and a wooden club on the other). The quintain turned on an axis so that the young horseman, if he did not manage his horse and weapon

71

with dexterity, would receive a wallop when the shock of his charge made the quintain spring round.[1]

Edward was being brought up to fight and to win his fights; losing could mean death, as happened to the young Thomas de Scales who was killed in single combat at the age of 15. There is a vivid description of mortal combat in *Tirant Lo Blanc*, the fifteenth-century novel written by a man who had fought such duels. It gives a real sense of the fight and helps us understand the fear and excitement:

> It was a most cruel combat, for Thomas was so mighty and smote such terrible blows that every time he swung, Tirant was forced to duck. Just when everyone thought Tirant was getting the worst of it, he began to fight back himself. Thomas struck his helmet and knocked him to one knee, but while he was kneeling, Tirant wounded his opponent in the groin, for Thomas had no chain mail beneath his armour. Tirant quickly rose and the battle waxed very fierce. Feeling himself bleeding, Thomas sought to end it quickly and hit Tirant's visor [covering the upper part of the face] with such force that his axe stuck in the beaver [covering the lower part of the face]. The blade touched Tirant's neck and, wounded though he was, Thomas dragged him across the field and pinned his body against the stands. ...

> [If] your arm, hand or foot goes outside the boundaries and the judge is asked to cut it off – under French rules – he is obliged to and at that point I would have given little for Tirant's life.

> But as long as they stayed as they were, Thomas could not knock him to the ground, so Thomas shifted his axe to his left hand and lifted Tirant's visor, keeping him pinned with his left hand and body.

> Then he slapped Tirant's face, crying: 'Confess your treachery, rascal!' Hearing no reply, Thomas tossed aside his gauntlet and reached into Tirant's helmet. He dropped his axe and other gauntlet and gripped Tirant's neck. When Tirant saw his hands free, though he still could not move his body, he raised his axe and struck Thomas's hands twice. Finding himself with neither axe nor gauntlets, Thomas drew his sword, but it availed him little against Tirant's mighty buffets.

There is much more of this and eventually: 'seeing Thomas's weakened state, Tirant raised his axe and brought it crashing down on Thomas's helmet, just above the ear. While his head was still spinning, Tirant struck him again and felled him with the blow.'[2]

That was what young Edward was being trained for and, up to this point, records hardly refer to him, but then why should they? He was a young man and insignificant in political terms; nevertheless as brother and companion to a great nobleman he had witnessed the achievements and trials of the last few years. He had watched the story unfold, but in December 1478, when he was about 20 years old, he joined the cast of major players.

His first proper – recorded – job was to take an embassy to King James III of Scotland who had come up with another marriage plan: Anthony should marry the King's sister, Princess Margaret. Edward's task was to negotiate a treaty centred on that; however, it was not only down to Edward, as his fellow ambassador was John Russell, Bishop of Lincoln, an experienced diplomat and civil servant, but one who would later be an adversary. (For good results, the idea of balancing a nobleman with a bureaucrat, or a politician with a civil servant was – and is – a well-established arrangement.)

The treaty was agreed with a dower of 4,000 marks but as King James had no money to pay that dowry, it would be deducted from the dowry agreed for Princess Cecilia's marriage. The idea of such a marriage again demonstrates that the King trusted Anthony. Arrangements were made for the wedding in October, but later the plan was abandoned because Scots cross-border raiding remained unchecked and King James prevaricated on dates.

In one sense it is surprising that after these two proposals for foreign-policy marriages, Anthony's second marriage was to Mary Lewis, a well-connected teenager with estates in Essex. Perhaps Gwentlian had died and Anthony did not want a foreign bride or had fallen in love. However, politics did play a part, for Mary had the blood royal and was Buckingham's half-sister. Her mother was a Beaufort, descended from John of Gaunt, and she was the daughter of Duke Edmund of Somerset, sister of the last two dukes and so first cousin to Margaret Beaufort, Henry Tudor's mother (whose father was Duke John, Edmund's elder brother). Her first marriage had been to Humphrey, Earl of Stafford, and Buckingham was the child of that union. Mary was the child of her second marriage. If Mary married Anthony then she would pose no political threat and was a good age for child bearing. All the Woodvilles would be hoping for an heir to the earldom.

The next time young Sir Edward features in the records is when he was one of those who sailed to Burgundy to collect the Dowager Duchess Margaret, the King's sister, for a holiday and foreign-policy discussions in England. They sailed in *The Falcon*, a tub-like ship under the command of 'trusty' Captain William Fetherston.

Edward took 12 servants of his own who were given 'jakettes of wollen cloth' in the York livery colours of 'murrey and blue', while Edward himself, for his jacket, received the 'yift [gift of] a yerde of velvet purpulle and a yerde of blue velvet'.[3] (Purple velvet cost £2 per yard and blue £1, so the gift was the equivalent to a standard suit of armour.) The voyage should have taken around three days each way, subject to wind and weather.[4]

They must have been a fine sight dressed in their finery under the fluttering pennants and streamers as they welcomed the Duchess aboard. For the festivities in England Anthony had a predictably grander role for which he was given three yards of 'white tisshue cloth of gold for one short gown'. On her return journey both Margaret and King Edward were entertained by Anthony at the Mote, his house near Maidstone in Kent.

While there are only occasional glimpses of Edward in the records, the people, events and prevailing political climate provide a good backcloth, even if there is not always an obvious connection. William Caxton is a good example. Under Anthony's patronage he was busy with his printing press, turning out a range of books such as *The Canterbury Tales*, *Chronicles of England*, *Mirror of the World*, *Reynard the Fox*, *Of Friendship*, *Declamation of Nobility* and many others. As for the last two, Caxton attributes their translation to the late – beheaded in 1470 – Earl of Worcester and gives him a panegyric. Interestingly it was probably Anthony Woodville who arranged this publication, as it fitted with his political agenda of emphasizing integrity, intelligence and commitment to the Yorkist establishment.[5] In *The Canterbury Tales* there are woodcuts that so graphically illustrate much of the period and it is probable that the printing of *Le Morte d'Arthur* was also due to Anthony; however, he was not acknowledged, as the book was printed after his execution in King Richard's reign.[6]

Anthony was then governor and ruler of the Prince of Wales as well as being the senior figure of the Prince's Council, which exercised direct control over Wales and the Marches. For efficient, good governance, it was helpful that the majority of the Council were Woodville friends and connections and, even at a lower level, the same names turn up. For instance, John Giles, the schoolmaster who worked for the Queen ten years previously, reappears as tutor to the prince.[7] While this may not have been universally popular, the arrangements worked. Mancini wrote a report on the 12-year-old prince: 'In word and in deed he revealed the fruits of a liberal, indeed a scholarly education, far in advance of his years. ... He was able to discourse most elegantly on literary matters; whatever book, whether prose or verse, came into his hands he was able to comprehend completely and declaim with clarity and feeling.'

Here is an Italian cleric and scholar who would now be described as a humanist clearly very impressed with the young prince. But then Anthony can also be described as a humanist. These were students of classical learning, a field that was related to educational reform and to a more disciplined training in the principles of good government. Additionally they seem to have had a purity of intention and piety. These were people educated in the classics, who were suspicious of dogma, thought for themselves and applied pragmatism where they could. Mancini approved of Anthony, whom he described as 'a kind, serious and just man and one tested by every vicissitude of life. Whatever his prosperity he had injured nobody, though benefiting many.'

Mancini also reported on Duke Richard of Gloucester who had been unswervingly loyal to his brother and 'kept himself within his own lands [the north of England] and set out to acquire the loyalty of his people through favours and justice'. Duke Richard was an able man, 'sharp witted, provident and subtle'. He also seems to have been a bundle of nervous energy, continually biting his bottom lip while thinking and always pulling his dagger half out of its sheath and pushing it in again.[8] During this period he was extending his influence in the north, probably more than his brother was aware of. He had acquired great wealth and wide lands through his wife, Anne Neville, Warwick's daughter, and even now was gathering up more land and followers. It was real power that could create a dangerous situation if the King's control faltered.

However, the King had no intention of losing control. He had the sensible policy of devolving power in distant places to trusted men and had no reason to doubt his brother. Duke Richard's methods were certainly ruthless, and while history has demonstrated his real ambition, there seems to be little sign of it at this stage, except in the acquisition of his wife's estates.

Neither is there any evidence to show he was at odds with either Anthony Woodville or Queen Elizabeth while the King was alive. Young Edward was still only a minor player, but working his way up. On 1 March 1480 the King gave permission for Anthony to assign one of his important commissions to Edward, who was then about 21. It was the governance of Portsmouth and custody of Porchester Castle, a key base on Southampton Water.[9]

The castle had been rebuilt 50 years before so that its cannon could properly guard the ships lying in its bay; the King could stay there in style – he visited in 1481 and 1482 – and its captain live in comfort. The outer walls, built by the Romans, still safely enclose the great marshalling ground of eight and a half acres (3.44 hectares). It was here that English armies assembled to go to war with France – Edward III before Crécy and Henry V before Agincourt. Now it was Edward's responsibility.

Royal favour had obviously helped in Edward's career, but of critical importance were the men on whom he could call, 'ones that ... were most devoted to the commander Edward' (Mancini's report). The brotherhoods of the sea and of soldiers were tight knit and Edward must have earned his acceptance shoulder to shoulder in hardship and, between time, in practising and training. Some of the talk would have been on the pressing issues of the day, with topics ranging from how to increase the range of cannon, the shortage of good yew for bow making, the war in Spain, Portuguese success in Morocco, shipbuilding techniques and the exploration of the oceans.

As commander of Porchester and governor of Portsmouth, not only was Edward the military commander but he also saw sea captains and merchants. Southampton was one of the ports of call for the Venetian galleys sailing to Flanders, while Genoese carracks came there with Eastern produce and other merchant ships on general trade. Edward might have heard intriguing tales of land sighted far to the west; he was living with ships and seamen at the dawn of the Age of Discovery. He was interested in ships and would later be appointed as 'the King's great Captain'.

His next appearance in the records is in the Scottish campaign of 1482,[10] where Duke Richard of Gloucester was commander-in-chief and his brother Anthony sent men. We know that Edward commanded 500 soldiers, the Rivers contingent, and was appointed 'to attend upon my lord of Gloucester'. He called at Coventry as he marched north and his visit was recorded, with the mayor and council giving him £20 as a contribution in lieu of men.[11]

It all started because the Scots were making constant border incursions, which worried the keepers of the border who pressed their overlord, Duke Richard, for action. He, in turn, had pressed the King, who was also irritated by Scots scheming and agreed to a campaign. He wondered about it for two years, during which King James seems to have known his thinking, and was getting ready. In October 1480 the Milanese ambassador in France reported that King James had asked King Louis for gunners and artillery. Surprisingly it was Sigismund of Austria who sent him cannon a year later.

Propaganda started with King James inveighing against 'The Revare [thief] Edward call and him king of Ingland'.[12] However, King Edward was still immersed in his convoluted deals with Burgundy, Brittany and France and was reluctant to engage on another front. He prevaricated about the timing and the leadership; perhaps he also worried about his health.

In May 1482 the English under Richard of Gloucester had made a *chevauchée* (major cavalry raid) that sacked Dumfries and infuriated the Scots. King James thought war inevitable and put 500 men to garrison Berwick Castle and another 600 into the border castles. King Edward decided on war and started recruiting – he wanted 20,000 men. Gloucester came south and was appointed lieutenant-general, although King Edward instituted a courier system so he could be kept closely informed of progress.[13]

A plan developed of installing King James's younger brother, Duke Alexander of Albany, as a puppet king. Timing was critical, for the army, which was probably nearer 15,000 than the proposed 20,000, was contracted for just one month (e.g. the contingent from York was paid from 14 July up to 11 August) although 1,700 of them were contracted for an additional 14 days. The cost of the campaign was some £13,000. Speed was essential and it seems a surgical strike was planned rather than anything longer term. Presumably King Edward had intelligence that Albany would be a popular substitute for his brother.

The campaign started with an advance into Scotland on 20 July 1482. The town of Berwick immediately capitulated and the army marched on, leaving the castle untouched. Then they began to pillage Roxburghshire and Berwickshire. King James hurried south from Edinburgh to take command of his army. But at Lauder his half-uncles and other nobles led by 'Bell the Cat', a.k.a. the Earl of Angus, stopped him.[14] They disliked him, his policies and his style – one report says he 'resorted to tears' to get his way – and they also probably thought it would be a mistake to fight this English army – much better to let it do its worst and go away.

They arrested King James on 22 July, dispatched him to prison in Edinburgh and hanged three of his advisors from the bridge, which may have been sensible but it left his unfortunate army without direction and so some dispersed while others shadowed the English. Perhaps the Scottish nobles knew Duke Richard had his army for just 30 days and so avoided an unwinnable battle. But Richard would have noted the speed and success of the coup de main where the King was captured, without fuss, by a determined man.

The English marched towards Edinburgh, ranging across the country as they went. On 24 July Duke Richard promoted Edward to the rank of Knight Banneret (field commander of knights and men-at-arms), which meant that there must have been good will between them.[15] The army reached and occupied Edinburgh on 1 August; they were starting a half-hearted siege of the castle when a delegation of Scottish nobles arrived to see Duke Richard.

They told him that, as far as they were concerned, the war was over and they had important domestic feuds to attend to. It was a brilliant negotiating position for the English, but Richard asked for no more than the return of 8,000 marks already paid on account for Cecilia's dower and the rehabilitation of Albany who, typically for out-of-touch exiles, had been much surprised to discover that none of his countrymen wanted him as king. With a treaty agreed on 4 August, the English marched back to Berwick, where on 11 August – the budgeted date – the bulk of the army was disbanded. The remaining 1,700 men besieged the castle, which fell after 12 days. The town has been English ever since.

Although the campaign had been expensive and distracted attention from the French problem, it had been a useful operation for Duke Richard – it had pleased the northern lords, a group he wanted to favour. Interestingly the treaty is regarded as being soft on the Scots[16] and it certainly looks that way. While this may be because Richard was a bad negotiator, it might also have been because he wanted new friends or just because he had to finish by 11 August. He was on a tight budget and against a deadline, which seems to be a good reason for getting the best he could within the available time. King Edward informed the Pope that the 'chief advantage is the reconquest of the town and castle of Berwick'. It was a reconquest indeed, as Margaret of Anjou had given it to the Scots in 1461 in exchange for aid.[17]

Meanwhile the King was busy with running his kingdom, but during the summer rumours had emanated from Calais questioning the loyalty of some people, in particular Anthony Woodville, Dorset and a friend of theirs, Robert Radcliffe, who was the Gentleman Porter of Calais and had been commanding the English naval squadron against the Scots in conjunction with Duke Richard's army.

These rumours had led to a certain John Edward being interrogated by the King and his Council at Westminster. The man withdrew the accusations he had made in Calais, agreeing that they sprang from 'his own false imagination for fear of his life and putting him in the brake [on the rack] at Calais'. It sounds as if Hastings, as Captain of Calais, had used Edward for mischievous tales. John Edward made a formal confession, of which copies were circulated by Anthony, who seems to have felt damaged by the accusations.[18]

Around the same time, Anthony complained to the King about Hastings and as a consequence Hastings was 'highly in the King's indignation'. The nature of the complaint is unknown. While it may have been related to the John Edward problem, there was also a concurrent rumour of treachery by Hastings who – in turn – suspected the source as Robert Radcliffe. But Radcliffe was away commissioning the King's ships, so Hastings vented his anger on his servants by throwing them out of Calais. This would have irritated the King.

It seems that there was long-standing ill will between Hastings and Anthony, whose unusual approach to life would not appeal to the old-school apparatchik. William, Lord Hastings, was one of the original Yorkists who had served King Edward's father, transferred his allegiance and had always been totally loyal. His service extended right into Edward's personal life where, according to Mancini, 'he was also the accomplice and partner of his [the King's] privy pleasure'. Another recorded 'accomplice' was Edward, so they would have known each other quite well.

Views of Lord Hastings are mixed, ranging from C.L. Scofield, 'neither a wise man nor a good man', while Commines describes him as 'a person of singular wisdom and virtue in great authority with his master whom he had served faithfully'.[19] However, Commines also records that he took a pension from King Louis of 'two thousand crowns which was double the amount the duke [of Burgundy] had accorded him'; not only that but Hastings refused to sign for it, saying, 'You will have neither letter nor quittance, for I am entirely unwilling, for my part, that it should be said, the Great Chamberlain has been a pensioner of the King of France, and that my quittance should be found in the Exchequer.' He was still paid the money.[20]

Nevertheless Hastings was unwaveringly loyal to King Edward and consequently had been generously rewarded with large estates and lucrative high offices. He was Master of the Mint, which paid a handsome dividend, and the King's Chamberlain, which meant many nobles, clerics and gentry paid him annuities or gave him presents for his influence with the King. He sounds like a streetwise old soldier, with his trotters in the trough, up for anything and the antithesis of Anthony, the intelligent but austere Champion.

At this stage Commines described the King as 'a fleshy and lazy man who dearly loved his pleasures, and it would have been impossible for him to endure the toils of making war in France'. He also observed that King Louis worked hard to avoid war, but had no intention of letting the Dauphin and Princess Elizabeth marry. Louis dissembled and paid out pensions in gold; in addition to King Edward, there were eight courtiers and officials who were recipients of pensions, 'all English envoys' who were given 'lavish gifts'.[21]

Meanwhile the Queen was in her mid-40s, busy promoting her family interests, and could review her work with satisfaction. There was an heir to the throne and a spare – in total a family of ten by King Edward. Her eldest son was the 31-year-old Thomas Grey, created Marquis of Dorset and exceptionally rich through his marriage. Her sisters were well married – one duke, three earls and two barons – although two brothers and her younger son from her first marriage were still unmarried.

There are widely divergent views of Elizabeth, but they seem to be determined by how the chronicler viewed the events of 1483. The Queen certainly had her admirers as well as her detractors. Edward Hall writing in the 1540s describes her as, 'a woman more of formal countenance than of excellent beauty, but yet of such beauty and favour that with her sober demeanour, lovely looking and feminine, smiling (neither wanton nor to humble) besides her tongue so eloquent and her wit so pregnant'.

She was certainly beautiful, probably manipulative and certainly enjoyed playing politics, with her son Thomas, known as 'Lord Marquis', as her lieutenant. After Clarence's execution 'Lord Marquis' became the King's chief representative in the south-west and an influential member of his Council, although he seems not to have been popular. As Mancini noted, he was a 'newly made man advanced beyond those who excelled in wit and wisdom'. Thomas More tells us he quarrelled regularly with Hastings 'over the mistresses whom they abducted, or attempted to entice from one another'. He was a drinking companion of the King and – by all accounts – an arrogant and shallow man, but was probably entertaining company. King Edward himself was not an ideal example. Mancini reported:

> He was licentious in the extreme; moreover it was said that he had been most insolent to numerous women after he had seduced them, for, as soon as he grew weary of the dalliances, he gave up the ladies much against their will to other courtiers. He pursued with no discrimination the married and unmarried, the noble and lowly: however, he took none by force. He overcame all by money and promises, and having conquered them, he dismissed them. Although he had many promoters and companions of his vices the more important and especial were ... relatives of the queen, her two sons and one of her brothers.

Edward was the brother involved and they must have had good fun. However, it is surprising that the King, in his late 30s, chose Edward, in his early 20s, as one of his boon companions. The King obviously knew Edward well but their companionship rather supports the theory that Edward had been with him – as Anthony's page and squire – through thick and thin. There was probably a lot of visiting the stews and bath-houses, where loose women and parties abounded.

Twenty years later Thomas More was writing that the Queen hated Lord Hastings because she thought him 'secretly familiar with the King in wanton company'. That means she had heard – like Mancini – that he was 'the accomplice and partner of [the King's] privy pleasure'. It was obviously difficult having a younger husband, and while she may not have known about her brother and her sons, she knew that her king was a serial philanderer. He loved the excitement of the chase through to the conquest but he usually abandoned his mistresses once he had enjoyed them, although he did have his favourites.[22]

There are well-known portraits of King Edward and Elizabeth. The only certain picture of Anthony is the one in the Lambeth library and there are

10. Happy times. A young man welcomes his lover to the bath;
outside there are couples and musicians.

no known portraits of young Edward Woodville. Perhaps the woodcut that
Chaucer published in *The Canterbury Tales* of his elegant knight (see plate 1)
is based on a Woodville, for he knew them well. Five years later the Spanish
chroniclers described Edward as witty, good looking and a stylish horseman
with a taste for fine clothes. One also reported that he 'found great favour
with the fair dames about the court'. His family were noted for being tall with
good looks and golden hair.

Property and position determined marriage and if Edward had been
driven by ambition then the Queen, his sister, would have found him an heiress. There was no pressure on penniless younger brothers. For instance, his

near contemporary young John Paston pursued women endlessly until he was 30, when he decided the time had come to settle down. He tried Katherine Dudley. His elder brother made his case to her but had to report, 'and she is nothing displeased with it. She does not mind how many gentlemen love her; she is full of love … [but] will have no one these two years.' Young John wrote, 'I pray get us a wife somewhere' and then fell in love with Margery Brews two years later. Five hundred years on, it is still moving to read their letters where the love is so strong.

One young nobleman fell in love with 'the Nut-Brown Maid' across the social divide. He pretended to be penniless and, even worse, on his way to exile.

> She: be so unkind to leave behind
> your love the Nut-brown Maid.
> Trust me truly that I shall die
> Soon after ye be gone
> For, in my mind, of all mankind
> I love but you alone.

Eventually he comes clean:

> I will you take and lady make
> As shortly as I can.
> Thus have you won an Earles son
> And not a banished man.[23]

Edward meanwhile was sowing his wild oats with King Edward, Thomas Dorset and his friends. In the England of that time they were drinking sweet wines, brandy and beer, while the women, 'though beautiful, were astoundingly impudent'. That is according to one Silesian nobleman who was visiting.[24] He also decided that the English 'surpassed the Poles in ostentation and pilfering, the Hungarians in brutality and the Lombards in deceit, while their virtues consisted of their wealth and hospitality, although their cooking was poor'.

But the English knew how to enjoy themselves. Elizabeth of York's privy purse accounts of 20 years later show her paying for players, dancers and other performers, as well as for minstrels and musicians. She kept greyhounds, bought arrows for hunting and played dice and cards.[25] But at least their souls must have benefited from the certainty of their faith, which was joined to a sensible directness. A prayer of the time says:

> Help us this day, O God, to serve Thee devoutly, and the world busily.

May we do our work wisely, give succour secretly, go to meat appetitely, sit there discreetly, arise temperately, please our friend duly, go to bed merrily, and sleep surely; for the joy of our Lord, Jesus Christ, Amen.[26]

In those halcyon days of the late 1470s and early 1480s England was at her best. It was when young Edward thought, talked, danced, loved, bathed, exercised and went hunting. There was music and laughter; it was when the sun of York shone on a peaceful and well-run country; when Shakespeare has Duke Richard tell us:

Now is the winter of our discontent
Made glorious summer by this sun of York;
And all the clouds that lour'd upon our House
In the deep bosom of the ocean buried.
Now are our brows bound with victorious wreaths,
Our bruised arms hung up for monuments,
Our stern alarums chang'd to merry meetings,
Our dreadful marches to delightful measures.
Grim-visag'd war hath smooth'd his wrinkled front:
And now, instead of mounting barbed steeds,
To fright the souls of fearful adversaries,
He capers nimbly in a lady's chamber,
To the lascivious pleasing of a lute.[27]

But the clouds were gathering and peace would be shattered. Edward was ready to take a leading role.

THE GREAT COUP

In early 1483 England was preparing for war with France, and Edward, the new knight banneret, would be eager for action. This was not a war of King Edward's choosing and had more or less been forced on him. Since the middle of 1482 his foreign policy had been in difficulties, the Scottish campaign had been expensive and little money was left for other ventures.

So when Maximilian of Austria, the Regent of Burgundy, appealed for help against France Edward prevaricated. Maximilian was in a weak position; his strength had come from Burgundy through his wife, the young Duchess, but she had recently been killed by a fall from her horse and the duchy was in chaos. Maximilian became regent but then fell out with the Members of Flanders who appealed for French help. King Edward understood the problems but calculated that King Louis, incapacitated after two strokes, would do nothing.

However, the French king, wily as ever, signed a treaty with the Members of Flanders at Arras on 23 December 1482. King Edward was enjoying Christmas in his palace at Eltham with its newly completed great hall where 2,000 people feasted under the magnificent oak hammerbeam roof.[2] He entertained and set new fashions, 'dressed in a variety of the costliest clothes very different in style from what used to be seen'.

The Treaty of Arras caught him by surprise and what he particularly disliked was the inclusion of an agreement for the heiress of Burgundy, Maximilian's small daughter, to marry the Dauphin, the French heir apparent. But the Dauphin was already engaged to the Princess Elizabeth, King Edward's daughter, so it was a blatant insult and, adding injury to insult, King Louis decided this was the time to stop paying the pension he had agreed at Picquigny.

An infuriated King Edward considered it rank betrayal by the Burgundians and a direct challenge by the French.[3] He may well have become fat and idle in the last seven years but he was not going to allow this. *The Crowland Chronicle* reports: 'The bold King was determined to give anything for revenge. Parliament was again summoned and he disclosed the whole series of great frauds and won over everyone to assist him to take vengeance.'

The misericord in the sovereign's stall in St George's Chapel, Windsor, depicts the Treaty of Picquigny. It is beautifully carved and shows the kings of England and France together in friendship. But King Louis has lost his head. Was the decapitation by Edward in his fury? Nobody knows but it seems probable.

By Easter the scene was set for a punitive expedition. Ever the tactician, King Edward covered his back by talking to Margaret Beaufort who was presently married to Lord Stanley. Henry Tudor, her son from her first marriage, was the last Lancastrian pretender; perhaps he might be brought back from exile and married to Princess Elizabeth? It was certainly a possibility that was discussed.

Military organization went ahead: the King instructed Sir Edward Woodville, the Captain of Porchester, to commission an expeditionary force of 2,000 men with a budget of £3,269-14s-3d. Sir Edward bought two new ships for £856-13s-4d, 2,000 new uniform jackets, extra ordinance – guns, powder, shot, arrows – 'most needed [to] be bought over the King's own stuff delivered out of the Tower'. He also arranged pilots for his fleet.

In the West Country where the Marquis of Dorset was the King's principal lieutenant, there was a Treasury allocation of £800 to pay for 1,000 men to be on standby against invasion for six months. Calais seems to have been a cause for concern, for an additional 500 men were dispatched there.[4] But at this crucial time King Edward fell ill. It was obviously serious, for there were premature reports of his death and a mass was sung for his soul at York while he was still alive.

The dying King tried to put his affairs in order; 'first, like a good Christian man, he reconciled himself to God ... then he made his will, appointing his sons as his heirs'. It is also believed that he added a codicil to his will appointing his brother Richard of Gloucester as Protector. But there is no hard evidence of this. It also appears he was worried about the rivalry between his in-laws and his friend Hastings, whom he begged to stop his quarrelling: 'Dorset, embrace him – Hastings, love Lord marquess.'[5]

King Edward IV was just over 40 when he died on 9 April, probably from a stroke. He has had mixed reviews as a monarch but it is worth remembering that during his reign some of the greatest Perpendicular churches were built. He was the first King of England to die solvent for more than 200 years. When he achieved the crown he assumed debts of around £370,000 and had annual royal revenues of just £24,000. During his reign he increased those revenues to £70,000.[6]

The shrewd Philippe de Commines summed King Edward up: 'not a schemer, nor a man of forsight, but of invincible courage, and withal the most handsome prince that ever my eyes did behold. Most fortunate was he in his battles, for he fought nine all on foot, and was always the conqueror.'[7]

His death was unexpected and it meant the King's Council was now in charge. Their main worry was how the French would react to news of King Edward's death. The Council ordered the embarkation of more soldiers to reinforce the Calais garrison. They did not question the decision to nominate Duke Richard as Protector and acclaimed the young Prince of Wales as king on the day his father died.[8] They were probably relieved that there was a clear-cut arrangement and they could pass executive responsibility on, particularly as it looked as if the kingdom now needed a war leader.

If the King had any deathbed fears about his brother's integrity then they would have been dispelled by his confidence in the well-balanced establish-ment he had built.[9] Duke Richard was the obvious choice to maintain political stability, as he was the only surviving brother and had demonstrated both his loyalty and his abilities. So while the country grieved for the dead King, at least they could be confident in a fine young heir with a supportive family.

The prince's youngest uncle, Sir Edward Woodville, was one of the escort to the coffin when the King was buried on 17 April, a public position in a very elaborate ceremony.[10] But behind the scenes of pomp and pageantry the Coun-cil still worried about France. Strengthened by the new neutrality of Burgundy, the French were becoming 'overbold'; in particular Philippe de Crèvecoeur, the Baron d'Esquerdes, a.k.a. Lord Cordes, was chasing and capturing English ships. Edward would have discussed the problems, the threats and the possible courses of action.

The Council met three days after the funeral to handle the routine busi-ness of running the kingdom and, in particular, deciding how to deal with the threat to the realm. Whatever plans there had been for attacking France were impractical without the King's leadership, so the Council restricted itself to commissioning a squadron of warships to stop the French making further depredations against English shipping and the coastal towns. Edward Wood-ville was appointed to command the squadron, presumably because he had been lined up for the main expedition, was 'a bold and valiant Captain' and already in control of the men, money and munitions, probably at Porchester.

The Council's instructions were perfectly clear, so Edward commissioned his squadron and recruited his men. His second in command was Robert Radcliffe, the Gentleman Porter of Calais so disliked by Hastings, an experi-enced naval officer who had commanded the naval squadron against the Scots in the campaign of 1482.

There were at least four ships, probably six, the nucleus being *The Trinity* and *The Falcon*, both Tower ships ('of the Tower' was the equivalent of today's 'HMS'). *The Trinity* was the same ship that Anthony Woodville had captured from Warwick at Southampton back in 1470 and may have been Edward's flagship.[11] She was 350 tons and her building had been authorized by Henry VI nearly 40 years earlier. In 1470 her captain was John Porter and then, in 1478, William Comersal. There is no further detail on *The Trinity* but the *Mary James* (bought in 1509) was a similar tonnage and, 20 years later, was manned by 85 sailors and 150 soldiers equipped with 200 bows, 500 bowstrings, 400 sheaves of arrows, 160 bills, 160 pikes and 130 harness (sets of armour).[12]

The Falcon was a ship that Edward knew, for he had sailed in her to collect the Duchess Margaret of Burgundy three years previously. Her captain was William Fetherston, who had recently received ten guns with 36 chambers 'for the apparel and defense of the King's ship Fawcon'.[13] In 1478 she had been employed for mysterious affairs of state, carrying 'certain secret persons ... to bring us knowledge of certain matters'; hence a *proper* Tower ship. Originally she was Spanish and bought by King Edward for £450 in 1475. Again, there is no other detail but she is assumed to be smaller than *The Trinity* and a guess would be around 100 to 120 tons, so perhaps similar to *The Lizard* of 1513, which carried 32 sailors and 60 soldiers. Perhaps there were a total of 200–300 soldiers on those two ships.

The two newly acquired carracks, which had cost £856-13s-4d, seem likely candidates for the squadron and then merchant ships were hired to make up the numbers. These merchantmen were chartered complete with sailing master and crew. They were given a military commander and soldiers at a ratio of two or more soldiers to one seaman and equipped with weapons of war: cannon, powder, shot and arrows. Quite often the merchant ships were foreign and on this occasion Edward hired at least two large Genoese carracks which probably carried some 200 soldiers each.

It took Edward and his team only nine days to commission, provision and make ready to sail, complete with captains, crews and fighting men, including 'ones that by every kind of tie were most devoted to the commander Edward'. The squadron sailed on the evening tide of 29 April and the following morning was out patrolling the Channel. Edward, who was looking for a fight with Lord Cordes, spent his time chasing and capturing French merchant ships. After a ten-day cruise he had certainly done damage to the French, in addition to taking a couple of prizes.[14]

He would have been unaware of the events unfolding at home. Mancini believed a story that Sir Edward had taken treasure from the Tower. In theory it was possible, but as Edward almost certainly sailed from Porchester, not London, and certainly before Gloucester had made any move, it seems most unlikely. Also and rather more importantly, there was no money in the Treasury: the cost of the war preparation had depleted the Exchequer and there was only £1,200 left, which was insufficient to pay for the King's funeral costs of £1,886.[15] No other source agrees with Mancini. Duke Richard and the Council knew there was no treasure in the Tower, so it was Richard's propaganda that gives us the clear understanding that the Woodvilles had helped themselves because they were 'greedy, selfish and unpublicspirited'.[16]

The same Council meeting that sent Edward off with his commission had to agree other plans which were not so easily settled. The date for the coronation was disputed. Queen Elizabeth and Dorset favoured government by the Council and an early coronation. This would follow the precedent set 60 years earlier, the last time a minor had been king. On the other hand, Lord Hastings believed his position would be jeopardized if the Queen's family gained control of the country through the Council and consequently wanted Duke Richard to assume unrestricted power.

Dorset proposed Sunday 4 May for the coronation but, much to his irritation, some of his colleagues on the Council said the decision should be postponed until Duke Richard arrived. Dorset at his most arrogant retorted, 'We are important enough to take decisions without the King's uncle and see they are enforced.' [17] When he suggested the new King should come to London with an army to escort him an exasperated Hastings asked if the army was to be 'against the good people of England or against the Duke of Gloucester?' Hastings went on to warn that if the escort was more than 2,000 men, he would withdraw to Calais. It is not clear where the number of 2,000 came from but it seems improbably high, and the thinly veiled threat of using the Calais garrison probably persuaded Dorset to accept the limit, which he did with little grace.

The young king-in-waiting and his uncle Anthony were at Ludlow Castle in Shropshire, the centre of Welsh and Marcher administration. It was from here that Anthony, as governor to the Prince of Wales, exercised the wide powers that the King had personally reconfirmed only six weeks earlier. At the same time, King Edward had made his youngest stepson, Richard Grey, effectively deputy governor and further strengthened Anthony's position by issuing him with a new patent that enabled him to raise troops in the Welsh March 'if need be'. These additional measures are clear confirmation of the King's decision to place his heir, together with Wales and the Marches, firmly in Anthony Woodville's safekeeping.

On 8 March Edward IV was certainly alive but there may have been unease about his health, as Anthony wrote to his lawyer, Andrew Dymmock, asking for the newly issued patents to be sent 'me by some sure man'.[18] That sounds as if he was worried about something; he had been responsible for the Prince of Wales since 1473 and there was no apparent threat, so why the patents by 'some sure man'?

News of the King's death reached Ludlow on 14 April. Nine days later, on St George's Day, a service for the Knights of the Garter was held there. The service could have been in the circular Norman church within the castle or, and this is more likely, in the huge parish church of Ludlow with its wonderful Perpendicular nave. The pageantry of the procession from the castle through the town to the church would show strength and calm at a time of uncertainty. After the service the Prince of Wales, his uncle Anthony and an escort set out for London.

Dorset had written to Anthony instructing him to bring Prince Edward to London by 1 May; the sharpness of the letter may have been due to Anthony's reluctance to become involved in the politicking. Queen Elizabeth and Dorset had a tight timetable that could have been driven by their interest in power, but it might simply have stemmed from the Queen's distrust of Richard, who had written to her expressing his devoted allegiance to her son. Did she distrust him at this date and doubt his devoted allegiance? It seems unlikely, as, according to Polydore Vergil, Duke Richard, 'in the meane sent most loving letters to Elizabeth the queen comforting her with many words and promising ...'

Thomas More says that Duke Richard persuaded the Queen it would be a mistake for a large company of armed men to escort the young King, because 'there was goodwill between all the lords and towards the young King'. It seems the Queen took his advice, for she sent word to Anthony, who consequently 'brought the King up ... with a sober company', or so More reports.

The size of the escort that Anthony took is disputed: was it near the limit of 2,000 men or a *sober*, i.e. moderate in number, company? It would be practically impossible to raise 2,000 men in the eight days available and it is also unlikely that a brave and experienced soldier like Anthony would have considered an escort the size of a small army to be necessary in a peaceful realm. Indeed most people would regard a troop of around 200 men as perfectly adequate for the task; King Edward had only taken 200 men as escort when great riots were widespread in 1467.[19]

The real questions are about Anthony's political instinct and his belief in Duke Richard's integrity. The Duke was on his way to London and had written, so reports Mancini, to the Council making his case: 'He had been loyal to his brother Edward, at home and abroad, in peace and in war, and would be, if only permitted, equally loyal to his brother's son and to all his brother's issue, even female, if perchance, which God forbid, the youth should die.' It was a good appeal and succeeded in 'winning many of them to his thinking'. He also wrote to Anthony suggesting that they meet en route for London.

The uncrowned King, Anthony and their entourage are recorded as arriving at Stony Stratford on 29 April 1483. Grafton, Anthony's family home, is just four miles north of Stony Stratford on the way to Northampton. There is nothing now to show that Grafton was once a place of great value and strength, except the site itself which is ten or so flat acres on a little plateau with the ground around falling steeply away to valley land. It makes an excellent defensive position, dominating the river Tove and the road that runs from Northampton to Stony Stratford. If Anthony was due to meet Richard at Northampton then it was the obvious place for them to spend the night, although tradition has them staying at the Rose and Crown in Stony Stratford.

That same day Duke Richard of Gloucester arrived with 300 men at Northampton. While there is no documentary evidence to show that Gloucester and Anthony had agreed a rendezvous, it would be a remarkable coincidence for both of them to arrive around Northampton on the same day, given their starting points of Ludlow and Yorkshire. If there was a rendezvous then Richard must have arranged it, and that raises the question: what was Richard's objective and when did he decide to pursue it?

As soon as Anthony heard of Duke Richard's arrival in Northampton, he left the young King and rode back alone to see the new Protector. It is ten miles from Grafton (or 14 from Stony Stratford); he rode as if to a friend and was 'greeted with a particularly cheerful and merry face' by the Duke, so he decided to stay for dinner and overnight.

Duke Richard remains an enigma. There are occasional glimpses of him, one from a visiting Silesian who describes him as 'very warm hearted' and physically tall, lean and fine boned – the Silesian was short and square.[20] Anthony certainly regarded him as a friend, and only a month before had agreed that Richard should be the arbiter in a property dispute where he was a litigant. There was friendship and trust between them, or so Anthony believed. But Richard had his own agenda: just nine months earlier he had seen the regime change in Scotland, executed without a hitch by Bell the Cat, a determined man. This may well have given Richard an idea.

In the inn Anthony and Richard talked, drank together and started dinner. Halfway through, Harry Stafford, Duke of Buckingham and Anthony's brother-in-law, arrived with an escort of 300 men and joined them at dinner;

was that another coincidence?

'Perceiving that the evening was merry he at once matched his spirits to the occasion. When supper was cleared away the three noblemen lingered over their wine. It was late evening by the time they rose from the table and, agreeing to ride together to Stony Stratford in the morning, Rivers left and went to his inn to bed.' [21]

He was fast asleep as dawn broke and armed men surrounded his inn and then rudely woke him. Thomas More relates what may be an imaginative account:

> When Lord Rivers understood the gates closed and the ways on every side beset ... comparing this manner present with this last nights cheer in so few hours so great a change marvellously misliked ... he determined upon the surety of his own conscience to go boldly to them [Gloucester and Buckingham were up and dressed] and enquire what this matter might mean ... they began to quarrel with him and say that he intended to set distance between the King and them. ... And when he began – as he was a very well spoken man – in goodly wise to excuse himself, they tarried no the end of his answer, but ... put him in ward [arrest].

So Duke Richard of Gloucester became 'the smyler with the knyf under the cloke'. He and Buckingham wasted no time and immediately rode on to gather up the young King. They arrived just as the boy was about to mount his horse, with his old tutor, Sir Thomas Vaughan, and his half-brother, Sir Richard Grey, beside him. Courteously Gloucester suggested they should all go back inside as he had important things to say. Once there, he told them he knew of a dangerous plot, one that had been hatched by Rivers, Dorset and Grey against him, the Protector! He continued on the lines that these Woodvilles were corrupting men who had brought about the King's death by ruining his health by involving him in their debaucheries.

The colour must have drained from their faces. There was shock and incredulity. The surprise was total. Gloucester dominated the scene, his words unnerving and his hostility suddenly apparent. In reality his ambition was driving him to exploit the opportunity that had been created by the King's unexpected death. This was the start of what Professor Ross has called 'the virulent and puritanical propaganda campaign by which Richard sought to discredit the Woodvilles'.

The King-to-be-crowned made a spirited protest in favour of Rivers and Grey: 'What my brother Marquis hath done I cannot say but, in good faith, I dare well answer for mine uncle Rivers and my brother here, that they be innocent of any such matters.' But this was unceremoniously brushed aside. Duke Richard was intent on his coup, not interested in the truth or the views of a 12-year-old. He put his nephew under 'protection', dismissed the royal servants and sent the escort back to Ludlow. Richard had won the first round. He took his prize back to Northampton while gallopers headed for London with the news that he had 'come upon him [the King] with a strong force at Stony Stratford and took the new King into his governance by right of his protectorship'.

The flavour of that report indicates that the escort was much smaller in number than the 600 men of Gloucester and Buckingham, and certainly not the 2,000 of popular history. Gloucester and Buckingham celebrated over dinner in Northampton and sent a dish of food from the table to the imprisoned Anthony who sent his thanks but, thinking of his companion, asked that the food be taken onto Richard Grey, 'who unused to adversity needed comfort the more. He himself was well acquainted with the fickleness of fortune.'

Reports of the abduction brought chaos in London. Hastings was delighted, Queen Elizabeth distraught. Archbishop Rotherham, the Chancellor, hurried to Westminster and found a scene of torch-lit confusion with crates, boxes, furniture and tapestries being dragged from the palace to the sanctuary. To speed the operation a hole had been knocked in the sanctuary wall to pass things through directly from the palace. The Queen was sitting 'alone, a-low on the rushes all desolate and dismayed'.

By the next day Duke Richard's advance guard had established control, with pickets patrolling the Thames and guards on the sanctuary gates. Four days later the King-to-be rode into London flanked by his uncles, the new Protector and Buckingham. The prince wore blue velvet and his escort of 500 men were all unarmed and dressed in black; but the column was led by four wagons loaded with barrels of armour, some of which was decorated with the Woodville crest.

Criers escorted the wagons and shouted that Earl Rivers had gathered this armour for use against the Duke of Gloucester. The Londoners were not impressed by the story or display, recognizing it as propaganda. Duke Richard had almost certainly lifted the barrels of arms from Grafton when he took his nephew into protection; it would have been the usual reserve of arms and armour kept by noblemen to equip their levies in time of war.

There is an odd snippet from the days that young Edward had spent with his uncles Richard and Harry. On the flyleaf of a book (now in the British Library) there is the signature 'R. Edwardus Quintus' (King Edward V). Some way beneath, as if to demonstrate service, his uncle has written 'Loyaulte me lie.

Richard Gloucestre' (bound by loyalty). Below again is 'Sounte me souenne. Harre Bokyngham' (Remember me often). The boy must have felt fortunate to have two such affectionate uncles.

Duke Richard had decided that the coronation must be postponed, but to allay fears that he had some secret agenda the peers and bishops were asked to swear loyalty to his nephew as King Edward V. He sacked Rotherham as Lord Chancellor and appointed John Russell, the Bishop of Lincoln and a career court official.

Anthony and his two fellow prisoners were sent north to different castles. The Protector at his first Council meeting proposed a charge of treason against them. There was not a shred of evidence, so the Council rejected the charges. None of the members could see any treason, but nevertheless the prisoners remained incarcerated. The Queen stayed firmly in sanctuary with her younger son and daughters but that did not concern Richard. He put guards on the doors, which effectively meant they were his prisoners. The Protector's immediate problem was Edward Woodville and his fleet.

On 9 May Duke Richard sent his own men to take over command of Edward's castle at Porchester and Anthony's at Carisbrooke. He also instructed that Dover and Sandwich be prepared to resist an attack by Edward – good anti-Woodville propaganda. The following day he commissioned 'Sir Thomas Fulford and one Halwelle to rig them to sea in all haste and go to the Downs [between Deal, on the Kent coast, and the Goodwin Sands] among Sir Edward and his company'.

Also on 10 May he wrote to the Mayor of Plymouth instructing him to hand over two French ships to his authority – might these have been captured by Edward? Then Duke Richard received news of the fleet being around the Solent, because, four days later, 'Edward Brampton, John Wellis and Thomas Grey' received writs 'to go to the sea with ships to take Sir Edward Wodevile'. This sounds more like a move against a small squadron rather than a 20-ship fleet. There were also further instructions to the new custodians of Porchester and Carisbrooke to victual and furnish those ships and the order for a soft line, 'to receive all that will come except the Marquis, Sir Edward Wodevile and Robert Ratclyff'.[22]

On the same day (14 May) the unsuspecting Edward sailed into Southampton Water and boarded a merchant ship. He was going about his business calling himself 'Sir Edward Wydeville knight, uncle unto our said sovereign Lord and great captain of his navy'. That was the description he used as he sequestered £10,201 of English gold coin that he had found on the ship. He signed an 'indenture ... that if it can be proved not forfeited unto the King ...

11. Flemish carrack by an artist known as WA, believed to have been drawn
around 1460. It shows the design and rigging of contemporary ships.

[Sir Edward] shall repay ... the value of the said money in English merchandise
within three month ... if the said money to be forfeited then Sir Edward to be
answering the King'.[23]

The sum of £10,201 was a fortune and would weigh some 350lbs (157kg).
It was enough to put an army in the field for a couple of months and the equivalent of some 15 per cent of the full annual royal revenue. The receipt implies

that Edward believed the gold belonged to the King and he was the best person to deliver it. The actual copy of this indenture that has survived came from King Edward V's Council, so Duke Richard would be well aware that Edward had the money. The ownership of the money remains a mystery; coincidentally £10,000 (about 50,000 crowns) was the annual payment due under the Treaty of Picquigny, so one possible source was King Louis, who, surprised by English war preparations, might have decided to send the suspended payments. However, this is pure speculation.

In London the change of policy was total. The Protector sent an envoy to 'the aggrieved Lord Cordes' to discuss a non-aggression pact and the mutual restitution of ships and goods. Only a month previously Lord Cordes had been dangerous and leading the threat to the realm; now he was the aggrieved. It seems the King's 'Great Captain' had fought the French, made damages and captured some of their ships. From the Protector's point of view he was a very dangerous man to have on the loose with his ships, men and a war chest.

The first squadron dispatched by the Protector had been unable to find Edward, which was hardly surprising as he was not in the Downs but in Southampton Water. The second was more successful but its leaders decided not to confront him. Instead, officers surreptitiously rowed out to his ships to subvert the crewmen and soldiers.

They told the soldiers and sailors that Sir Edward was a traitor and offered a big reward for him, dead or alive. They said his officers would be outlawed and the ship owner's goods confiscated, unless immediate allegiance was given to the Protector. The reaction was mixed; the English soldiers remained loyal to Edward but the Genoese officers and seamen of the hired ships were in a quandary. Mancini relates:

> For the purposes of that war the Genoese merchants trading in London had lent these vessels for a fixed time and manned them with Genoese sailors and captains ... yet on hearing of the proclamation they realised they could not reasonably remain at war, not indeed without losing their wares and imperilling their countrymen. ... They had all the more reason for fear since on these two ships had been put a sprinkling of picked English troops, ones that were most devoted to the commander Edward.

Having decided where their best interests lay, it was then a question of how to get rid of the soldiers and to escape from Edward. One of the captains of the two Genoese ships was 'a man excelling in wisdom and audacious resolution', who concocted a plan. He arranged a special dinner for the soldiers on board, which was served along with copious quantities of wine and beer. Once the soldiers were happily fuddled, he left them saying he was going to look at the stars and climbed to the forecastle.

The carousing continued until suddenly the captain shouted down. He pretended he had seen new weather, 'as though by unexpected chance favourable winds began to blow'. He ordered his men to make ready to sail and told the soldiers to clear the decks and go below. After some time the soldiers were called up again on deck and so they came, one by one, up through the hatches. But as they emerged, they were knocked out and tied up. A similar ambush on the other Genoese ship was equally successful. Once the Genoese had control of their ships they hoisted their colours, blew their trumpets and set sail. The rest of the squadron was thrown into confusion and the fleet broke up, with some ships sailing for port.

Edward was left with two ships, *The Trinity* and *The Falcon*. It is remarkable that the officers, seamen and soldiers of these two capital ships remained loyal to him and so became proscribed men. For instance, 'one William Slater now goone to the see with Sir Edward Wodevile' was stripped of his office of parkership of Whitemede Park, and on 19 May Sir Robert Radcliffe was deprived of his two farms in the Calais marches. Also on that day Lord Lovell was appointed Chief Butler in place of Anthony, while the park at Grafton had been handed over to a new custodian on 14 May, the day Brampton was commissioned to find Edward.[24]

The Protector again commissioned ships to seek out Sir Edward and demanded that Earl Rivers be indicted for treason. But the Council refused to accept the proposed charge of treason, although they did agree to postpone the coronation to 24 June. *The Crowland Chronicle* reported:

> The powerful Lord Hastings, Chamberlain of Edward IV, who seemed to oblige the Dukes of Gloucester and Buckingham in every way and to have earned special favours from them, was overjoyed at this new world, declaring that nothing more had happened than the transfer of the rule of the Kingdom from two of the Queen's relatives to two of the King's. This had been achieved without any killing or any more spilling of blood than that from a cut finger.

Archbishop Rotherham started to worry about Gloucester's motives, but Hastings, whose loyalty was not in doubt, assured him there was no danger for the young King to whom both he and Gloucester had sworn fealty. Hastings had never been so well off or so powerful. He had even taken into his protection the late King's mistress, the beautiful Jane Shore, who had been very special to King Edward, 'for many he had but her he loved'. She was 'the merriest' of the King's mistresses, 'ready and quick of answer' as well as being 'proper she was and fair'. Lucky Hastings, but around this time his trusted lieutenant Sir William Catesby switched allegiance and started to work covertly for the Protector.

Duke Richard needed to know the strength of Hastings's commitment to the young princes. It was Catesby who was sent to test his loyalty and 'found him so fast [to them] ... that he durst [go] no further'. This attachment did not suit the Protector. It meant that Hastings was not only loyal to the young King, but in the medium term would be reconciled to the Woodvilles because he would know that the young King could not give up all his mother's family.

Meanwhile the Protector, with the enthusiastic help of Buckingham, was drawing together the reins of power. On 10 June he secretly sent to the North for military help, 'against the Queen, her blood, adherents and affinity which have intended to murder and utterly destroy us and our cousin the Duke of Buckingham ... by their subtle and damnable ways ... and also the final destruction and disinheritance of you and all other men of honour, as well of the north parts as other countries that adhere to us'.

It was a brilliant letter accusing the Woodvilles of murder, treason, rebellion and sorcery and appealing to the citizens' sense of honour, their instinct for the sanctity of inheritance, their regional sentiment and loyalty.[25] In reality Richard had made certain that the Woodvilles were incapable of posing a threat to anyone. Even the clerical brother, Bishop Lionel, who seems to have been more interested in university business than state politics, had scuttled straight into sanctuary when he eventually arrived in London.[26]

A meeting of the Council was called for Friday 13 June, but different instructions were issued to different people. Lords Hastings and Stanley, Archbishop Rotherham and Bishop Morton of Ely were to meet at the Tower, the others at Westminster. Thomas More wrote that Hastings, on his way to the meeting, saw a herald he knew at the Tower wharf where they discussed a previous chance meeting at the same place: 'In faith man,' said Hastings, 'I was never so sorry, nor stood in so great dread in my life as I did when thou and I met here. And lo, how the world has turned: now stand mine enemies in the danger, as thou mayest hap to hear more hereafter, and I never in my life so merry, nor never in so great surety.'[27]

It seems that Hastings was hinting that Anthony's fate was on the Council's agenda. He then passed on to join the meeting that opened well enough, with the Protector in fine spirits: 'My Lord of Ely, when I was last in Holborn I saw good strawberries in your garden there; I do beseech you send for some of them.' He then left the meeting and returned an hour later, looking grim. 'I pray you all, tell me what they deserve that do conspire my death with devilish plots!'[28]

There was a moment's silence and then he accused Hastings and the two bishops of treason, a dread word. There was shock and fury, shouts of 'treason' and armed men rushed into the room. Stanley very sensibly fell to the floor. Hastings was grabbed, held by guards and told he was to be executed immediately.

'For by St Paul I will not to dinner till I see thy head off,' said the Protector. It would be interesting to know if he shouted, was matter-of-fact or hissed this terrifying statement.[29] The soldiers took Hastings out to the little green by the Tower chapel. As he stood on the grass and watched life for the last time he must have felt foolish and bitter. He had failed to see Gloucester's brutal ambition and now there was more blood to be shed than 'from a cut finger'. He was there and then beheaded. More wrote his epitaph: 'Thus ended this honourable man, a good knight and a gentle, of great authority with his prince, of living somewhat desolate [dissolute] ... eth [easy] to beguile ... a loving man and passing well beloved; very faithful and trusty enough, trusting too much.'

For their part, the bishops and Lord Stanley were imprisoned in the Tower. The Protector's attention now turned to the nine-year-old Prince Richard who was with his mother, safe in sanctuary. There had been a debate on the use of sanctuary, with the Protector arguing that it should only be used as a refuge, not for detention. In his view, the Queen was detaining the young prince, who should be free for his brother's imminent coronation.

It was just a matter of putting things together. Having dealt with Hastings, the Protector took his party of soldiers from the Tower and rowed upriver to Westminster, where he joined the remaining members of the Council in the Star Chamber. Duke Richard's dominance was total, so it is hardly surprising that the rump of the Council agreed with him. The Archbishop of Canterbury, Lord Howard and the soldiers marched on to the Abbey for a discussion with the Queen.

Soldiers stood guard at the entrances while the Archbishop, the boy's great-uncle, went in to talk to the Queen, Lord Howard with him. He made a persuasive case and the Queen, swayed by his categorical assurances for the boy's safety, agreed. She relinquished the prince.

At this point she cannot have known of Hastings's summary execution and presumably calculated that the best chance for the boy was for the Archbishop to take personal responsibility. She would have had no doubt about the Protector's determination and probably believed that he would, if necessary, break into sanctuary to get his way, as he had at Tewkesbury.

She said unto the child: 'Farewell, my own sweet son, God send you good keeping, let me kiss you once yet ere you go, for God knoweth when we shall kiss together again.' And therewith she kissed him, and blessed him, turned her back and wept and went her way, leaving the child weeping as fast.[30]

So Prince Richard left sanctuary and was taken for a talk with his uncle Richard before being sent downriver to join his brother at the Tower.

Under the flurry of activity round the Abbey, Dorset chose his moment to slip out of sanctuary and escape. The sentries did not notice but an officer discovered soon after; they thought he was hiding locally so sent for help to ring the nearby cornfields with soldiers and dogs. They beat the fields to catch the fugitive 'just as hunters do' but Dorset had eluded them and was clean away.

By this time the Council was little more than a facade for Duke Richard's ambition. *The Crowland Chronicle* reported, 'Thus, without justice or trial, the three strongest supporters of the new King had been removed, while his remaining followers were fearing something similar.' He now felt strong enough to override the Council's refusal to indict Anthony; he simply decreed the death sentence, including Sir Thomas Vaughan and Sir Richard Grey for good measure. Having physically ambushed both potential rivals – Rivers and Hastings – he then justified his illegal acts by claiming a conspiracy, and finished the job by comprehensively blackening their characters.[31]

Anthony was informed he was to be executed the next day. Why? Because, he was told, his sister the Queen, had been plotting against the Protector. That night he prayed and wrote his will:

I, Anthony Wodevile, in the castle of Sheriff Hutton, ... bequeath my soul unto the great mercy of Jesus Christ ... my heart to be buried (if I die south of Trent) before our lady of Pewe [the chapel rebuilt by Anthony at Westminster Abbey] ... bequeath all my lands that were my father's to his right heirs; with my cupp of gold of columbyne ... and such lands that were my first wife's the Lady Scales, and Thomas Lord Scales's, her brother, to my brother Sir Edward, and his heirs male ... before he took possession thereof, to deduct 500 marks to be employed for the souls of the said lady and her brother, and the souls of all the Scales's blood, &c. and to find a priest for one year to pray for them, his own soul and all Christian souls, at our lady of Pewe; and another priest to sing at the chapel of the Rodes, in Greenwich, for his own soul and all Christian souls.

His wife Mary was left silver plate, silks and feather beds, together with her wedding provision and presents. He instructed that manors and land should be sold to build and endow a hospital at Rochester for 13 poor folk. He directed that his clothes and tournament armour should be sold and the money used to buy shirts and smocks for the poor. He listed various debts to ensure they were paid and gave instructions for the rewarding of his servants and others: 'my servant James have £10 ... Tybold my barbo have £3. ... My gown of tawny cloth of gold I give to the Prior of Royston.' [32]

He appointed several executors including his lawyer, Andrew Dymmock, and Robert Poyntz, who was married to his natural daughter and had been his lieutenant at Carisbrooke. He also composed some wry poetic musings:

Somewhat musing
and more mourning
In remembering
The unsteadfastness;
This world beeing
Of such wheeling,
the contrarying,
What may I guess?

Methinks truly
Bounden am I,
And that greatly,
To be content;
seeing plainly
Fortune doth wry [turn aside]
All contrary
From mine intent.

I fear, doubtless
Remediless
Is now to siege
My woeful chance;
For unkindness
Withoutenless [to speak plainly]
And no redress
Me doth advance

With displeasure
To my grievance
And no surance
Of remedy.
So in this trance
Now in substance
Such is my dance

Willing to die.

My life was lent
Me on intent.
It is nigh spent
Welcom fortune!
But I ne'er went [never thought]
Thus to be shent [cut off]
But so she ment
Such is her won [custom].

The verses are interesting for the strength of voice and the absence of any obvious reference to God. The metre is 3:1:3:1, possibly in honour of the Trinity and the text has assumptions such as *This* world. It helped to while away the night, his last before execution.[33]

On Tuesday 24 June the young King should have been crowned, but instead his uncle, his tutor and his half-brother were brought together at Pumfret (Pontefract) Castle and there beheaded. After the execution, Anthony was discovered to have been wearing a hair shirt beneath his finery, an uncomfortable garment to remind him of pain and humility; this was later taken to Doncaster church and venerated by generations of worshippers.

He had no children by either of his wives, 'but by a beloved mistress called Gwentlian, only daughter of Sir William Stradling of Glamorganshire ... he had a daughter Margaret', who married Sir Robert Poyntz, his friend and one of the executors of his will.[34] The Stradlings were a distinguished Anglo-Welsh family but this Sir William was the son of a cadet branch.

An early sixteenth-century copy of an entry in the Garter Book shows Earl Rivers's coat of arms, crested by a man brandishing a scimitar over his head. The left supporter is a fully armoured knight also brandishing a scimitar; on the right is a leopard standing on his hind legs and grinning broadly. The shield is divided into six sections covering the heraldic range, from the silver scallops to a golden griffin. (Fess and quarter gules of Wydeville; Escallops of Scales; Griffin sergeant of Rivers; Lion rampant of Luxembourg: Vair of Beauchamp; Sun rayonny of Baux.) There is also a short biographical note celebrating Anthony's jousting fame and lamenting that this 'courageous Knight and gentill' was 'piteously put to dethe at Pumfret'.

While these terrible events were unfolding William Caxton was printing *The Canterbury Tales* with 26 cheerful woodcuts, amongst which there is one of a dashing knight on his charger. Might this have been modelled on his patron, or perhaps his patron's young brother who was presently sailing the Channel wondering what to do?

Duke Richard's propaganda campaign now turned full strength to legitimizing his position. A sermon was delivered from St Paul's Cross, the standard place for outlining government policy. The preacher was a Cambridge theologian who denounced Duke Richard's mother, the Dowager Duchess, as an adulteress and his dead brother, King Edward, as a bastard.[35] Apparently the Duchess Cecily had agreed to this and some people take this as legitimizing Richard's claim. But it is far from proven and still left Edward Plantagenet, Clarence's son, as senior in line to Richard, although it might be argued that he was disqualified by his father's attainder.

On the point of legitimacy, it has been argued that Edward's father was away campaigning at Pontoise when he should have been fathering Edward. Maybe, but the Duchess was at Rouen, and Pontoise is only 60 miles away, no more than a hard day's ride. The Duke was overseeing the siege, so time was on his hands; why should she not have visited her husband there or he returned for a night or two? (Mary, Queen of Scots once rode 60 hard miles in a day to see Lord Bothwell, and Edward III averaged 55 miles a day from London to York in 1336.) Perhaps the strongest argument for legitimacy is that Duke Richard accepted Edward as his firstborn. A letter written by Edward and his brother to their father starts, 'as we your trew and natural sons'.[36] This expression has been accepted as evidence of legitimacy in other cases. If the Duchess had strayed then her husband had been very accommodating, and that is not how people regarded the Duke. It is all rather far-fetched, a typical exercise in character assassination.

After the sermon from St Paul's Cross the Protector imposed a curfew in London and instructed its bishop to make the beautiful Jane Shore do penance as a harlot. She walked barefoot through the streets carrying a lighted taper in her hand and wearing only a shirt. This was his dead brother's favourite mistress, and while some Londoners may have enjoyed the spectacle others sympathized with Jane rather than applauding the Protector, who had two illegitimate children of his own. Life also changed for his little nephews: 'after the removal of Hastings, the attendants who had previously administered to the young King's needs were all kept from him. He and his brother were transferred to the inner chambers of the Tower.'

At this opportune moment Bishop Stillington of Bath and Wells suddenly remembered that the marriage between King Edward and Elizabeth Woodville had been illegal because the King had previously been engaged. Actually there was no evidence of any earlier pre-marital arrangement with the lady, who was long since dead; however, the Bishop remembered with absolute

12. The Protector is offered the crown by the citizens. John Leech's view
of the event in *The Comic History of England* (1879).

certainty. This was a surprise.

There is anecdotal evidence that Bishop Stillington's memory was helped by
inducement: the French had the opportunity of interrogating his son when he
was their prisoner. Commines recorded that the Bishop was a 'courtier' with
an illegitimate son whom 'he dearly loved' and that King Richard 'wished to
bestow great benefits on him [the son] and have him marry Elizabeth of York'.
That would be an impossible marriage for a bishop's bastard unless there was a
very high price. But the plan came to nothing because the boy, who had been
given accelerated promotion with the command of an English warship, was

captured off the coast of Normandy. He was 'imprisoned in the Petit Châtellet in Paris where he died of hunger and deprivation'. Presumably he was interrogated before he died, so Commines would have known all he had to tell.[37]

In June 1483 the Bishop's revelation was just what the Protector needed. He may have wrestled with his conscience but concluded that his nephews and nieces were bastards. It is odd that he forgot about the ecclesiastical courts, the correct place to deal with such matters, and decided on his own authority that as a bastard the young King was unable to succeed his father, whose legitimacy was not now in question.[38]

Apparently Duke Richard was untroubled by his own position. As Clarence had been married to Isabel Neville, his own marriage to her sister, Anne, was consequently between brother and sister-in-law. That was contrary to Leviticus Chapter XVIII. Papal dispensation would be required to permit such a marriage and it was far from certain that it could or would be given. They were also cousins, related in the 'fourth degree', although that was not such a problem. There can have been no misunderstanding. But Duke Richard never asked for papal dispensation; his son was thus illegitimate and so he was living the lie.[39]

Buckingham made a persuasive speech to the mayor and aldermen of London and treated the Lords to the same on the following day. They all, 'fearing for their own safety, decided to declare Richard King and request him to assume the duties of government'. He accepted and the nation was told that there would still be a coronation, but it would now be the Protector who would be crowned. The full argument and logic of Richard's right to the throne was then set out in a bill, *Titulus Regius*, which Professor Ross describes as a mixture of specious moralizing and deliberate deceit.

There was no word about the poor little princes, but Mancini, who was recalled to France immediately after the Protector's coronation, reported, 'I saw many men moved to weeping and lamentation at the mention of his name. However, I have not yet been able to establish whether he was done away with and, if so, by what means.'

The princes were never seen again. They had been in the Protector's care and he had absolute power. His contemporaries believed he was guilty of murder, and one of the more reliable of the London chronicles has a persuasive report: 'as the said King Richard had put to death the Lord Chamberlain and other gentlemen ... He also put to death the two children of King Edward, for which cause he lost the hearts of the people.'[40]

Nevertheless the Protector was crowned King Richard III, by the grace of God and with great ceremony, on Sunday 6 July. The master of the ceremony was the Duke of Buckingham, but his wife, Catherine Woodville, Edward's and Anthony's sister, was absent. Margaret Beaufort, Henry Tudor's mother and married to Lord Stanley, carried Queen Anne's train and kept her thoughts to herself. After the coronation they sat down to a dinner that was served on dishes of gold and silver. During the second course Sir Robert Dymmock, the King's Champion, entered, armed and on horseback. He proclaimed: 'Whoever shall say King Richard the third was not lawfully King, he would fight him at all hazards,' and to ratify the engagement, threw down his gauntlet. The hall resounded: 'King Richard, God save King Richard.' Sir Robert repeated his challenge three times, then drank wine from a gilded cup which he carried away as his fee.[41]

But the coronation posed questions for honest men. Lord Dynham, in command at Calais, wrote to the new King asking how the officers were to square his accession to the throne with their previous oaths of loyalty to Edward V. King Richard replied with the full text of *Titulus Regius*, which seemed to do the trick, but others were unconvinced. Many of his brother's lieutenants and retainers had supported Richard while they thought he could provide stability, but once they knew he had betrayed his nephew, then they would only acquiesce until there was an alternative.

On 23 July Anthony's will was disregarded and the Scales lands were granted to the Duke of Norfolk. Edward Woodville, lurking in the Channel, can have had no doubt about the state of the nation. His two ships had eluded the Protector's squadrons but the news was very depressing. There were his nephews, the little princes, locked up in the Tower; his brother Anthony executed or rather murdered, together with his old playmate Richard Grey; Hastings summarily executed; bishops locked up and, to cap it all, Duke Richard of Gloucester crowned king. What a litany of disaster.

However, he had £10,201 in gold coin, two good ships[42] and a company of soldiers who were 'most devoted to the commander Edward'. So there he was, cruising in the Channel, wondering what to do next.

EXILE IN BRITTANY

'**Y**ou have witchcraft in your lips, Kate; there is more eloquence in a sugar touch of them than in the tongues of the French Council.' So, according to Shakespeare, said Henry V, King of England, to Katherine, Princess of France, when he was wooing her after his brilliant victory at Agincourt.[2] Henry won her but died after only two years of marriage, leaving a beautiful widow and a very young heir.

There was little agreement on how to run the country but at least there was agreement about the Queen — public interest required the hero's widow to be on a pedestal, out of the reach of man. However, from a modest background in Wales came a young man with a twinkle in his eye, Owen Tudor, who took employment as a Clerk of the Wardrobe in the Dowager Queen's household. According to Vergil he was 'a gentleman of Wales, adorned with wonderful gifts of body and mind, who derived his pedigree from Cadwallider, the last King of Britons'.

One of the better stories has Owen at a dance. The music was fast, the drink flowed, the dancers whirled and Owen, distinctly the worse for wear, collapsed into the Queen's lap. It was a good way of gaining her attention. Elis Gruffydd, the Welsh chronicler, has a different story: the Queen first saw Owen swimming in a river on a summer's day. He caught her watching, grabbed her and tried for a kiss. In the scuffle that followed her cheek was scratched, which caused blushing and embarrassment when he was serving her at dinner the following day. Whatever the truth of their courting, Owen and Katherine married secretly and had three children, Edmund, Jasper and Owen (a fourth died young).

French Kate died in 1437 and the Council suddenly discovered that their hero's wife had not only remarried but had married someone of 'neither birth nor property'. They were furious and threw Owen into gaol, but he escaped by 'hurting foul his keeper'. When recaptured he seemed unable to prove the marriage; nevertheless the young King Henry VI, who had no other family, decided to recognize his half-brothers. Edmund, the eldest, was made Earl of Richmond and was later provided with a rich bride; Jasper became Earl of Pembroke, while Owen became a monk.

Edmund's bride was Margaret Beaufort, but he did not enjoy his luck for long and died soon after, leaving a heavily pregnant 13-year-old widow. Their son was Henry Tudor, the new Earl of Richmond, born in 1457 in Pembroke Castle. Through his mother he had a distant but flawed claim to the throne of England, as his great-grandfather was the legitimized bastard son of John of Gaunt.[3] It was enough to make him a pawn in the power game and after the Lancastrian defeat at Towton, Lord Herbert discovered Henry at Pembroke. He took the boy in charge and was granted the – lucrative – wardship, so young Henry spent the next few years in the Herbert establishment at Raglan Castle.

Then came Warwick's invasion in late 1470. Henry's uncle Jasper returned and collected Henry from Raglan. However, the battle of Tewkesbury put paid to his plans and Jasper was forced to retreat to Pembroke taking Henry with him. With King Edward's men following hard on his heels, Pembroke Castle became unsafe. They rode over to Tenby and took a ship for France but bad weather blew them off course to Brittany.

Duke Francis thought his unexpected visitors could be useful and welcomed them. His mother, Jeanne, a daughter of King Charles VI of France, was sister of the late Queen Katherine so Henry was his first cousin, as well as being a cousin of King Louis of France. Vergil observed that he was 'the only imp now left of King Henry VI's blood', which was not true, but what a court historian might be expected to say.

The news reached London where King Edward 'had intelligens that therles [the Earls] of Pembrowgh and Richmond were transported into Bryteyn', so he sent an ambassador with instructions to bring them to London. 'The duke [of Brittany] herd willingly King Edwards ambasage and when he understood therles were so rich a prey he determynyd not to let them go.'[4]

They stayed in Brittany, sometimes under protective custody in the massive octagonal tower at the Château de Largoët, but at other times in almost complete freedom. But they were prisoners and pawns for Duke Francis to use in his diplomatic manoeuvring. However, he also protected them and gave allowances according to their importance: Henry, being (nearly) of the blood royal, received substantially more than Jasper.[5]

Henry of Richmond, this cousin of kings and princes and possible pretender to the English throne, was 26 in 1483. His mother was now married to her fourth husband, Lord Stanley; she was rich, ambitious for her only child and unconcerned by an old proviso that barred her family from the royal succession.[6]

Henry appears to have been a natural leader with considerable charm, although he was totally unproven, having spent most of his life kicking his heels in exile. His portrait shows a bony, intelligent face with a big nose, shrewd calculating eyes and a generous mouth. Polydore Vergil, his court historian, wrote, 'His body was slender but well built and strong; his height above average. His appearance was remarkably attractive and his face cheerful especially when speaking; his eyes were small and blue.'

King Edward would have liked those Lancastrian earls back in England and under his control but Duke Francis refused to part with his pawns. Anthony had been commissioned to bring them back when he was there in 1472 but had failed. At least the Duke had given King Edward an undertaking that Henry and his uncle would not be allowed to make mischief in England.

However, ten years on and King Edward's view of the threat seemed to be changing. The previous June he had given permission for Henry to inherit lands worth £400 a year, provided he returned to England 'to be in the grace and favour of the King'. Perhaps more importantly, there had been a discussion between the King, Margaret Beaufort (Henry's mother), her husband Lord Stanley and Bishop Morton about a marriage between Henry and the Princess Elizabeth of York.[7] Nothing had come of it and now the King was dead while Henry was still the Duke's 'guest' (Vergil says Henry was released from 'prison' as soon as Duke Francis heard of King Edward's death).

Into this fertile territory sailed Edward Woodville in June 1483. *The Trinity* and *The Falcon* had sailed out of the Solent in late May and we know he was in Brittany because on 13 July one of King Richard's clerks, Thomas Hutton, 'a man of pregnant wit', was commissioned to go to Brittany and discuss areas of mutual interest but particularly to 'feel and understand the mind and disposition of the Duke about Sir Edward Woodville and his retinue, practising by all means to him possible to search and know if there be any intended enterprise out of land upon any part of this realm, certifying with all due diligence all the news and disposition there from time to time'.[8]

The arrival of the ships with some 200–300 well-armed soldiers and around 130 seamen to join the neglected earls would have caused a sensation. These two Tower ships were brightly painted in vermilion (bright red), gold, russet, bice (sky blue), red, white etc, with standards and long streamers flying and their sides lined with pavesses (wooden shields) decorated with coats of arms in brilliant colours.[9]

While there is no documentary evidence that tells how Edward arrived or who was with him, circumstantial evidence has him arriving in *The Trinity* and *The Falcon*. Both he and those ships were last recorded escaping from

English waters in late May.[10] King Richard knew he had a retinue with him and was worrying what he might do with it. Importantly, around then there was a marked increase in Henry's credibility which coincides with Edward's arrival at the ducal court and the addition of 200–300 unnamed Englishmen recorded in Vannes.

These men were not there before. Presumably they came from *The Trinity* and *The Falcon*; Edward is the only commander who – with his soldiers – is known to have left England at that date. There is some confirmation in the cases of William Slater (or Sclatter) and William Comersal. In June 1483 Slater had been dismissed as keeper of the park at Whitemede because he had 'gone to sea with Sir Edward Wodeville'.[11] The next time Slater makes the records is after Bosworth, in September 1486, when he is reappointed park keeper at Whitemede and also becomes 'bailiffe of Chadlyngton'. Later, in March 1488, he was appointed a Yeoman of the Crown.

William Comersal was captain of *The Trinity* in 1478 and, while little else is known of him, it might be assumed he was still her captain in 1483 and so went to Brittany. He was appointed 'Clerk of the Ships' in August 1488, the key job of controlling the King's naval organization. Henry Tudor favoured those who had been with him in Brittany and this would account for the appointment of an ordinary sea captain to a top job.

If *The Trinity* and *The Falcon* docked in Brittany then presumably the ships remained there to form the core of the Tudor navy, rather than going back to face King Richard's anger. What of the 156.8kg of gold coin? The only reference is rather oblique, Mancini believed Edward had taken the treasure from the Tower, but there was no treasure in the Tower to take. However, perhaps Mancini heard that Edward had taken treasure in a general sense and been told, or assumed, the Tower was the source. Duke Richard would certainly be worrying about Edward and his war chest.

We have no idea where the gold came from or how its owner reacted to the sequestration.[12] Did Edward deliver it to the new King-in-waiting, use it to pay his men while they waited or squirrel it away? The records are silent but if the ships and men did stay with Henry, which is probable, then the cost of paying and feeding all those soldiers and sailors would be at least £60 per week, or £3,120 a year. There is every reason to suppose that Edward was an honourable knight and so he would regard himself bound by the terms of his receipt. He was the custodian of the gold and responsible for it to the *legitimate* king. But that was not Richard and, until he knew better, it was his nephew, Edward.

The arrival of *The Trinity* and *The Falcon* heralded the start of the 25-month rush which took Henry from – effectively – being a prisoner, dependent on whim and goodwill, to the crown of England. Edward and his retinue[13] had suddenly given the Tudor cause real credibility and wherewithal.

Meanwhile in London, King Richard was alert to the dangers of a Tudor and Woodville alliance. His new Lord Chancellor, John Russell, drafted a sermon to parliament: he would cover the issues facing the nation and in particular he spoke of 'fluctuacion' with 'gret waters and tempestous Rivers'. But the sermon was not given. This was the same Bishop John Russell who had been with Edward in Scotland four years before. Now the Bishop must negotiate with Brittany, as his master wanted Edward Woodville.

Thomas Hutton, who had been given the task under cover of a trade mission to agree such matters as action against piracy, should particularly 'feel and understand the mind and disposition of the Duke about Sir Edward Woodville and his retinue'. From this it is clear that Sir Edward and his retinue were considered a threat, one that was capable of undertaking an enterprise against England. This is confirmation that they were professional soldiers. As important or perhaps more so, Hutton was to persuade Duke Francis to deliver Henry of Richmond into King Richard's tender care.

Duke Francis mulled the matter over. It was tricky; while King Richard was unknown to him, Edward Woodville was a friend. The Duke remembered how important Anthony's military help had been 11 years before and now – according to French records – the Bretons called Edward 'Lord Scales, in memory of his brother'.[14] (It seems more likely they called him Scales because his badge was the silver scallop which they knew from his brother's 1472 expedition.[15])

However, the Duke could not afford to alienate England so he dispatched an envoy to King Richard offering the 'Lord of Richmond'. However, he pointed out that the consequence of the gift would be a French invasion, so the price had to be high – 4,000 archers at England's expense. He ignored the request for Edward and was probably not surprised when his offer was turned down.

As the diplomatic manoeuvring progressed, Henry 'the Lord of Richmond' and Edward presumably reached agreement. They were joined in opposition to King Richard. The only difference might be over the crown, but in that June and early July there was no reason to think the young princes were dead, only that their wicked uncle had locked them up and was a usurper.

Edward's aim was to put his nephew back on the throne, and while Henry may have been the Lancastrian pretender, he might happily agree to something less than the crown. Better to be a great earl in England than a penniless pretender in exile. That would be the logical conclusion to the talks his mother had pursued with the late King Edward, which had been witnessed by Bishop Morton.

In the château at Vannes and the halls of the newly built ducal palace at Nantes they discussed insurrection and invasion. How would the arrangement be structured? What resources were available? How were they to keep Duke Francis supportive and what would be required to defeat Richard the usurper?

Men, money and munitions have always been the essential ingredients of any such project. They and their contemporaries were well aware of that. In the near contemporary novel we have the hero Tirant Lo Blanc advising, 'In war three things are necessary and those who lack any one of these will fail ... [these are] troops, money, and provisions.'

Henry's formidable mother was providing information and intelligence, so Earl Henry could feel confident of Lancastrian support, some help from the Stanleys and financial backing. Edward had his soldiers' and his family's support; he also had his war chest and two capital ships. Meanwhile 'The people of the southern and western parts of the Kingdom began to murmur greatly and to form meetings and confederacies in order to deliver the two princes from the Tower.'

The Dowager Queen Elizabeth was urged to smuggle her daughters out of sanctuary and abroad, but this plan was discovered and a heavier guard put on the door. Many of the dead King's officers and friends decided Richard had gone too far by seizing the crown. They were prepared to rebel. There was a groundswell of dissent amongst the southern notables in which the remaining Woodvilles, their relations and dependants were deeply involved.

It was at this point that the Duke of Buckingham, previously Richard's most fervent supporter, had a startling change of heart – he joined the conspiracy. *The Crowland Chronicle* reported, 'He was repentant of what had happened and was to lead the enterprise.'

What triggered his change of heart, this Damascene conversion? What drove Buckingham to risk all on a wildcard like Henry Tudor? The general view is that the wily John Morton, Bishop of Ely, was responsible. He was comfortably imprisoned in Buckingham's castle at Brecon where he had been sent after his arrest at the Tower and would have had ample time for discussion. Interestingly, it was Buckingham who had asked to take responsibility for Bishop John.

In their conversations the Bishop could have pointed out that Buckingham was second only to the King in power and also had a blood claim to the throne. Was it a coincidence that Rivers and Hastings had been two of the most powerful men in the land but had lost their heads? Could it be that King Richard did not like powerful magnates? Would it be Buckingham's head next on the block?

These would be persuasive arguments for a nervous man, perhaps followed by a question about the little princes?[16] The Duke's young wife was Edward's sister, Catherine Woodville, and she could have joined the discussion. Perhaps the contrast between King Richard's courtiers[17] and the pragmatic Bishop made Buckingham aware of the breadth and depth of feeling against the usurper king. Did raw fear drive him to rebel? Either that or something else persuaded Buckingham to join the conspiracy, perhaps the confirmation that the little princes were dead.

In human terms this was a tragedy, but in political terms it was a disaster, as it removed the focal point of the rebellion. What next for the plotters? Buckingham may have considered himself for the role of successor, being a direct and legitimate descendant of Edward III.[18] However, Bishop John seems to have persuaded him that Henry Tudor had a better chance. The Bishop had been present at the meeting between King Edward and the Stanleys where the possibility of Henry marrying Princess Elizabeth was discussed. He may have told Buckingham that there was some form of existing betrothal and, if that is correct, then it would explain why Henry's claim was accepted so easily. The Bishop was clearly a formidable operator.

Again on the Bishop's advice, Margaret Beaufort was told of Buckingham's commitment to the cause. It was certainly helpful, for she had a plan that was coming together. There was encouraging news from Brittany and so she sent her doctor, 'one Lewis a Welshman', to talk to Queen Elizabeth (Woodville) in sanctuary.

The Dowager Queen was deeply depressed; her world had collapsed, her husband was dead and her sons probably murdered. She looked as if she needed a doctor so Lewis the physician was allowed past the guards. Once alone, he delivered the proposal for Elizabeth, her eldest daughter, to marry Henry Tudor, Earl of Richmond. The Queen undertook to 'do her endeavour to procure all her husband King Edward's friends to take part with Henry so that he might be sworn to take in marrying Elizabeth her daughter after he shall have gotten the realm, or else Ciciley the younger if the other should die before he enjoyed the same'.[19] This was a crucial endorsement, for it meant there could be a popular focus for rebellion against King Richard. It was now a matter of organization and timing.

Duke Francis was supportive but, mindful of his antipathy to France and the consequent importance of good relations with England, proposed only covert help. He offered the use of his naval squadron that was being assembled to combat piracy. It was due to patrol the Channel from 1 September to 30 November 1483 and within this time the ships could be used for one month for 'the passage of the Lords Richmond and Pembroke'.[20]

Additionally Duke Francis would contribute hard cash for wages and provisions. But he also wrote on 26 August to his envoy in England with instructions to start negotiating with King Richard for joint action against the French, as soon as he should hear of King Louis's death. He died on 30 August,[21] so the Duke was running two policies that were potentially in conflict. Margaret Beaufort had no problems of conflicting interest. She borrowed money in the City and sent it to Brittany with her chaplain, Christopher Urswick. He was also to discuss the plans and bring back news.

On 22 September Bishop Lionel Woodville, Edward's brother, was staying at Buckingham's grand manor at Thornbury, eight miles north-east of Bristol, where they plotted. Two days later Buckingham wrote to Henry in Brittany asking him 'to hasten over to England as soon as possible for the purpose of marrying Elizabeth, eldest daughter of the late King, and at the same time, together with her, taking possession of the throne'.[22]

Bishop John having masterminded the Welsh end of the plot slipped away, telling Buckingham he would raise men in Ely. The coup was set for 18 October but an over-enthusiastic group in Kent started a week early, which alerted King Richard to the plot. Moving 'in no drowsy manner', he gathered his forces, priced the traitors' heads and issued a proclamation devoted to blackening the characters of the rebels. At the top of the list was Dorset, '[who] not fearing God ... hath many and sundry maids, widows and wives damnably and without shame devoured, deflowered and defiled, holding the unshameful and mischievous woman called Shore in adultery'.[23]

The Duke of Buckingham stuck to his plan, raised his standard and recruited his tenants, then set off in a rainstorm towards England, taking his wife and their two sons with him. The local Welsh gentry could hardly believe their luck; the Duke's castle was undefended so they sacked it and took his daughters as a bonus. Meanwhile the rain did not stop. The Duke and his men reached the river Severn where they were stopped by floods and there the army waited for a week in continuous, torrential rain with the flood water rising. Provisions ran out, everyone was soaked and the men deserted.

The weather defeated the Welsh side of the rebellion before it had even started. Buckingham was picked up hiding in a servant's cottage. He snivelled and told all he knew of the plot before he was executed on 2 November. King Richard now understood his enemy's plans, in particular that Henry Tudor was due to land at Poole. News of Buckingham's failure reached the other conspirators in England, who packed up and went home, but Henry and his little invasion force were unaware and under sail for England. King Richard set a trap.

Henry's fleet had been held up by the same storms that had disrupted Buckingham's plans but they probably sailed on 1 November.[24] In October Duke Francis had provided Henry with 13,000 livres for wages and provisions and later an additional loan of 10,000 crowns at Paimpol, a port in north-west Brittany. The expedition sailed but almost immediately ran into a westerly gale which blew them on to the Normandy coast. The Breton ships decided to return home, leaving Henry with two ships (perhaps *The Trinity* and *The Falcon*?) to sail on to Poole harbour where they found the quayside lined with soldiers.

The soldiers shouted that the rebellion had prospered and they had come from the Duke of Buckingham to take Henry to his camp. For some reason Henry and his advisors smelled a rat. They sailed out of the harbour and on to Plymouth where they discovered the rebellion had been nipped in the bud. King Richard and his army marched to Exeter hoping to catch them, but he was too late.[25] There is no hard evidence that shows Edward was there but, on the balance of probabilities, he was. Where else would he be?

Although the rebellion had failed, the adventure established Henry as undisputed leader of the opposition to King Richard. Some of the conspirators now fled to Brittany, among whom were the Bishop of Exeter, Lord Dorset, a dozen of King Edward's important adherents, knights such as his Master of Horse, Sir John Cheyne, some Lancastrian sympathizers and some gentry from across the south of England, including three sheriffs and 33 justices of the peace. Bishop Lionel Woodville took sanctuary at Beaulieu,[26] as did Robert Poyntz, Anthony Woodville's son-in-law (who sued for a pardon the following year but then fled to Brittany). Polydore Vergil lists the main men in Brittany at the time, and 'Edward Woodville, a valiant man of war, brother to Queen Elizabeth', was 'amongst that company'.

Meanwhile Catherine (Woodville), Duchess of Buckingham, was taking no risks with her eldest son; she dressed him as a girl and hid him with a gentleman's family. Her youngest she took to London where her late husband was being denounced as a 'rotten member of the body politic' and one of 'the great and principal movers, stirrers and doers of the said offences and heinous treasons' who were then attainted by parliament.

At Rennes in Brittany, Earl Henry chaired a council of war. It lasted several days and then, on Christmas morning 1483, in the huge Gothic cathedral, there was a service where he swore an oath to marry the Princess Elizabeth.

13. Sea fight. Two ships come together with English archers
on the left and crossbowmen on the right.

To do this he would have needed a papal dispensation, because they were related within the fourth degree, and also her consent; presumably he had the latter. There were 423 exiles who knelt and paid him homage as if he had been crowned.

Promises to God to complete tasks if events went the right way were standard. If Edward made a vow – an agreement with God that he would do something in return for God granting his prayers – then this could have been the time. The agreement might have been that once Richard, the usurper and murderer, was dead, then he, Edward, would fight for God, undertake a crusade or some such, just as his brother had.

Throughout that winter England and Brittany skirmished at sea. Perhaps *The Trinity* and *The Falcon* engaged in some light piracy. A 'John Porter of Calais with other evil-doers' are recorded boarding a ship of Hamburg and carrying off most of her cargo on 20 January.[27] Unsurprisingly the 423 exiled Englishmen were straining the Breton exchequer.[28] The composition of the group is unclear. Henry's immediate entourage was perhaps a dozen or so. The Marquis of Dorset probably had some people with him but there were few other nobles. There were about 20 named knights, around 40 county figures together with a bishop and a few clerics, other adherents and Edward's 200–300 soldiers. It must have been difficult maintaining morale and cohesion and there are always problems with any group of soldiers with time on their hands. On one occasion Duke Francis paid out 200 livres in damages to poor Georgette le Cutt because her husband had been killed in a brawl with some Englishmen.

By March 1484 King Richard's position seemed to be stronger and he had convinced the Queen Dowager, 'after frequent entreaties as well as threats', that the Tudor enterprise was doomed. She was having a nervous breakdown and agreed that Princess Elizabeth of York and her sisters should leave sanctuary. However, she insisted that King Richard must first give an undertaking that the princesses 'would not suffer any manner of hurt ... nor imprison within our Tower of London or any other prison'.[29] She was also persuaded to send for her eldest son, to recall Dorset from Brittany, and he, weak as always, set out for home. He was soon missed and Henry's emissaries rode out. They hunted down every route to England and eventually Sir John Cheyne found him at Compiègne in Flanders. He was persuaded to return.

In England conspiracies were about. A Wiltshire gentleman – amongst others – was 'abbreviated shorter by the head and divided into four quarters'. He had nailed 'bills and ballads of seditious rhyme' to the doors of St Paul's and corresponded with Earl Henry. It was the celebrated attack on King Richard and his cronies, Catesby, Ratcliffe and Lovell: 'The Cat, the Rat and Lovell our Dog, Rule all England under the Hog'.[30]

They may have ruled, but events were taking over and control was becoming harder. King Richard needed to know what was happening and when. *The Crowland Chronicle* reported, 'he observed the new method, introduced by King Edward at the time of the last war in Scotland, of allocating a mounted courier to every 20 miles ... these men carried messages 200 miles within two days'. He also 'provided himself with spies overseas ... from whom he learnt almost all the movements of his enemies'.

But despite the organization, King Richard was struggling on several fronts. He was short of funds and trusted men and had been obliged to impose northerners on the southern counties to replace the sheriffs and others who had fled to Brittany; inevitably his men were loathed. Even his Scottish policy came to nothing: his overtures of the previous year had been overtaken by a French embassy led by an ex-patriot Scot called Bernard Stewart, Lord d'Aubigny, who was high in French favour. King James agreed a new Franco-Scots alliance and when Stewart returned to France he took with him 'eighteen companies of Scots foot'.[31]

It seemed that England could be fighting a war on two fronts, so any focus for internal rebellion had to be neutralized. King Richard dispatched another embassy to Duke Francis, this time proposing action against France and hard cash to buy Henry Tudor. The envoys were received by the Duke's Treasurer, Landois, who knew just how badly Brittany needed England's help against France. He also wanted to stop the drain on the Treasury caused by the Tudor contingent and, as the Duke was again ill, he negotiated a deal.

Bishop Morton in his Flanders exile heard of the danger and dispatched Christopher Urswick to warn Earl Henry. The source of his intelligence is unknown. However, Urswick was the confidential agent of Margaret Beaufort, whose husband Lord Stanley was a senior member of the King's Council.[32] At this time Margaret was landless, as Buckingham had implicated her in his plot, so her lands had been confiscated and given to Stanley, who was then made responsible for his wife's behaviour.

Earl Henry, well aware of his vulnerability, sent Urswick straight on to the new King of France asking for asylum, which was immediately granted (11 October 1484). He decided a few important people would slip away with him – uncle Jasper, presumably the Bishop of Exeter and Dorset – and, without waiting for the answer from France, announced that he was going to visit Duke Francis who was convalescing on the French border. Away he rode with 12 companions, and once they were clear of the city he changed clothes with his groom.

The Treasurer saw the English gold disappearing and sent armed guards in hot pursuit but they were just one hour too late. The companions and their groom had crossed the border into France. Duke Francis recovered and, over-riding his Treasurer, sent for Edward Woodville, John Cheyne and Edward Poynings who had remained in Rennes with the main party. The Duke believed he had an obligation and, being a man of honour, provided passports and money for the 411 Englishmen to follow Henry. The level of pay-out reflects the Duke's view that Woodville, Cheyne and Poynings were important, the others not.[33] But he did not override the main agreement; he needed England's goodwill, irrespective of who was on the throne.

King Richard probably congratulated himself on closing Brittany to the Tudors. To reinforce the arrangement, he sent Lord Grey of Powys with 1,000 archers to Brittany, ostensibly to deter a French invasion. It was lucky for Henry that his crisis coincided with an urgent French need for a clever move. The Regent, Anne de Beaujeu, and the 13-year-old King Charles VIII[34] were under considerable pressure; a new alliance of Burgundy, Brittany and England had been formed, which looked dangerous and there were internal problems with a recalcitrant group of French noblemen known as the Feudal League.

In addition King Charles strongly disapproved of King Richard, believing he had 'barbarously murdered his two nephews to whom he had sworn allegiance' and 'caused the daughters to be degraded and declared illegitimate'.[35] Consequently he made a show of refusing to answer King Richard's letters or see his ambassadors. This was not just a foreign-policy matter but an issue of the sanctity of kings and the precedent that King Richard had set must not be allowed.[36] The result was an enthusiastic welcome for Earl Henry and an immediate cash payment with promises of more to come.

The exiled Englishmen proposed an invasion but they were lacking an experienced army commander. Henry had commanded nothing and uncle Jasper's experience had been confined to guerrilla warfare. He had only once commanded a division in action and that had been at the disastrous battle of Mortimer's Cross, while at Tewkesbury he had failed to get his men to the battlefield in time.

Edward Woodville had commanded his fleet but did not have the political stature or experience to be the army commander. The obvious choice was the Earl of Oxford, an experienced general and a committed Lancastrian. However, he was a prisoner and, for the last ten years, had been incarcerated at Hammes, one of the two fortresses defending the English Calais enclave. He loathed King Richard who had bullied, threatened and robbed his old mother in a disgraceful case ten years earlier.[37] Oxford had become increasingly frustrated by his imprisonment and at one point had tried to escape by leaping off the walls into the moat. He got stuck in the mud up to his chin and had to be rescued by his gaolers.

The Captain of Hammes was Sir James Blount, one of Hastings's lieutenants, who had no illusions about King Richard. He was happy to release Oxford and join the Tudor cause himself, leaving his wife and a garrison of 52 men behind. A detachment was sent from the main garrison at Calais to recover the castle but Lady Blount and the soldiers at Hammes decided to pull up the drawbridge and appeal to Earl Henry for help. The newly liberated Oxford took a company and prepared to attack the Calais detachment, but rather than have a fight they decided to allow Lady Blount, the garrison and their baggage to march off and join Sir James and Lord Oxford. This shows just how precarious was King Richard's hold on the situation, and morale must have been at rock bottom with his regular troops.

While Oxford's presence helped persuade the Regent of France that an invasion was worth backing, what really convinced her was the news of 'six thousand hostile archers heading for Brittany'.[38] It was this supposed action by the anti-French alliance coupled with danger from the dissidents in the Feudal League that made her decide on solid support.

King Richard had miscalculated by squeezing Henry Tudor out of Brittany and into the arms of a more effective sponsor. However, in England he was managing matters with apparent success and, aware that the 16-year-old Princess Elizabeth of York was critical to Henry's plan, brought her to court and paid obvious attention to her. *The Crowland Chronicle* observed: 'but let it not go unsaid that during this Christmas festival [1484], an excessive interest was displayed in singing and dancing and vain changing of clothes by Queen Anne and Lady Elizabeth, the eldest daughter of the late King, who were of similar complexion and figure'.

Queen Anne died in March 1485 and King Richard then indulged his niece, so tongues began to wag. The gossip was that he had poisoned his wife in order to marry Elizabeth. It seemed logical because if he could marry her then it would wreck the Tudor plans. When the rumour reached France it 'pinched Henry by the very stomach', but, fortunately for Elizabeth, Richard's trusted northerners disapproved of incest.

Many of them had originally been Warwick's men who had transferred their allegiance to Richard because of Anne Neville and they were becoming uneasy. *The Crowland Chronicle* reported that others 'put so many obstacles in the way through fear that if Elisabeth became Queen it might be in her power some time to avenge the death of her Uncle, Earl Anthony [Rivers] and of her brother, Richard [Grey]'.

The rumours were probably untrue but the strength of them forced the King to make a humiliating public denial and look for an acceptable wife. He wrote to a distant cousin, King João of Portugal, asking for his sister, the 'Infanta Joana', as a bride. However, Joana was in a nunnery and happy there. She told her brother the marriage would be pointless because – she forecast – King Richard would be dead within the year.[39]

Meanwhile the Tudor high command considered its invasion plans. A Welsh landing was attractive because of family connections, lack of central authority and the fact that there had not been an effective Welsh overlord since Anthony Woodville. Additionally the Stanleys, whose support was hoped for, had their strength in North Wales and the North West, so a meeting in the West Midlands would be expedient. The arguments of inaccessibility and of King Richard anticipating such an obvious choice were dismissed and Pembrokeshire was chosen for the landing of the invasion.

On 23 June 1485 King Richard ordered his Chancellor to again issue a proclamation (the previous one had been six months earlier) against 'Piers Bishop of Exeter, Jasper Tidder son of Owen Tidder calling himself Earl of Pembroke, John late Earl of Oxon and Sir Edward Widevile with other rebels and traitors ... who have chosen to have as their captain one Henry Tidder, who of his insatiable covetousness ... usurpeth upon him the name and title of royal estate of this realm'. This confirms that King Richard regarded Edward as a key figure in the equation and also that Henry was short of impressive names. The proclamation went on to tell its readers that Henry 'Tidder' was a bastard on both sides of his family and to remind Englishmen that he would be brought to these shores in French ships crowded with foreign soldiers. It is a fine example of 'the politic, manipulative side of an insecure monarch who sought to deploy the arts of propaganda to steady his regime'.[40]

In France Henry Tudor 'tarred and rigged his navy at the mouth of the Seine', or so reported Vergil (was this *The Trinity* and *The Falcon*?). Henry believed his opportunity was coming and would have heard from England that King Richard was not providing the stability that would make people support the establishment. Henry's mother believed the Stanleys would fight for him, and her agents had reported lively sympathy for the Lancastrian cause in Wales and England. On the Yorkist side, the exiles were confident that their friends in England would rise for Princess Elizabeth's future husband.

Perhaps more importantly, the French government was now committed to the project, but for pragmatic rather than altruistic reasons. The Regent decided a serious diversion was needed and the Tudor enterprise was in the right place at the right time and, in the scheme of things, it only needed minimal assistance. She agreed to lend Henry 40,000 livres (but only paid 10,000).

Henry borrowed a further 30,000 livres commercially, although he had to leave two noblemen in Paris as a pledge; unsurprisingly he chose Dorset to be one of them. As a 'Marquis' he was valuable, but being completely unreliable was better out of the way. So Henry managed to borrow around £4,400, as presumably the lenders thought he had a reasonable chance of success. The Regent would also have insisted on an unequivocal commitment to good Anglo-French relations and support for France should Henry be successful.

If Edward had been paying his men a standard rate for the last two years then there might be around £4,000 left in his war chest. While history does not relate what happened to the £10,000, if there was any still around, it would certainly be needed, as would any additional funds Margaret Beaufort could arrange – one of her people had recently arrived with coin from England. There might also be something left from Duke Francis's contribution.

There has been much debate about the composition of the Tudor army. If Edward's company was there then it would form the professional core, to which the exiles and the Hammes garrison would be added, making a total of some 500 Englishmen. There was a French division of 1,800 commanded by Philibert de Chandée.[41] Of those foot soldiers, 1,500 had (probably) been discharged from the army camp at Pont de l'Arche and may have been trained pikemen. For the last six years Swiss *reislaufers*, or petty officers, had been training the French infantry which was reorganized on the Swiss model, so these pikemen should have been well disciplined, presumably discharged simply for the invasion, and were outside formal French responsibility.

Although that seems probable, it may be that they were simply redundant and coincided with Henry's need. Seigneur d'Esquerdes, a.k.a. Lord Cordes, now a Marshal of France (with an annual pension of 12,000 livres, the second highest in France) was responsible for the base at Pont de l'Arche and there is some form of confirmation in his funeral epitaph where he is described as having been the veritable arbiter of Henry of Richmond's fate. Cordes was certainly a powerful man in the hierarchy, a foreign-policy hawk and quite capable of arranging whatever Henry needed.

As part of the French contribution, there were – according to two Scottish sources – Scots companies totalling around 1,000 men. These presumably came with King James's blessing and were a part of the 18 companies of foot that Bernard Stewart raised when he was in Scotland the year before.[42] So 500 exiled Englishmen, 800 professional French soldiers and 1,000 Scots, together with a few Breton adventurers and men from the Normandy gaols, made up the invasion force. (Apparently the criminals had been offered the choice of rotting in prison or fighting in England.)

The Regent had oscillated between strong and weak support as the threats to France increased and decreased until, at last, on 4 May the final commitment was set out in the royal decree that triggered the invasion. According to Molinet, shortly before sailing, a further 1,800 joined, which would bring the force up to a total of around 4,000. Given the size of the French loans this seems unlikely, but given Cordes's interest it is possible, and those additional men could have come from Pont de l'Arche, which is only just upriver from Honfleur. However, this report is more probably post-event French double-counting, to exaggerate the support they provided. On balance, the probable number that sailed from France in Henry's army was between 2,000 and 2,500.[43]

The economics seem to support that figure: conventionally hired foot soldiers would be paid three months in advance, so 2,500 infantrymen would cost around £6,000.[44] The leaders and officers would, at the very least, need their expenses but would probably want more, certainly the French and Scottish officers. The expedition would also need a war chest for rations (a budget figure for rations for 2,500 men for three months would be £2,000), munitions over what the French supplied, supplies, intelligence, bonuses and bribes. If the war chest had £4,400 from the French, the £4,000 remaining from Edward's money and some from Margaret Beaufort, it might total around £10,000, which could be just enough.

'One could not find a more evil lot,' remarked Commines, the French contemporary diarist. There were probably 15 ships to ferry them and, while it may not have been an impressive force, it was still bigger than King Edward's invasion force of 1472. The exiles sharpened their swords and arrow-heads and prepared themselves. King Richard was dismissive: 'an unknown Welshman, whose father I never knew, nor him personally saw'.[45]

Henry Tudor with Edward Woodville and the others sailed from Honfleur, at the mouth of the Seine, on 1 August 1485 with a soft southern wind. Coincidentally William Caxton was finishing his first printing of *Le Morte d'Arthur*, the story of King Arthur and his heroic knights which is set with lavish tournaments, jousts, intrigue, beautiful ladies, betrayal and battles to the death. Sir Thomas Malory had written and compiled the book while he was imprisoned ten years before, in the 1470s. Malory's full title for the book is, 'The Birth, Life and Acts of king Arthur, of his noble Knights of the Round Table, their marvellous Enquests and Adventures; th'Achieving of the

Snagreal, and in the end the dolorous Death and Departing out of the World of them All.'

BLOOD AND ROSES[2]

A week of good weather brought the fleet to Pembrokeshire on a Sunday afternoon. They waited until dusk and then sailed into Milford Haven, landing at Mill Bay, where Henry knelt and prayed:

Judge me, O Lord, and defend my cause against the unmerciful people: Deliver me from the deceitful and wicked man.[3]

So Edward and his men were back after two years. That night they camped around the nearby Castle de Vale (now Dale), owned by a Tudor cousin, and in the morning Henry knighted some of his companions. Then they marched to the county town of Haverfordwest, where they heard that the garrison of Pembroke Castle had recognized Uncle Jasper as its *natural* lord, but the confidence of the invaders was shaken by rumour of enemy forces at Carmarthen.

Scurriers (mounted scouts) were sent to investigate and found a false alarm. The army started its march north, through Cardigan and into mid-Wales. Henry rode under the Dragon banner of Cadwallader, exploiting his connections and claiming descent from long-dead Welsh kings. But despite this, the number of recruits was disappointing – no more that 500 or so.

Just four days after the landing, news reached King Richard 200 miles away in Nottingham. He immediately sent out his call to arms. Meanwhile the Tudor army marched on, through the hills towards England, with Henry dispatching a stream of letters. He had learned the power of propaganda: 'that homicide and unnatural tyrant that now bears dominion over you'.

Messengers rode out to likely supporters: 'Right trusty and well-beloved ... we desire and pray you, and upon your allegiance strictly charge and command you ... with all such power as ye may make, defensibly arrayed for war ... ye fail not hereof as ye will avoid our grievous displeasure and answer unto your peril.'[4]

But many prevaricated, which was worrying for Henry; however, some did not. Recruits started trickling in and then the flow increased, men from South Wales, men from Gwynedd. Rhys ap Thomas arrived with 'a great band', then Sir Gilbert Talbot, guardian to the young Earl of Shrewsbury, assembled a force and by the time he joined Henry at Newport in Shropshire had 500 men, the first serious support from an English magnate. Not only did Henry need the men but the majority of his army was French or Scots, some 2,000 of England's traditional enemies, which did not look good.[5] To balance them there were only 1,400 or 1,500 Welsh and English by the time they reached Shrewsbury.[6]

At Stafford Sir William Stanley turned up for a clandestine meeting. His brother was Lord Stanley, Henry's stepfather, who was crucial to the invasion's success but seemed loyal to King Richard, possibly because his eldest son was being held hostage.[7] Few people knew what was happening or who to support and rumour was rampant.

King Richard quickly mustered some 6,000 men, mainly from the Midlands and East Anglia, with the northerners still to arrive under the Earl of Northumberland. The royal army marched out of Leicester on Sunday 21 August 1485 and a fine sight they must have been.[8] Mounted men-at-arms and archers of the vanguard preceded the King, who was wearing his crown and riding his charger 'White Surrey'. His banners flew above him and then came the mainguard with ranks of peers, knights, men-at-arms and thousands of foot soldiers.

That night they camped at Bosworth, a village about ten miles west of Leicester. The Scottish ambassador, who had a servant named MacGregor, told a story of the evening before the battle. Richard was in his tent and sent for his crown. He set it upon his head, declaring that he would wear it into battle and win, or die 'crownit King of England'. But then he was interrupted by a commotion outside. He and his attendants rushed out, leaving the crown unguarded. MacGregor found himself alone in the tent and could not resist the chance to steal the crown. He was caught red-handed and explained:

> 'I had realised early in life that, like my fathers before me, I would be hanged for theft and I resolved that I would not die for just a sheep, or for cattle but for something of great value. It would be a great honour for my kith and kin if I could be hanged for the rich crown of England, for which so many honourable men have lately died; some hanged, some beheaded, some murdered, some killed in battle and for which King Richard had, within the hour, offered to die himself, before his enemy Harry got it off his head.'

> At the words of the highland man that could not speak good English but every word was 'ane mow' and he spoke so quick causing the English lords to laugh and made them so merry and rejoyst at his speaking that they obtained him grace from the King's hands ... with safe conduct to Scotland.[9]

This incident may have contributed to the King's terrible last night when he is supposed to have dreamed 'of bloody deeds and death'. First light did not improve morale: 'At dawn on Monday morning the chaplains of King Richard's army were not ready to celebrate mass, nor was any breakfast ready which would restore the King's ailing spirit.' Furthermore the Duke of Norfolk woke to discover a nasty poem stuck on his tent, according to Hall:

Jack of Norfolk be not so bold,
for Dykon thy master is bought and sold.

And during the night Sir Simon Digby, one of Henry's officers, had crept into the royal camp to gather intelligence. He saw the army preparing to move and then slipped away at four o'clock to report.

The King was wearing the highly polished suit of armour he had worn at Tewkesbury; he left his tents standing and marched his army to take the high ground before his enemy was on the field. On the hill he rode through the ranks wearing his crown, showing his banners, probably led by a gold processional cross held high by a priest.[10] He was trooping his colours. He gave an invigorating speech, telling his soldiers he owed the crown to their wisdom and he had proved a just king. They must fight like lions because the devil was in the heart of an unknown Welshman who was aided by a company of beggarly thieves. Henry of Richmond was a milksop without courage or experience, his men traitors and runagates and the French braggers and cowards.

On the opposing side Henry rode to a little hill to encourage his army (according to Hutton): 'If the Almighty had ever assisted a just cause then this was the one and you can be certain of victory. Richard was a murderer and his guilty followers were avaricious villains ... though our numbers be few the greater will be our praise if we vanquish and if we fall the more glorious our death.' (This sounds like Shakespeare's Henry V before Agincourt.)

The Tudor army was now some 5,000 strong. The majority were in the vanguard under Oxford, which is where Scottish tradition has its contingent. The whereabouts of Edward and his soldiers is not recorded but *The Crowland Chronicle* describes the vanguard as 'a large body of French and English troops'. Edward's status as one of the leaders – with his own troops – would put him in the vanguard, commanding that part of the line.

'The leaders of the opposing army were first and foremost Henry, earl of Richmond, whom his men called King Henry VII; John Vere, Earl of Oxford; John, Lord Welles; Thomas, Lord Stanley and his brother William; Edward Woodville, brother of Queen Elizabeth and a most courageous knight.' Then follows a list of nine further names without any comment. From this extract it is clear that the *Crowland* chronicler, who may have been Bishop John Russell writing in 1486, recognized Edward as one of the top men in the Tudor army. (The Stanleys were not, in fact, part of the opposing army but given their subsequent behaviour and importance it was the correct place to list them.)

The royal army stood on Ambion Hill, facing southwest, watching the Tudor vanguard advance towards them up the old Roman road from Fenny Drayton. There were three other armies in the area: Northumberland with 3,000 men was hanging well back 'to watch Stanley', or so his messenger told the King. Lord Stanley with 3,500 men was waiting by Dadlington village, half a mile or so to the south of Ambion Hill, and Sir William Stanley with 2,500 men a little to his west on a small hill by Stoke Golding. There is now little doubt about the layout of the battlefield but the sequence of events is still uncertain.[11]

The Tudor vanguard halted 1,000 paces from the royal army. Richard sent to Stanley demanding his immediate attendance with his troops. According to Hutton his message also threatened, 'or by God your son shall instantly die.' 'If the King stains his honour with the blood of my son,' replied Stanley, 'I have more, but why should he suffer when I have not lifted a hand against him?'

The sun shone, standards waved and armour gleamed as the Earl of Oxford arranged the Tudor vanguard in an extended line. The royal artillery began its bombardment. The Tudor vanguard started to advance through the corn-fields.[12] Halfway to the enemy they paused for their archers to shoot. Then they wheeled north, probably to avoid a swamp, present a smaller target and put the sun was behind them. They moved on, through the flights of arrows and cannon fire. Part of the royal army swung south to face them. The two divisions crashed together and fought.

Polydore Vergil tells how the Tudor vanguard executed a very disciplined manoeuvre: during the fight they disengaged, withdrew a few paces, regrouped and attacked in a tighter formation, probably wedges designed to cut through the extended royal line. The manoeuvre would need experienced men who had fought and drilled together – such 'a model advance would have earned praise from leading exponents of fifteenth-century continental warfare'.[13] Norfolk, commanding the royal force, was unable to respond with the same level of coolness and expertise.

Perhaps the wedges cut through the royal line and isolated some sections. Norfolk's son, the Earl of Surrey, was fighting the veteran Sir Gilbert Talbot and became separated from his ranks but fought on, even though surrounded. There was an attempted rescue by two knights who were cut to pieces. An ordinary soldier tried to take him prisoner but Surrey hacked off the man's arm. Eventually he surrendered to Talbot.[14]

Apparently Oxford and Norfolk came face to face. They were first cousins and set to with their swords. Norfolk wounded Oxford who then smashed the visor from Norfolk's helmet. As Oxford retreated a few paces – disdaining to fight an unguarded adversary – an arrow hit Norfolk in the face and killed him. Oxford later commented, 'A better knight could not die, though he might in a better cause.'[15]

Ferocious hand-to-hand fighting lasted maybe an hour. Perhaps it was now that Richard realized that Stanley and Northumberland would not fight for him and he gave instructions for Stanley's son to be killed. But the order was never executed, a sign that discipline in the royal army was breaking down and victory for the king looking unlikely. Maybe this was when Richard was brought a fresh horse and urged to fly. Certainly not! 'The Ballad of Bosworth Field' has him say:

> Give me my battle-axe in my hand,
> Set the crown of England on my head so high!
> For by him that shaped both sea and land,
> King of England this day will I die!

It may also have been the point when Henry, his standards and his escort left their safe position behind the mainguard. They cantered towards William Stanley. Perhaps Henry was going to plead for Stanley to join him, but he could have been the bait for a trap. Henry was in open ground and appeared vulnerable. Richard saw the chance to kill Henry and, demonstrating true Yorkist courage and dash, led his household troops in a charge down the hill, straight at his enemy.

It may have been a straight cavalry action or Henry might have taken refuge with some French pike men who had formed a 'hedgehog'. There is a fragment of a letter from one French soldier: 'he [Henry] wanted to be on foot in the midst of us, and that is partly the reason why the battle was won'.[16] Whether contrived or accidental it was the opportunity William had been waiting for. He launched his red-coated cavalry. The King saw them bearing down on him and shouted 'Treason! Treason!'

The three groups collided and there was savage fighting. Richard hacked his way towards Henry and killed his standard-bearer. He engaged Sir John Cheyne. But his troop was being overwhelmed. His horse became stuck in the bog and a Welshman felled him with a halberd. In the main battle Sir William Catesby was looking for the Royal Field Commander:

> Rescue! My lord of Norfolk, rescue rescue!

> The King enacts more wonders than a man,
> Daring an opposite to every danger.
> His horse is slain, and all alone on foot he fights,
> Seeking for Richmond in the throat of death.
> Rescue, fair lord, or else the day is lost! [17]

Then *The Crowland Chronicle* reports: 'King Richard, after receiving many mortal wounds, died a fearless and most courageous death, fighting on the battlefield.' The last Plantagenet king, ruthless in the pursuit of power, was dead. His body was stripped naked and thrown over the back of a horse like a dead animal for later display. The battered crown was retrieved from under a thorn bush and placed on Henry Tudor's head by Sir William Stanley while the soldiers shouted, 'God save King Henry, God save King Henry.' The 'Song of Lady Bessie' chants, 'They hewed the crown from his head, knocked him down, beat his basnet [basinet, a conical helmet] into his head, dashing his brains out, then carried him to Leicester.' [18]

The body count was 1,000 from the royal army, most of whom were killed after Richard's death in the mopping up which ranged over two bloody miles. On the Tudor side, a mere 200 were dead. King Richard, the betrayer, had himself been betrayed, certainly by the Stanleys, by others who were unconvinced he would or should win and by Northumberland who had never moved his men up to the action. He now came forward to kneel in homage to King Henry, but not all the defeated were able or quick enough to do that.

> Treason doth never prosper.
> What's the reason?
> Why, if it prosper,
> None dare call it treason.

So wrote Sir John Harrington, an Elizabethan wit whose great-grandfather had fought for King Richard, having previously been 'granted a parcel of lands' for capturing the Lancastrian King Henry for Edward IV. But now the ancestor was on the wrong side and so in his descendant's view 'he was fool enough to loose them'.

King Henry made a triumphant entry into Leicester where King Richard had so recently been cheered out. The innkeeper at the White Boar, where Richard had stayed and left his bed, hastily painted the boar on his inn sign blue, thus converting it to a Lancastrian badge.

The *Crowland* chronicler quotes a poem that finishes, 'the tusks of the Boar were blunted and the red rose, the avenger of the white, shines upon us'. But the red rose was only shining on the battlefield and it was important for

Henry to establish his authority throughout the country. The God of battles had confirmed his hereditary right to the throne and acclamation on the bloody field itself had rounded off the procedure, but there were loose ends. Edward of Warwick, Clarence's young son, was secured and sent to the Tower while Princess Elizabeth of York was brought out from custody and restored to her mother. Twenty-eight of Richard's close followers, dead or alive, were attainted.

Henry started to run his new kingdom, which must have been difficult, for it was completely outside his experience. It took 12 busy days to reach London where the first ceremony was a procession to St Paul's Cathedral with a formal presentation of his three battle standards: the banner of St George, the red fiery dragon of Cadwallader and the dun cow painted upon 'yelowe tartene'.

Henry seemed to have an instinctive grasp of *realpolitik* and quickly gathered together the threads of government, but never having ruled anything he would need to be well served by professionals who guided and perhaps even made policy. His first secretary was Richard Fox and in expanding his executive team he presumably relied on character assessments by those he trusted, such as Edward. There was considerable patronage at his disposal and he used it to reward those who had served him 'by yonde the see as over this side' and who had been exposed to 'great charge, labour and jeopardy'.[19] Uncle Jasper became Duke of Bedford, Thomas Stanley Earl of Derby, Edward Courtenay Earl of Devon, and Richard Woodville (Edward's elder brother) was confirmed as the third Earl Rivers, while lower down the ladder a number of Welshmen were given jobs at court.

Edward himself received two grants. The first was his original holding of the castle, forest, warren and town of Porchester, together with governance of the town of Portsmouth and the wages to pay the staff. The other was Captaincy of the Isle of Wight, together with the lordship of Carisbrooke Castle and all the King's castles, lordships, lands and franchises there. This was a new grant and uniquely it was 'in tail male', which meant it was his to leave to his son, should he have one. Both the deeds are dated 16 September 1485, just three weeks after the battle.[20]

Carisbrooke was of great strategic importance, a castle of such strength that the French had failed to capture it when they invaded 100 years before. Anthony had further strengthened the castle and had the Woodville and Scales badge carved high above the entrance gate, which was 'flanked by two noble towers' (a part of the badge is still visible). An indication of rental value comes from a grant in 1495 to a Sir Reginald Bray of roughly the same thing, 'with manors, rights and privileges at an annual rent of £308-17s-8d'.

The castle and holdings in the Isle of Wight were a handsome reward that also generated revenues from 'fees and advowsons, frankpledge, wreck of sea and other liberties'. But it also carried responsibilities, such as inquiring into a complaint from merchants of 'Rone' in Normandy, now that France was an ally. Their vessels carrying salt and other goods had been boarded and plundered by two English ships which had 'cast her men ashore in Normandy [unharmed], taken her to the Isle of Wight and there distributed her cargo'. Edward was commissioned to arrest 'the pirates' and compel restitution. If they refused then he was to take them before the King in his Council.

Edward's own disposable wealth seems to have been remarkably small; the only record is dated 24 September 1485, a week after these grants, and refers only to an annuity of £50. It was presumably the annuity he had taken in exchange for the manor his mother left him in 1472. The will says that if Edward should die 'without heirs of his body begotten' then his brother Richard would inherit, a sensible consolidation of family wealth, but if Richard should die without an heir then the annuity was to be divided between his poorer sisters and a niece: Anne, Margaret, Joan and Elizabeth, the daughter of the deceased sister, Mary. If they all died without heirs then it went to his rich sisters, Elizabeth, Queen Dowager, and Katherine, Dowager Duchess of Buckingham. This is sensible and – such as it was – the inheritance would be split between those who needed it most, unless the head of the family produced children.[21] This seems a complicated arrangement for an annuity of just £50 a year but it was all he had.

There was a spectacular coronation of Henry on 30 October 1485. Everyone was decked out in great finery[22] and at the banquet that followed Sir Robert Dymmock, still the hereditary Champion, again threw down his gauntlet and challenged all comers to dispute King Henry's rights. There were no takers. Once crowned, the new King had his realm to govern and there was a backlog of business. The coronation tournament was postponed to allow his first parliament to sit and affairs of state be dealt with.

The papal envoy reported great activity: Northumberland and two bishops were released, Surrey was still under arrest, the Princess Elizabeth had been declared Duchess of York and 'the king will marry her', and ambassadors had arrived from France, Austria and Brittany.[23]

Only 18 nobles had attended the coronation out of the total peerage of 30; the others were dead. The ruling class had been much depleted by the last 35 years of war, even though there had only been some 13 weeks of actual fighting. The 'Cousins' War' (or arguing over the crown) had resulted in the violent deaths of three kings, one prince of Wales, nine dukes, one marquis,

13 earls, 24 barons, innumerable knights and many soldiers. There was a gap at the centre of the kingdom and that presented Henry with the opportunity of shaping a new form of government.

Those who survived made the best of it and the extant Woodvilles were once again close to the centre of power. A week after the coronation Jasper married Catherine, Edward's sister and Buckingham's widow, a good strategic arrangement that put the late Duke's considerable power firmly in the royal family's hands.[24]

In January 1486 King Henry married the Princess Elizabeth, Edward's niece. In her portrait she appears pretty, blonde and curvaceous.[25] A Venetian called her 'very handsome' and the Portuguese ambassador reported that she was 'of medium height with large breasts'. The three-month period had given just enough time to get papal dispensation for the marriage, canonically necessary as they were related (in the fourth degree from John of Gaunt) and also to reverse Richard's law, which had declared her a bastard. Perhaps it also allowed time for a little wooing.[26]

Immediately after the wedding Edward asked King Henry for permission to go to fight the Moors in Spain. It was a curious request for a man who had been in exile for the last two years and would be needed by his new king to help run the country. There is a strong echo of his brother's decision to go crusading back in 1472. One wonders if it was in fulfilment of a vow made during the hard times. But what of Anthony's will? Did Edward not care about his inheritance? 'I, Anthony Wodevile, in the castle of Sheriff Hutton, bequeath ... the lands that were my first wife's, the Lady Scales and Thomas Lord Scales her brother's to my brother Sir Edward Wodevile.'

Andrew Dymmock, the family lawyer and man of business, was an executor of the will and is described in it as capable of proving and protecting the titles to the Scales estates, which Anthony had acquired through his first wife, Elizabeth, the Scales heiress. Dymmock had worked for Anthony for nine years and 'documents show him to have been one of the most busy and versatile men in the earl's employ'.[27] Interestingly King Henry made him Solicitor General on 15 November 1486, an appointment that surprised the author of *Judges of England*, who wrote 'it has always been a puzzle why Dymmock, well born though he was, should have been promoted so promptly by Henry to the place of law officer of the Crown'.[28]

There could have been no better recommendation than Edward Woodville's when the new King was looking for an able lawyer. It is also interesting that within a couple of months of Bosworth, John Alcock, Bishop of Worcester, was appointed Chancellor of England. He was a close Woodville friend and had been tutor to the late Prince of Wales under Anthony.[29]

It was presumably Andrew Dymmock who properly enrolled Anthony's will in the Prerogative Court of Canterbury, but there is no subsequent entry recording the granting of probate. It was also presumably Dymmock who on 13 October arranged for the writ of *diem clausit extremum* (the old equivalent of probate) to go to the escheators of Northampton, mid-Kent, Essex, Bedfordshire and Buckinghamshire 'as to the possessions and next heir' of Anthony Woodville.[30]

Edward, one of the heirs, was high in royal favour and the executors were very much alive, but it seems that Edward was uninterested in that inheritance. It is too long ago to be sure of the reason but it does suggest that Edward was not driven by lust for property or power. Perhaps he was thinking of higher things.

What happened to the Scales lands? They went to third cousins of Anthony's late wife, great-great-granddaughters of a Lord Scales who had died more than a century before. What happened to Edward? He went crusading.

Edward sailed for Spain with 300 men in January or early February 1486. Presumably these men, or the majority of them, had been with him at Bosworth, in France, in Brittany and in *The Falcon* and *The Trinity*. While a vow may well have driven Edward, what of his men? Did they follow him for love or money? Probably both!

But why did he go crusading? He must have been driven by a vow – his side of a bargain made with God when he was in exile, when the future was bleak, his brother and nephews newly murdered and the perpetrator of the crimes on the throne of England. God had answered his prayers and so now Edward could fulfil his side of the agreement.

If this was the case then he would following the precedent set by Anthony who – presumably – made a similar arrangement with God when his and King Edward's fortunes were at their lowest ebb, back in the autumn of 1470. He too had gone crusading once the re-establishment of King Edward was achieved. Perhaps his friend, Antoine, the Great Bastard of Burgundy, who had taken 2,000 men to fight the Moors in 1464, had inspired him because he had gone crusading to redeem a pledge his father had made publicly ten years earlier. It is also likely that the Spanish monarchs had offered to pay handsomely for an English nobleman and three companies of infantry. There is no evidence that Edward had any money of his own and it would be surprising if Henry had volunteered to pay.

LOCAL AFFAIRS

Edward arrived home from his crusading in August 1486, having been away for seven or eight months. He had fulfilled his vow and lost his front teeth; a few of his company were dead, some were missing, but most were home safe and sound.

The soldiers would have been paid for three months in advance before they sailed but would now need to have their pay made up to date, if that had not been done in Spain. It had been a costly operation: six pence per day per man totals £5 or £6 per man; 'peti-captains' were paid double; officers would earn more or they might just be there for the experience; ships were hired; mouths fed and munitions bought, so the full expedition would have cost over £2,000, a princely sum. If Edward paid, then where did he find the money, or was he provided with funds? The records are very patchy but at the time Ferdinand and Isabella were hiring professional soldiers and – on balance – it seems probable that Edward's company was on a contract.

His first duty on returning home was to report to the King who would want to be briefed on events and politics in Spain and Portugal. Most kings gathered information from travellers as well as ambassadors and King Henry was an avid collector of intelligence. He would also want to know how the Spanish monarchs viewed him, a newcomer to kingship.

The problems of the late Castilian King Henry IV ('the Impotent') and the validity of Isabella's right to his throne were grist for the mill, as was the offence caused to Isabella by King Edward's rejection of her hand 20 years earlier, particularly as he had chosen instead Edward Woodville's sister, 'a mere widow of England'. King Ferdinand of Aragon's antipathy to the French would be of particular interest, as would both of their views of English politics and King Henry himself.

The King and Edward discussed a possible engagement for one of Queen Elizabeth's sisters to the Portuguese heir apparent and they must also have talked about the Portuguese expeditions down the African coast and their newly discovered gold mine. King Henry asked Edward what had impressed him most in Portugal. The answer was, 'The sight of a man who took orders from nobody and was obeyed by all.' [2]

King Henry would need to know about any English dissidents lurking in Portugal, men such as Sir Edward Brampton, who had been sent by King Richard to capture Edward's ships in the Solent but, since Bosworth, had lived in Lisbon. He would need watching and it later transpired that his wife had taken a page called Piers or Piris with her to Lisbon. This Piers later became Perkin Warbeck who claimed to be Duke Richard of York, Edward IV's youngest son, having miraculously escaped from the Tower. Whoever the page was, he was going to give King Henry much worry during the 1490s. [3]

Of particular interest would be the current campaign in the Reconquista and the fighting abilities of the Spanish soldiery. Edward could tell the King how effective the Spanish artillery was at siege warfare and how the infantry had suffered during the march from the Moorish light horsemen. More importantly, he might have had views on how useful the light Spanish cavalry, the *genitors*, were at reconnaissance and harrying the enemy. He had also seen the result of progress in the manufacturing of hand-held guns which had enabled the Spanish to turn raw recruits into soldiers within weeks, in contrast to the English system where bowmen trained from birth (and would be a declining resource).

However, while musketeers could be quickly trained and the smoke and noise from a volley of shot was terrifying, there was a drawback. A musketeer could only fire about once every three minutes, while an archer could shoot up to ten arrows in one minute. There was also the matter of accuracy: a distance of 10–12 paces from the target was recommended for hand-held guns and only about one shot in 500 hit the target. [4]

As well as weapons and tactics, Edward may have remarked on the quartermastering and nurturing of the troops, all of which was overseen by Queen Isabella. He had left at least one of his men in her care, a Rupert (possibly an officer). On 20 April 1487 there is an entry in her accounts: 'To Ruberte, the Englishman, who came with the Count of Escales and stayed behind wounded, 4,000 mrs.' [5] Perhaps Edward commented on the morale of the troops and – as an aside – he might have mentioned Columbus, the Genoese navigator with the ambition to sail west to China and make a fortune for his patrons.

That September, a month after Edward arrived home, William Slater was appointed 'bailiffe of Chadlyngton'. He was the man who last appeared in the records in 1483 as 'gone to the see with Sir Edward Wodevile'. Presumably he had been with Edward ever since and seen service in Spain. King Henry obviously liked him, as Slater was on 4 March 1488 appointed a Yeoman of the

Crown and also 'bailiffe of Chadeworth'.

Edward's own responsibilities would claim his attention. The attainder on Anthony was reversed that November. Perhaps he paid an early visit to Carisbrooke and Porchester to settle some of his household troops for light duties and building work; the majority of them would be paid off. Then he was back at court to celebrate the birth of his great-nephew, Arthur, the first-born of King Henry and Queen Elizabeth. At the christening 'the Lord Edward Woodville' and three others 'bore the canopy' over the prince. Afterwards 'all the torches were burning, the king's trumpets and minstrels playing' and the young prince was carried to the King and Queen, while 'in the church yard were set two pipes of wine'.[6]

Edward wrote to King João following up the suggestion of an engagement for one of his York nieces with the Portuguese heir[7] and the records show him being paid 36 marks at Easter,[8] so he did something else – unknown – that was a particular service for King Henry.

There was peace and calm across the country. Edward's sister Catherine and her new husband Duke Jasper of Bedford were enjoying Buckingham's estates.[9] The administration ran smoothly, with King Henry's supporters installed in the key jobs; meanwhile he continued to tighten his grip on power. Many Welshmen arrived at court; a story current at the time had St Peter reduced to despair by a sudden influx of the Welsh into heaven, driving everyone mad with their incessant talk. St Peter arranged for an angel to stand outside and shout 'Caws Pob' (baked cheese, or Welsh rarebit). The Welsh charged out to get the delicacy and the gates were slammed behind them, much to everyone's relief.[10]

In March Edward had been granted four manors in the Isle of Wight to hold during Edward of Warwick's minority and in November he was being referred to as 'the beloved and faithful Edward Wideville, knight' when he was granted the right 'to present a suitable literate person' for the next vacancy in the cannonry at a collegiate church in Leicester.[11]

Life was good, the country was at peace, rural activities continued and the careful Treasury records of five years later[12] show how the King enjoyed himself: there were payments to minstrels of 13s-4d; to clerks for making lists for a tournament of £24-2s-10d; to paying the King's debts where he 'lost at buttes with his cross bow' of 13s-4d; where he lost at cards of £40; to maidens of Lambeth for May of 10s; for a pair of tables and dice of 16s; to the young damsel that danced of £30; to Pudsey Piper on the bagpipe of 6s-8d; where he lost again at cards of 40s; to a Spaniard, the tennis player, of £4; for tennis balls of 2s; where he lost at tennis of 27s-8d; to the challengers at the jousts of

14. Gentle activities. Four scenes: crossbows in the butts,
hawking with a lover, judging and book work.

£66-13s-4d and the same to the defenders; and so forth.

This was not a parsimonious or starchy court; that happened later in the reign. Now it sounds good fun and, indeed, some of the costs seem rather high, e.g. £30 for a dancing girl seems generous when compared to more mundane expenditure such as, four years later, paying Cabot £10 for discovering North America. The King clearly liked his gambling and girls. Edward was about and presumably joined in with some of these activities. It was a happy and idyllic time, but suddenly in November a rumour spread across England – Warwick will rise!

Over the next three months these rumours gained such strength that the King was obliged to react. Everywhere there was whispering: Edward of Warwick, son of the executed Duke of Clarence, blood royal of England and grandson of the Kingmaker, was to lead an invasion from Ireland.

King Henry tried to quash the rumour by displaying an 11-year-old boy who, he said, was the real Warwick and had been kept safely locked up in the Tower. But there was a convincing pretender, also aged 11, who had assumed the name of Lambert Simnel and had been coached, so we are told, by a 'subtle priest' named William Symonds. History is uncertain about who was the real Warwick, but the Tudor view was unambiguous: the Warwick in Ireland was the impostor. The real Warwick was the one who walked from the Tower to St Paul's in February 1487, heard mass and talked to people in the nave after the service.

John, Earl of Lincoln, King Richard's nephew and his appointed heir, had been Lord Lieutenant of Ireland.[13] Soon after Bosworth he had made his submission to King Henry but now he decided to support the Irish Warwick. Why he should remains a mystery, but either he accepted the young man's identity or regarded him as a useful stalking horse. Anyway, Lincoln sailed to Burgundy for talks with his Aunt Margaret, the Dowager Duchess of Burgundy, who had loved her brother Richard and consequently 'pursued Henry with insatiable hatred and fiery wrath'.[14]

On this occasion the hatred manifested itself in the form of 2,000 prime German and Swiss mercenaries led by a redoubtable Commander, Martin Schwarz. The Dowager Duchess had cast about for someone to provide suitable help and found Schwarz, the archetypal military entrepreneur. He had started his career making shoes in Augsburg but, finding that dull, followed the drum and decided military enterprise was much more to his taste. He had fought for Burgundy at the siege of Neuss and then captained 200 Swiss mercenaries in the Low Countries. Recently he had moved up a grade and was now able to contract with the Dowager Duchess for 2,000 trained soldiers. Contracts of the time required the payment of three months' wages for each man in advance, so the Duchess's hatred would have cost her something in the order of £5,000.[15]

She obviously felt that her late brother King Richard was worth that or she had a particular interest in the boy, perhaps both. There had been rumours that she had an illegitimate child but there is no obvious substance to them. The mercenaries were recruited and added to the hard core of Richard's men, followers who had escaped to Burgundy. These included the once powerful Lord Lovell, 'the dog', who had already organized one small revolt while

Edward was away in Spain, and a captain from Calais who, with part of the garrison, had refused to take the oath of loyalty to King Henry.

In England free pardons were offered to any plotters who turned King's evidence. The Council was worried and the Dowager Queen Elizabeth was suspected of involvement, but while there was no evidence or logic to support this the Council felt that she would be safer in retirement in a convent in Bermondsey. Fear and rumour were about and on 3 June a proclamation was issued ordering the pillory for anyone telling 'untrue and forged tidings and tales'.

Lincoln and his army arrived in Dublin on 5 May 1487 and were greeted by Gerald Fitzgerald, the great Earl of Kildare, who had effectively been viceroy since the death of Clarence in 1478. The Irish, always eager to discomfit the English, crowned their Warwick in the early Gothic splendour of Christchurch Cathedral with a gold circlet borrowed from a statue of the Virgin Mary. Lambert Simnel, a.k.a. the Earl of Warwick, was paraded through the streets as the new King Edward VI on the shoulders of d'Arcy of Platten, the 'tallest man of his time', and Irishmen enlisted with enthusiasm. Henry considered the pre-emptive strike of invading Ireland. Kildare and the Irish peers considered trying to lure him there, but then the thought of feeding Lincoln's army while they waited for Henry put paid to that plan and they hurried their King Edward VI and the invaders on their way to England.

On 4 June the invasion landed at Piel Island and occupied the castle that guards the deepwater harbour of Barrow-in-Furness. Lambert Simnel, as Edward of Warwick, declared himself king and knighted some of his followers, rather as Henry had done two years previously. They moved on to Barrow, a short walk at low water, and camped by Ulverston.

Christopher Urswick, the King's chaplain and intelligencer, was already in Lancashire, where he had been brought up. Vergil reports that he was inspecting the Lancashire ports to see which ones the invaders might use and he was around there when they arrived, so immediately sent the news south. He also reports that King Henry promptly arrested the Marquis of Dorset, observing, as he sent him to the Tower, 'if he were a true friend he would not take offence'. (Afterwards Dorset was released with an unblemished character but King Henry was always suspicious of him.)

The King had moved his court north to the huge castle of Kenilworth in Warwickshire where he started to plan and muster support. Towns were instructed to lay in food and drink which would be bought at a 'reasonable price' for the army. A proclamation was issued enforcing public order and military discipline, i.e. no robbing churches, no ravishing women, no stealing

15. Cavalry. Mounted men-at-arms and soldiers on the move with two trumpeters.

meat, no illegal lodging and so forth.

There were detailed orders for the cavalry: at the first blast of the trumpet the trooper must saddle his horse, at the second put the bridle on, at the third mount up and await orders; there was to be no unauthorized shouting or horn blowing. Vagabonds and 'common women' were not permitted to follow the King's host.[16]

The cavalry was to be divided into two wings, the leading or right wing to be commanded by 'the Queen's uncle, Sir Edward Woodville Lord Scales'. This wing was to be formed immediately. The only surviving instructions for any kind of organization in these proclamations are for the cavalry, Edward's area of command.

The order of battle was predictable: the Earl of Oxford 'besought the king to have the conduct of the Forward, which the king granted',[17] with Jasper, Duke of Bedford, commanding the mainguard. The left or rearguard would be made up of Stanley troops under Lord Strange, the heir to Lord Stanley who had been King Richard's hostage at Bosworth.

Troopers for the first cavalry wing were drawn from the young gallants at court and the surrounding counties. Kenilworth was a good recruiting centre in the heart of England and easy for Edward, as Grafton, where he would know many of the locals, was only a day's ride away. As soon as he had recruited his wing, he took them north to Yorkshire where the invading army was expected. Information on Lincoln's plan was excellent, 'for the King was in his bosome and knew every hour what the Earl did'. The Reverend Urswick was clearly a good intelligence gatherer.

Edward found the invaders outside Doncaster and launched a harassing action. He had limited numbers, perhaps 500 men (see note 18), so there can have been no question of a pitched battle. He was to delay them to enable the King to gather his forces. It was an ideal opportunity to use the cavalry tactics he had learned in Spain, where the lightly armed Moorish horsemen had dashed in to attack the army on the march and the Spanish *genitors* had shown their worth. Here the enemy was very short of cavalry, so it was easy to harass their wretched infantry.

Edward's prickers (light horsemen or skirmishers) galloped at a marching column of foot soldiers and while they may have caught an occasional straggler, more importantly, they disrupted the line of march. When they swooped, the infantry were forced to stop marching, regroup to form a defensive hedgehog and prepare to receive cavalry. The prickers then irritated the captains by riding away and not fighting. They ambushed supplies and foraging parties; they were always watching, waiting for a weakness.

The action lasted for the three days it took the enemy to march from Doncaster to Sherwood Forest, just north of Nottingham. There Edward and his cavalry broke off their harassment and joined the royal army which had arrived just south of Nottingham. In those three days the enemy had only managed to cover some 35 miles, 12 miles each day, which was slow for a small medieval army in a hurry, particularly one that had been averaging 25 miles each day when they had marched from Barrow to Doncaster – 150 miles in just six days. But that rate of march was before Edward had started work.

Molinet, with his Burgundian sympathies, implies that the invaders had the best of these encounters but the facts do not support this. Rather they show how effective Edward was in holding up the invaders by reducing their average daily rate of march by half. The King had needed extra time and Edward provided it.

There had been a supportive response to the King's call to muster. Lord Strange had 5,000–6,000 men; Northumberland had 4,000 and other noblemen with their followers, in all making up to around 12,000 men. The rebels numbered only 8,000–9,000, having failed to recruit in England (they were still substantially larger than the Tudor army of two years earlier). Martin Schwarz believed he had been let down by Lincoln and Lovell who had promised to raise substantial support that had not materialized. King Richard had exhausted the goodwill for the house of York and there was no appetite for further civil war. The captain of the mercenaries could do nothing other than fulfil the terms of his contract and grumble. He and his men had taken their pay.

King Henry should have been set for an easy victory, but for some reason morale appears to have been low and the troops unsettled. It seemed to them that the King kept disappearing and this gave rise to rumours that he had run away. There were some desertions but the English captains held the army together and the King was back in place to do the traditional dawn-of-battle business on 16 June.

He knighted suitable young men, attended early church and made a pre-battle speech, or so Bernard André writes: 'Most trusty Lords and most valiant comrades-in-arms who have experienced with me such great dangers on land and sea, behold again we are assailed against our will in another battle.' He laid the blame squarely on 'the perfidious' and ungrateful Earl of Lincoln and the 'silly and shameless' Duchess of Burgundy who were 'unjustly and spitefully in contention' with him. 'As God is my witness I have laboured unceasingly for the safety and peace of the realm and it is the Devil himself who has thwarted my efforts. Nevertheless just heredity will be stronger than their iniquity.'

Here he conveniently forgot his own suspect lineage but he ended the speech robustly, ordering his men to have faith: 'God himself, who made us victors in the previous battle will allow us now to triumph over our enemies.' The final exhortation was to attack fearlessly, 'for God is our helper'.

The royal army was up at the crack of dawn and started its march up the Fosse Way. Molinet reports that Edward, 'Le Seigneur d'Escales', was 'at the left wing of the vanguard in command (*en chief*) with two thousand horse'.[18] In reality he was on the right wing, according to the herald's report, and probably with nearer 500 horse, which, on the advance, would have provided a reconnaissance screen well ahead of the marching men. At around six o'clock in the morning his scurriers found Lincoln's army drawn up on a ridge across the Fosse Way just south of Newark.

The vanguard under Oxford arrived at nine o'clock and shook themselves out from line of march into battle order, i.e. ranks facing the length of the enemy front. The mainguard arrived and started to take up a position to the left, but they could do no more than watch as the rebel army was arranged in a tight knot, offering a front that was too small for anything but the vanguard to confront. Lincoln and Martin Schwarz had decided that this knot formation was best suited to their mixture of experienced, well-armed German mercenaries and wild, ill-equipped Irish. But they had not considered its weakness when their opponents had longbows.

The invaders and the vanguard stood and faced each other in silence while the rest of the royal army sorted itself out. The vanguard then advanced with measured tread to the beat of the drums. Schwarz's crossbow men fired a volley at the vanguard, which halted and loosed a flight of arrows. The tight enemy formation presented a perfect target for the archers who were beyond the range of the short Irish bows and arquebuses,[19] while the crossbows were slow to crank back and load. The bowmen in the vanguard stood and shot flight after flight of arrows at the enemy who could do nothing.[20]

The invaders' casualties were terrible, particularly amongst the Irish who had no armour, so that many of them were 'shot through with arrows like hedgehogs'. While they were strong on courage, they were weak on discipline and could not take such punishment without reacting. The Irish ranks suddenly erupted and charged down the hill at their tormentors, catching Lincoln and Schwarz totally unprepared – their battle plan included no headlong heroic charge. But on seeing most of their army streaming down the hill towards the enemy, all they could do was to sound the general advance.

The Germans charged after the Irish, down the hill into Oxford's vanguard that reeled under the impact, but then steadied and held its ground. There was fierce hand-to-hand fighting. The Germans fought solidly but the poor 'half naked' Irish, though they 'fought hard and stuck to it valiantly', were no match for armoured professionals and were slain like 'dull and brute beastes'.

It could not last for long. The invaders wavered and withdrew back up the hill. Again the archers took their opportunity and sent terrifying flights of arrows into their enemy. Oxford sounded his advance and led the vanguard forward and up the hill. Edward and his cavalry were on the right and they charged the enemy's exposed left flank. The vanguard reached the hill top where there was hard fighting. After an hour or so, the invading army was no more, with only a few small groups of die-hards left on the hill while most of the men had been pushed back, over the hill and down into a ravine still called the 'Red Gutter'. There was terrible slaughter.

Half the invasion force was dead – between 4,000 and 5,000. One estimate puts the King's losses at around 3,000, another puts it at only a few hundred. The latter seems more likely. The Earl of Lincoln[21] and Martin Schwarz were killed in the battle and the Irish Warwick was caught. In the afternoon great trenches were dug for the corpses, and cavalry rode out to round up fugitives. The English and Irish rebels were hanged and the mercenaries discharged, i.e. sent home. (Molinet reported that only 200 rebels survived but, again, that is probably an exaggeration.) Letters were dispatched telling people, 'how Almighty God had sent the king victory of his enemies and rebels, without the death of any noble or gentleman'. The German mercenaries had fought their best but the odds had been against them:

> These, in the day when heaven was falling,
> The hour when earth's foundations fled,
> Followed their mercenary calling,
> And took their wages and are dead.[22]

At the post-mortem King Henry and his Council considered the young prisoner. They agreed his name was Lambert Simnel[23] and decided to put him to work turning the spit in the royal kitchens. Through industry he was eventually to rise to the post of royal pastry cook. It was a shrewd move as it showed clemency, but was spiced with a heavy helping of contempt. The policy was to ridicule the opposition.

Piel Island, where Simnel landed and was declared king, was given its own 'king', one who rules even now. He is also the local publican, the landlord of the Ship Inn, and by tradition he can create a 'knight of Piel', and so King Henry's ridicule still runs.

Two years later the absurdity of a commoner aping royalty was still the narrative when some Irish peers came for an audience. The King reminisced happily, 'My masters of Ireland you will crown apes at last.' [24]

However, the uprising had frightened the King, so the fate of the wretched young Warwick in the Tower was sealed. He was executed ten years later once he was old enough. After all, it was only evil men like King Richard who killed children.

CHAPTER TEN[1]

ONWARDS TO GLORY

After his victory King Henry toured the north and then marched back towards London. At Leicester he was met by French envoys who congratulated him effusively on his success and, having flattered him, moved smoothly on to ask for his understanding for their king who had 'a similar problem'. In reality, this meant France was going to attack Brittany and wanted a clear run. This was the start of what the French later christened *La Guerre Folle* or 'The Mad War'.

The envoys had come to remind Henry of his debt to France and to dissuade him from aiding Brittany, England's traditional ally. Her dukes paid fealty to the Kings of France, but it was nominal, as they stood 'erect and armed' when they pledged and 'recognized no creator or sovereign save God Almighty'. Duke Francis of Brittany was not a strong man but he had a tough chief minister, the hawkish Pierre Landois, who was 'intelligent, industrious and astute' but also 'arrogant, avaricious, violent, suspicious and vindictive' and, even worse, 'his humble origin made him odious to all classes'.

This meant that the nobles loathed him and were joined in opposition to anything he did. The Marshal de Rieux led the group that took a dove-like line on France because Landois was a Francophobe. However, the real problem for Brittany was the deterioration in the Duke's mental health (inherited through the maternal line from his grandfather, Charles VI of France) and the need for an advantageous marriage for the heir apparent, his eight-year-old daughter Anne.

In France government was in the hands of Anne de Beaujeu, King Louis's daughter and elder sister to the young King. She was 24 years old and noted as handsome, although she looks rather forbidding in her portrait. Anne was proving a very capable regent, with her father's grasp of *realpolitik* and – unfortunately for Brittany – she had decided France would have the duchy. The *Rosier des Guerres* ('Rosebush of Wars') written in 1481–82 for the instruction of King Charles when he was Dauphin, under the direction of King Louis, states 'the noble kings of France have always aimed and worked to expand and enlarge their kingdom'. Anything other than the total subjection of Brittany would be unacceptable.

The French Minister for War put the analysts to work and produced a reasoned exposition of the French claim, along with an appreciation of how best it could be achieved.[2] They knew the duchy's annual revenues were around 1 million livres (£110,000) even after defence costs; there were about 12,000 men who were capable of carrying arms and some 600 ocean-going vessels.

No attempt was made to minimize the difficulties and the report started from the premise that the claim would be so unpopular in the duchy that success was doubtful. Even if the Breton nobles could be persuaded to accept French claims, the exercise would be pointless as the nobles were unreliable. The conclusion was to use overwhelming force to take the duchy.

Landois was well aware of French aspirations and had been working hard at a new alliance. He had signed up Maximilian of Austria, Regent of Burgundy and recently elected King of the Romans, and was hopeful of Spain and England. He had allies within France itself, as Brittany was providing refuge to a cousin of the French King, Duke Louis d'Orléans, 'a young prince and very handsome but much addicted to his pleasures'.[3] Orléans was a natural athlete in his mid-20s, next in line to the French throne but a leader of the Feudal League, a group of disgruntled nobles. He had recently tested the Regent's power, lost and fled to Brittany.

Anne de Beaujeu had dealt with the Feudal League and Maximilian's military incursions, she had neutralized England by aiding Henry Tudor and now turned her attention to Brittany. The opposition needed little encouragement and the Marshal de Rieux executed a palace revolution. Landois was caught and hanged, the Marshal took over government and immediately signed a friendship treaty with France. This fuelled the argument about the duchy's future and who should marry the heiress (according to Voltaire she was 'one of the finest women in her time and in love with the Duke d'Orléans').

Landois had wanted Orléans to marry her, although he was already married – against his wishes – to his crippled cousin, King Charles's younger sister. The Duke liked the widowed Maximilian of Austria, while de Rieux, now effectively the chief minister, supported Alain d'Albret, the head of a powerful Gascon family, whose late wife was a distant cousin of the Duke.[4] But d'Albret, known as 'Le Grand', was old (48), ugly and had a nasty reputation.

Once de Rieux was in power he suddenly understood France's territorial aspirations. He thought he could re-negotiate the friendship treaty by writing to the Regent and telling her a new arrangement was needed. If she would not agree then, 'He would regard his promises as dissolved and deem himself free to terminate his friendship with the King.' To this the Regent sent the splendid reply, 'The King of France has no friends and will have Brittany.'[5]

Duke Francis appealed for English help, which put King Henry in a difficult position. While Brittany had been his refuge for ten years of exile, it was France that had actively helped him take the crown; indeed the Regent had provided the money and the men that gave him the throne. So, in Vergil's words, 'between these two extreme calls on his goodwill he decided for a time to hold a middle course'.

At the very least, the Regent would have extracted an unequivocal commitment to neutrality over Brittany. On the other hand, as King of England it was not in his interests for Brittany to become part of France. Fortunately he did not have to commit himself, as the Regent 'cunningly' asked him to mediate between the two.

David Hume, the eighteenth-century Scottish historian, believed it was Bernard Stewart who was sent to London to persuade Henry to mediate. Stewart had provided 1,000 Scots infantry for the invasion and was in a strong position to persuade Henry, who agreed and commissioned the ubiquitous Christopher Urswick to find a diplomatic solution.

The last French attack had been a probe against Nantes just three days after the battle of Stoke (19 June 1487). France had already taken Vannes, Dinan, Châteaubriant and Ancenis but Nantes had not yielded by the autumn, so the French army withdrew to their winter quarters. In March the Marshal de Rieux woke them up with a series of surprise attacks and re-captured all four places. The Regent and her Minister of War were not pleased and decided the time had come to sort out the question of Brittany. This marked the start of the so-called 'Mad War'.

They prepared a full-scale invasion. Louis de la Trémoille was appointed commander-in-chief with instructions to take the whole duchy. He was 28, methodical and a first-rate strategist who was to become one of France's great generals. This was his first major command.

Coincidental to the French preparations, Ambassador Urswick set out for Paris and Rennes on his mission of reconciliation while King Ferdinand of Spain and envoys from Brittany urged King Henry and their English friends to take firm action. Urswick found the Regent very receptive to the offer of mediation, which was 'readily embraced'. However, his reception in Brittany was less enthusiastic.

He was reminded that the Duke had acted as protector and guardian to Henry during his youth and adverse fortune. He expected from 'a monarch of such virtue' proper aid and assistance in his present difficulties. But all he was getting was 'a barren offer of mediation'. That would not stop the French army. If Henry's gratitude was insufficient, then his prudence, as King of England, should make him well aware of 'the pernicious consequences attending a French conquest of Brittany'.[6]

Urswick reported this to King Henry but they concluded that, with more time, the Bretons might accept a negotiated settlement. So back went Urswick for more negotiations. Some time around then King Henry was staying with Edward in his castle of Carisbrooke[7] where the main subject of discussion must have been the deteriorating situation in Brittany and the fact that Urswick was making little progress.

King Henry had been playing for time but it is not clear what he hoped to achieve by this; perhaps he hoped the problem would solve itself. He and Urswick must have known that the Regent was dissembling in Paris while her army prepared for war. In Brittany Duke Francis was ill so it was the Duke d'Orléans who spoke to Urswick. He was furious with his cousin, the Regent, who had out-manoeuvred him. He wanted war – no compromise for him. It may have been unconnected but at about this time King Henry ordered the construction of two new big Tower ships, each to be 600 tons, one of them to be built at Southampton.[8]

Foreign policy may have been difficult but life at the English court was undisturbed. The King ran the country and dealt with a predictable range of problems, petitions and so forth. It is good to see William Slater reappearing in the records on his appointment as a Yeoman of the Crown. Furthermore one recent proposal interested the King: it was the offer from Christopher Columbus to sail westward to India under the English flag. He sent his brother, Bartholomew, who arrived in February 1488, for an audience with the King. An almost immediate audience meant he had a powerful friend at court and Edward is the likeliest candidate.[9] Perhaps Edward had met Christopher in Cordoba, as they were both there at the same time, or he could have overlapped with Bartholomew in Lisbon.

According to Hakluyt, the King was taken with the plan and 'accepted the offer with joyful countenance'. He dispatched Bartholomew to bring his brother to England. But Bartholomew got lost for six years, by which time Queen Isabella had commissioned his brother, 'and so the West Indies by providence were thus reserved for the Crown of Castilia'.[10]

Meanwhile all was not well in Brittany. The situation suddenly deteriorated, the French recaptured and razed Châteaubriant and Ancenis, then moved on to besiege Fougères and St Aubin. Maximilian of Austria, the Duke's ally and Regent of Burgundy, was unable to help because he was imprisoned by the burghers in Bruges, one of his daughter's cities.

Duke Francis, recovering from yet another bout of insanity, was in despair. If Maximilian could not help, then English help was critical. He sent two special envoys to King Henry who arrived on 'St George's even'. They were in time for the investiture of new Knights of the Garter and the attendant celebrations.

On 27 April 1488 'Sir Edward Wydville called Lord Wydville' was formally invested with the Order of the Garter. In those days the garter was of light blue silk and the members wore the velvet surcoat, mantle and hood. Edward became one of the 25 members and his coat of arms was now circled with the garter (the near contemporary depiction of his coat of arms does not include the scallop of Scales).[11]

Bosworth had made vacancies in the ranks of the Order and Henry had appointed six new knights while Edward was away in Spain (the Earl of Oxford, Sir John Cheyne, Lord Dynham, Giles Daubeny, Sir William Stanley and Lord Strange); then, 'after 30 September 1487', Edward and the Earl of Shrewsbury were appointed and installed on 27 April 1488.[12] Certainly Edward was a paladin, one of the trusted friends of the King.

It was a splendid ceremony, followed by matins and then a dinner where the nine knights present had their own special table: 'that day the hall was marvellously ordered and served'. The next day saw a parade where the knights made offerings: 'Lord Wodvile his helm and crest' (which was standard). There was then a further mass. The herald reported[13] and also recorded the special song used for the celebration:

England now rejoice, for joyous may thou be,
To see thy king so flowering in dignity.
O most noble king, thy fame doth spring

and so forth for some 50 lines to:

Much people present to see thee, King Henry.
Wherefore, now Saint George, all we pray to thee,
To keep our sovereign in his dignity.

A few days after the ceremony the two Breton envoys were, at last, able to see the King. One was Guillaume Guillemet, who had been the envoy sent to England in 1472 to explain to King Edward IV that Henry Tudor could not be handed over to him. 'Why not?' King Edward asked. Guillaume's answer was simple. Duke Francis had given his promise of protection and that was sacrosanct. He would also have brought messages from his brother who had been

Henry's guardian for seven years. The envoys now pleaded for English help.

The language of the Bretons and the Welsh is similar so there would have been sympathy and much talk in the mother tongue around the corridors of court. The envoys would have reiterated the case that honour demanded action and, if that was not enough, England's defence required it. Henry reluctantly decided he could not or would not help. Hume says that he was 'desirous of preserving the appearance of strict neutrality'. Instead he sent an order to all ports prohibiting any Englishman, on pain of death, from leaving the country without his express permission, which was noted by the French with satisfaction – they were having their pound of flesh.

Sir Edward Woodville KG disagreed with King Henry, doubtless reminding his monarch of debts and honour owed to Duke Francis. Vergil reported that 'Edward Wdeuyll, brother of King Edward's wife Elizabeth, an impetuous man, trained to bear arms and incapable of languishing in idleness, besought King Henry for permission to lead a small band of soldiers to the aid of the Bretons', and asked for leave 'to try a fall with the old enemy' (Edward's own reported words).

Edward Hall, the Elizabethan historian, recounts: 'Sir Edward, Lord Woodville, uncle to the Queen, a valiant captain and bold champion, either abhorring ease and idleness or inflamed with ardent loyalty and affection towards the duke of Brittany, desired very earnestly of King Henry that he, with a convenient number of good men of war, should transport himself to Brittany to aid and defend Duke Francis, the King's good friend.'

Edward understood the King's problem and proposed stealing away privately 'without licence or passport'. But King Henry was still confident that peace could be made by political persuasion and by 'the wise intentions of his elected Ambassadors'. He would not agree to Edward's 'hot, hasty and wild desire'. 'Yet, Lord Woodville, despite being forbidden by the King, could not rest and determined to make his own arrangements without the King knowing. The King strictly prohibited Woodville from attempting any such enterprise but he [Edward] went straight to the Isle of Wight, of which he was ruler and captain, and there gathered together a crew of 400 tall and hardy men.'

But this is only part of the story. The Breton ambassadors decided not to press the matter with the King, an odd decision in the circumstances. Instead they left court and went straight to the Isle of Wight where they met Edward in the first week of May. We do not know if King Henry agreed to support the Bretons by covertly turning a blind eye to Edward's plans or if Edward really did disobey his king.

Whatever happened, there was a serious ruction and Edward stalked off to the Isle of Wight where the Breton ambassadors found him. They provided Edward with 'funds in silver' to buy arms, munitions and equipment and recruit men. They told him that four Breton ships would be ready at the Isle of Wight on 20 May, two weeks later. Events were moving fast.

Two weeks is a very short time to find 400 men and dress them for war. Edward started recruiting. It is locally recorded that he 'selected 40 men at arms and 400 of the strongest from among the common people, whom he armed with pikes, bows and arrows and dressed them in white tunics bearing the red-cross'. In all probability many of them were Edward's troops from his old campaigns, but some were locally recruited, including one boy, 'Diccon Cheke of Mottiston', who went as Edward's page.

At the same time, William Paston, the contemporary letter writer, was reporting what he knew to his brother:

> It was said that Lord Woodville and others would go over to Brittany to help the Duke. I cannot tell you about that but on hearing the rumour many men went to wait for him [presumably they liked 'the valiant captain and bold champion'] at Southampton where it was said he would take ship.

> When Woodville was refused permission, those that were there still waited in the hope there would be a licence [to go to Brittany]. Once they knew there was no likelihood of a licence, two hundred of them boarded a Breton ship that had just come over with salt. They told the master to take them to Brittany.

> They hadn't sailed six leagues [18 miles] when they saw a French ship, which made over towards them. The English were frightened that the French might not meddle [fight] with them, so all the English went under the hatches. Only the Breton men were visible to cause the Frenchmen to be keener to meddle with them.

> The Frenchmen boarded them and all the English came up from under the hatches and captured the French ship. They took the men, ship and all to Brittany. Also on the ship there was an ambassador from the King of Scotland who is now in great trouble, together with his son and other Scots Lords.

To the French this was an act of piracy but the English were delighted with themselves.

The main party, Edward Woodville and his 440 'tall and hardy men', had 'prosperous wind and weather' for their trip to Brittany in the four ships the Duke had provided. So the English force that massed in Brittany was at least 640 and the best estimate is '700 or 800 strong'.[14] Hall continues the story: 'The rumour of this doing was soon blown into the French Court, which

16. A ship under sail. A *nao*, or typical sailing ship of the period.

made the Ambassadors of England not smally abashed.' Vergil remarked, 'the English ambassadors began to be fearful for their safetey'.

On 25 May the Archbishop of Bordeaux reported a rumour to General de la Trémoille: 'Mons de Squales' had arrived at Saint Malo and did not have many men, 'Dieu mercy'. Four days later Trémoille received word that 'Scalles' had passed through Honfleur (100 miles to the east, in France) 'without many people'. This sounds like an additional party of Englishmen, for on the same day the French commander at Dol, Viscount d'Aunay, ambushed yet more Englishmen outside Dinan.

The Viscount boasted to King Charles, who informed Trémoille on 31 May, that the English had been in the town when they saw 30 French horsemen galloping past; they had rushed out in disorder and chased the horsemen for a mile and a half. Then they ran straight into the ambush laid by d'Aunay and his troop of 120 men who had killed 240 *and more* while taking 114 prisoners. This sounds a gloriously exaggerated claim, but there probably was a skirmish where some English were taken prisoner.[15]

Nevertheless by 5 June Edward and his Englishmen were in Rennes enjoying a lavish reception which, judging from the drink consumed, turned into a serious party. 'Two barrels of claret were broken open in their honour in the rue Haute, and two barrels of white wine in the Bout de Cohue square. There the English soldiers, who were being triumphantly paraded through the streets, stopped, ate and drank while a band of musicians serenaded them and a young boy entertained them with his acrobatics' (*tours de souplesse*). 'Then a great banquet was offered by the town of Rennes to Wydeville and all English officers, in the private apartments of the Ducal Chateaux. At this banquet were eaten, among other things, one and a half calves, two and a half sheep, three kids, two hares, twenty-eight young rabbits, eight goslings, thirty-six chickens, twenty-eight pigeons, and so on. ... One barrel of white wine, one of claret, and seven *estamaux d'hypocras*[16] were drunk.'

Interestingly that was the day King Henry gave instructions for 'fortifying of certain our ships of war yet being upon the sea' and 11 days later the Master of the 'Mare Guldeford' was commissioned to recruit soldiers and sailors and victuals for 'an armed force being about to be sent in resistance of the King's enemies congregating at sea'.[17] What the threat was or who the enemy were is unknown. It could have been for surreptitious support for Brittany.

News of the arrival of Edward with his Englishmen and the partying became public in Paris. Tempers flared, the young bloods threatening violence to the English embassy. 'The French King suspected King Henry was responsible but messengers came from him declaring, by most evident tokens and argument, that Lord Woodville without his knowledge or consent had sailed to Brittany with so small a number of men that it did not become a Prince to send them. And neither would they be of any great help to the Bretons.' The envoy also brought a letter from King Henry:

Most High, Most Excellent, and Most Powerful Prince, Most Dear and Most Beloved Cousin ...

no one of our subjects had been in Brittany; and that was the truth, for we had forbidden, under the pain of death, anybody to go there. ...

However, we have just been informed that the Breton ambassadors ... have gone to the Isle of Wight to Sir Edward Woodville ... and have by their subtle ways and intrigue so much exhorted and seduced him, that to our very great displeasure he went away with them to Brittany ... with ... some 300 men, most of whom he extracted from places of asylum where they had been for several years on account of their crimes and misdemeanours; most of these men went without armour. ...

we did not know of it until after their departure. ... Sir Edward Woodville has asked us many times for a permission to go and we not only have never given him permission, but we have expressly forbidden him to go there so positively that he knew he would incur our indignation, and we would never have believed he would dare to infringe our order. ...

There was also a young knight ... who made ready to go after the said Sir Edward; but as soon as we knew it, we seized his ships and his company and caused him to be arrested, and because, Most High Most Excellent, Most Powerful Prince, Most Dear and Most Beloved Cousin, we are certain that these things will come to your knowledge, and we know not in which way you would accept or interpret them ... we apprise you willing of the truth (etc). ...

we shall know by the result that Edward and his people have been badly counselled in making such a foolish attempt. ...

we send to you our Garter King of Arms, by whom you will be able to know the exact truth, praying you to believe him and to put faith in what he will say to you, and to inform us by him of your good news and if there is something you desire to be done by us, we shall accomplish it most willingly, as the good Son of God helping, Most High, Most Excellent, Most Powerful Prince, Most Dear and Most Beloved Cousin, and may He have you in his Holy Protection and grant you the full accomplishment of your good desires.

Written in our Castle of Windsor the 27th day of May,
    Your good cousin
        Henry

It was hardly surprising that, in Hall's opinion, 'The French King did not believe a word of the denial but he hid his anger and dissembled (according to the French custom) with a flattering smile.'

The English ambassadors had a difficult time in Paris and an easier one when they visited Duke Francis. They then returned to England with their assessment of the situation. They thought both sides were posturing, and thus King Henry reasoned that the French would not move quickly against Brittany, because the Regent's action against the Duke d'Orléans, the heir presumptive, would be 'very faint and slow' and she knew that Maximilian was again at liberty so would be quick to help the Bretons.[18] Also there was late news: the French had just agreed to a short truce, which seemed to confirm this analysis.

What he did not know was that the truce was a subterfuge to demonstrate French good intentions and coerce those Frenchmen who were sympathetic to Brittany and the Feudal League. It convinced the Breton army, who were all volunteers, to take immediate advantage of the 'temporary cessation of hostilities' and go home. The Duke was horrified and announced a general inspection for 12 June. This had no effect, so Edward and his Englishmen were almost the only organized force capable of defending Rennes against a French raid. If the French had moved then, they might have walked in, but either they observed the truce or were not yet ready.

By the beginning of July the Bretons had gathered their harvest and suddenly 'realising the danger which threatened their homeland, the gentlemen and irregular troops gathered in Rennes to the number of about 7,000'. They joined Edward's troops while other foreign contingents were arriving: 1,500 Swiss *lansquenets* (halberdiers) from Emperor Maximilian, 1,000 Spaniards from King Ferdinand and 1,500 Gascons, who had landed near Quimper under the leadership of Alain d'Albret. The Breton army assembled at Rennes in early July totalled around 11,500 men, of whom 4,600 were English, German and Spanish.[19]

The French army had stayed firmly in Brittany during the truce. The Regent and King Charles had no intention of giving up, even though the English ambassadors returned to Paris to tell them an English army would be sent to Brittany if the French dared attack. Unfortunately for Duke Francis, nothing was done to back up the threat, and negotiations for an Anglo-French peace treaty continued at the same time, which sent a very different message to the French.

Hall reports: 'King Charles had as little regard for the English threat as the biting of a flea. He knew his army was powerful and strong and that the Bretons had but a few Englishmen with the Lord Woodville, for whom he cared little, and seeing England had not yet sent an army for the Duke's help, he judged that his army would do great exploit before either the Duke should be provisioned or any aid sent.'

King Charles was proud of his army. Long gone were the feudal levies. They had been replaced by regular infantry organized on the Swiss system with 18ft (5.4-metre) pikes, crossbows and non-commissioned officers. His father had hired Swiss training teams and established a new army, he and his sister had continued the arrangements and now it was time to put the training into practice. Additionally the Regent had just hired a large contingent of prime Swiss mercenaries. Not only that, but France had the best artillery train.[20]

The King was keen to put them to work, and on 14 June wrote to General de la Trémoille enclosing copies of letters 'which our cousin the King of England wrote to us by Jarretière, his herald of arms from which you will see the whereabouts of Lord Scales and the small number of English ... who did it regardless of the prohibitions. ... [King Henry] is not pleased ... be on your guard as to what you might have to do and notify us of what happens, send news often.' He wrote again on 1 July: 'Their [the Bretons'] policy is one of dissimulation, and we see no prospect of achieving good results but by force. They have requested another ten days' truce, which we have peremptorily refused ... make war as vigorously as you can.'[21]

Trémoille did and, according to Hall, 'sore oppressed the country of Brittany, burning and destroying towns and besieging the town of Fougères so that the Duke of Brittany was encouraged by the Duke d'Orléans and other rebels of the French King to fight and give battle to the French army.' Fougères was one of the strongest places in Brittany and well garrisoned; however, these new cannon were a worry. Some of the council thought it should be relieved with the full force of Breton arms as a demonstration of strength; others were not convinced.

The wily Marshal de Rieux recommended masterly inactivity. He thought the French would run out of enthusiasm and go home in the autumn but Trémoille was piling on the pressure, which made de Rieux's approach look weak. The huge fortress of St Aubin was also under siege and, to make matters worse, the French ambassadors working on the Anglo-French peace treaty in England had persuaded King Henry to sign on 14 July. While it was separate to Breton affairs, it gave the French good reason to believe that the English would stick to the bargain and not intervene in Brittany. There was thus no reason to hold back – rather the opposite.

It seems that Ferdinand and Isabella were also worried about the English

17. Siege of a city. On the left is the Earl of Warwick instructing a gunner with a breech-loading cannon on its wooden bed; below is a ship with its cannon. English soldiers are above the town with their bills; the defenders are around the town.

position and well aware that Edward had fallen out with King Henry. On 15 July they wrote to him: 'the Count de Scalas had gone to Brittany without permission from King Henry. As he is a faithful servant of Ferdinand and Isabella they beg the king to forgive the count. Sepalveda [the Spanish envoy who carried the letter] will give all necessary explanation by word of mouth.' [22]

Ten days later Duke Francis held a council of war in Rennes where the seven leaders, Edward being one of them, were called to speak. There was a consensus for immediate action and so the army marched to the relief of Fougères and St Aubin. However, by the time they arrived the French siege guns had destroyed the defences and both strongholds had surrendered after just one week. Nevertheless the Bretons decided on battle. Molinet reported:

> It came about that on 28 July [1488] an arrow's flight from La Roche Troolet, the Duke d'Orléans, the Prince d'Orange [a nephew of Duke Francis], the Count of Dunois in charge of the Swiss companies and the Lord Descales with a number of English, all on foot, together with the Lord d'Albrecht and the Lord de Rieux came down from a hillside to engage the French commanding their battles [battalions] and artillery as best they could.

> The French, who were holding St Aubin, decided to fight; they prepared their armies and assembled their garrisons to engage the Bretons. Starting from St Aubin a great procession set forth which comprised the Bailly of Dijon, leader of the Swiss, and Claude and Jacques de Salli, captains of archers in the King's own guard ... and other warlords all very highly experienced.[23]

The Marshal de Rieux positioned his army on a ridge about a mile south of Mézières, facing south across some moorland towards St Aubin, with the Wood of Usel to the forward left and the forest of Haute Sève on the right. He took command of the 2,400 men-at-arms in the cavalry wing of the vanguard, although he seems to have positioned himself with d'Albret and 5,000 infantry in the middleguard. The rearguard was commanded by Châteaubriand and formed the reserve, but was 'comprising more vivandiers [sellers of provisions and liquor to the soldiers] and servants than combatants'. The cavalry were divided between the two wings, i.e. they were on the outside flanks of the battle line up.

Edward commanded the foot soldiers in the vanguard, over 2,000 men, all wearing the red cross of St George. This is the first time English foot soldiers are recorded wearing the red cross. Hall explained: 'To make the French believe that they had a great number of English, notwithstanding there were but four hundred with the Lord Woodville, they dressed one thousand seven hundred Bretons in coats with red crosses after the English Fashion' (the Bretons normally wore the black cross).[24]

They waited, drawn up in their lines along the ridge. The French marched out of their fortress and along the road. Trémoille reckoned the Bretons were well north of Mézières, maybe six miles further away, and his army of 15,000 professional soldiers, 'well appointed in which the artillery and the heavy cavalry were conspicuous', came ambling along the narrow road beside the Wood of Usel. They were in file and without order.[25] The artillery train rumbled along; most of the cannon were bronze, drawn by horses and so able to keep up with a marching army.

The Frenchmen tramped round the corner of the wood and suddenly saw their enemy lined up in full battle order. The surprise must have been palpable and the Bretons should then have taken the advantage and attacked then. A charge was demanded but, at that moment, d'Albret decided to change his dispositions and vetoed the idea. Marshal de Rieux pleaded with him to allow the vanguard to attack, presumably echoing an urgent demand from Edward.

It is surprising that Edward, who knew an opportunity when he saw one, did not lead his men in his own charge. But it would have been unsupported and he had recently seen Lincoln defeated as the result of an indisciplined charge at Stoke. However, he must have seethed with rage as he watched Trémoille deploy his army into a fighting formation and the advantage disappear. He exercised remarkable restraint and perhaps remembered that campaign in Spain when he had lead an unexpected and successful charge into the enemy flank.

Once the French were properly arrayed, the infantry and cavalry lined up and, with cannon arranged, the battle started. The French and English accounts – Molinet and Hall – produce a mixed picture of the battle, which opened with an artillery duel: 'there was a heavy exchange of artillery fire, very damaging to both sides'. The Bretons shouted 'Sant-Sanson' and the Swiss 'Sant-Lautrois'.[26] 'The sun shone brilliantly on the arms of the French.' 'Both the vantgardes joined together with such a force it was a marvel to behold.' [27]

The infantry of the Breton vanguard, English or Bretons dressed as English, led by Edward, advanced 'en pointe' against the enemy, i.e. they charged in arrowhead formation, presumably behind the banner of the scallop of Scales with Edward as the leading man. 'The French right flank went to meet it en masse.' The Marshal de Rieux, beside d'Albret, watched from his horse and must have known the charge should have been made earlier. 'The battle was hard and furious ... bodies fell, blood flowed.' Edward, the man at the point of the arrowhead, presumably hacked his way through the French but perhaps he hacked too hard and became isolated.[28]

The action was reported by Molinet: 'The English archers showed great courage, for each of the opposing parties fought for victory. ... The mêlée developed into a hard and rough free-for-all; bodies fell, blood flowed.' In the face of this assault the French pulled back 100 paces but Edward had been killed there. 'Lord Descales together with a large number of English were killed there, near a wood called Selp.'

On the edge of the wood there is now a bed of pine needles and around a carpet of heather. Somewhere there Edward lay with his blood soaking the ground; a dead paladin, a knight driven by honour and obligation.

He was dead but there were still other Englishmen. There was a break in the hand-to-hand fighting and the French drew back for breathing space, the English holding their ground. At this point the archers saw their opportunity and shot flight after flight of arrows into the French whose front ranks, already heavily knocked about, tried to pull back out of range. They scurried back to the reserves where their horsemen were. The rearward of the French, seeing the retreat, started to flee, but, luckily for Trémoille, his captains grasped the situation, subdued the panic and were able to regroup their men.[29]

Meanwhile the Breton mainguard was moving into the attack under a barrage from the French artillery. It seems that one of the German captains in the Breton line, keen to avoid cannonballs and grape shot, moved his men forward too quickly and while this may have saved his men, it made a gap in the line. 'But a kink formed in the Breton centre by the fault of the Chief German Bühler. A Neapolitan adventurer in the French Service, Jacques Galliota, with four hundred mounted men-at-arms and two hundred others, attacked to the back. Galliota was killed but the breakthrough was made.'

King Charles had particularly recommended Galliota to Trémoille who was using him as his military advisor.[30] He had been one of Duke Charles of Burgundy's leading (mercenary) captains and fought in the last disastrous campaign against the Swiss, so he had useful experience. There seems to have been a question over his eyesight, but there was nothing wrong with it that day.

Part of the French line had been in deep trouble as a result of Edward's attack and Galliota had been watching for an opportunity to change the balance. He saw the break in the Breton line and asked Trémoille if he could mount an attack. With permission, he gathered together 400 men-at-arms and charged the gap created by the German mistake. His troop smashed through the Breton lines sending shock waves along the ranks. The Breton cavalry waiting on the wings should have been dispatched to deal with the incursion but they only watched, doing nothing to help their foot soldiers who were terribly exposed.

Despite his death, Galliota's horsemen, 'threw themselves on the artillery, killing the soldiers [manning the guns]. They raced over to the rearguard and fell on the vivandiers and valets, spreading death and disorder everywhere.' A French infantry company, in their turn, penetrated the open gap in the Breton lines, then turned and attacked the mainguard in the rear.

It was disastrous, and to make matters worse this coincided with a huge explosion in the wood behind the Breton lines. Their magazine blew up, probably hit by a stray shot. It was all too much for the untrained levees and the Breton lines just dissolved into groups of frightened individuals.

A question mark hangs over d'Albret. The gap arose in the centre of his division and that, together with his earlier refusal to allow the charge, would take some explaining at a court of inquiry, as would de Rieux's failure to order his cavalry to charge Galliota's incursion. The main body of French infantry regrouped and, in conjunction with their cavalry, mounted a full-scale attack against what was left of the Bretons. They 'set fiercely on the Bretons and slew the most part of their footmen'.

'The Ducal rearguard ran away. The mainguard broke up. The Breton cavalry scattered or ran away as did the Chief Marshal [de Rieux] with d'Albret whilst the archers were annihilated. The wearers of the Red Cross, Bretons like the English, were sacrificed.'

The Breton army entered its death throes. 'When the [survivors of the] vanguard of the Bretons saw that neither their horsemen nor the Germans were coming forward [to fight] they provided for themselves and fled.' 'In conclusion, the Frenchmen obtained the victory and slew all such as wore red crosses supposing them to be English.' The French mopping-up operation turned into 'a hunt which went as far as the village of Masières in the area of Barbase. ... In this conflict were slain almost all the Englishmen and 6,000 Bretons, Lord Woodville was found amongst the dead. The French losses were 1,200.'[31]

On a count by the heralds the French dead were estimated at 1,400, most of whom were killed by the vanguard. Included among the figures of the Breton dead were the Spanish contingent, all 1,000 of them killed. Marshal de Rieux and d'Albret were safe as they had galloped away with the cavalry.

The Duke d'Orléans and the Prince d'Orange had been on horseback but the Breton infantry distrusted them, believing they would gallop away if the battle went badly or they might betray the cause, 'wherefore they dismounted and put themselves in the German *battle* [battalion]'.[32] Things did not go well for them. Orléans was captured in the Wood of Usel trying to rally the stream of fugitives, and Orange, having thrown off the Black Cross of Brittany, was pretending to be dead. Unfortunately for him, he was recognized by a French soldier who had once served under him and took considerable pleasure in making the arrest.

King Charles wrote, 'Never within living memory was there so wonderfully complete a rout.' Two weeks later General de la Trémoille received the surrender of St Malo, one of the articles of capitulation being, 'All the goods, arms, ships, horses and other things belonging to the late Lord Scales which are in the said town and its harbours and roadsteads are to remain at the disposition of the Sieur de La Trémoille'.[33]

These were the spoils of war and of no more use to Edward. He had died in the service of a ruler to whom he owed no allegiance, only friendship. His death was regarded as sufficiently important for the Spanish chroniclers to record. Bernáldez wrote, 'in her [the Duchess of Brittany] support there came the Count of Scalas, the Englishman, who was at the capture of Loja, who died in a battle between the French and the Bretons', while Pulgar reported, 'and there died many Bretons, Englishmen and Castillians who had gone to help them. And there died fighting the Count of Escalas, since he would not surrender and be imprisoned.'

There is now a grey stone monument that records the end of Breton independence and catalogues those who fought for Brittany and died on 22 July 1488: 'The Earl of Scales and 500 English archers.'[34]

They are listed together with 6,000 Bretons, Gascons, Spaniards and Germans from the Holy Roman Empire. A hundred yards beyond through the pinewood, a rocky outcrop rises up out of the scrub with a battered old stone cross firmly embedded in its top. There on the ridge, a mile south of Mézières, with the woods to left and right and moorland sloping down 'an arrows flight', was where Edward Woodville had stood, watching the battle unfold and from where he had led his last charge. Beyond is a dark pinewood encroaching the field where the bloody battle was fought and Sir Edward and his archers died.

What drove a man like Edward? Was it the sheer excitement of fighting death and hoping to win? Earlier in the fifteenth century Jean de Beuil wrote:

> How seductive is war! When you know your quarrel to be just and your blood ready for combat, tears come to your eyes. ... Alongside him [your friends], one prepares to live or die. From that comes the delectable sense which no one who has experienced it will ever know how to explain. Do you think that a man who has experienced that can fear death? Never, for he is so comforted, so enraptured that he knows not where he is and truly fears nothing.[35]

On 20 August King Henry was in Southampton inspecting *The Sovereign*, one of his two brand-new Tower ships of 600 tons; it was also the day Duke Francis signed the Treaty of Sable. With this bitter pill the Duke formally accepted defeat, acknowledging himself to be a vassal of France. He agreed to a French veto on the marriage of his daughters and he surrendered territory. Three weeks later the heartbroken Duke died, leaving Marshal de Rieux as guardian of his children.

Rennes, with the huge new ducal château and state-of-the-art defences, had never surrendered and the fighting was renewed. The Duchess Anne and her guardian appealed to King Henry for help, while King Charles also wrote to his 'beloved cousin':

La Roche Talbot, the 29th August, 1488

Most High and Most Powerful Prince, our most dear and most beloved cousin.

We have received the letters which you wrote ... we thank you also for what you inform us by your letters concerning the late Sir Edward de Woodville, who called himself Sieur de Scales. ... we well knew, the expedition of the late Lord de Scales and of your subjects whom he had brought with him to Brittany was made without your knowledge and permission and regarded by you on your account of your love for us with a very great displeasure; and we never had a single doubt of that; besides, since our last letter we have, with the help of God and the works of our good and loyal subjects, won the battle against the Bretons and our other rebellious subjects.

The towns and the fortress of Dinan and St. Malo have fallen also into our obedience and notwithstanding all these things we have made peace with our cousin the Duke of Brittany, although if we had wished it was in our power to take into our hands the rest of the said country of Brittany and its fortresses, but we were content in assuring to ourself for the future the right which we claim over them in driving away our rebellious subjects who had retreated there. ...

Most High and Most Powerful Prince, our most dear and beloved cousin, our Lord have you in His holy guard,

CHARLES

But it was not that simple. English blood had been shed and it looked increasingly likely that France would absorb Brittany. King Henry began to think about war. Four months later he sent an embassy to Spain[36] and was telling the papal legate that, 'He was not meditating anything against the King of the French but he is compelled to defend the Breton interests, both on account of the immense benefits conferred on him by the late Duke in the time of his misfortune, and likewise for the defence of his own kingdom.'[37]

The legate also reported on Henry's preparations for war: three embassies dispatched, parliament summoned to provide £100,000 over three years for 10,000 men.[38] In practice he was hearing about the Treaty of Redon, concluded in February, where Henry would lend the Duchess 6,000 soldiers for defensive purposes. The Bretons would pay the cost and hand over some strongholds as an earnest. It was to fund this expeditionary force that Bishop Morton developed his celebrated 'fork' to raise the money. He extracted benevolences from all, from the ostentatiously wealthy because they could obviously afford to pay, and from the parsimonious because they were careful with their money. It seems King Henry was remembering his obligations to Brittany, always provided the duchy could pay.

In the spring of 1489 Spain and England agreed the Treaty of Medina del Campo, which was about good relations. Coincidently they acted on Brittany; King Henry sent 6,000 soldiers and King Ferdinand 2,000. However, it was too little and too late. Twelve months later the troops were still there and King Henry was declaring he would not make peace or truce with France unless the Duchess be included. However, the duchy was doomed and the young Duchess at odds with de Rieux over whom she should marry. Not only that, but she had run out of money, sold her jewels and her country was sick of war. So when King Charles marched his army to Rennes and proposed marriage there was little she could do but accept. This ended the 'Mad War'.

The wedding took place on 6 December 1491; the Duchess may not have enjoyed it. According to Voltaire, she had fallen in love with the handsome Louis, Duke d'Orléans, while he had been at her father's court. But that day her bridegroom was Charles of France who had won her with rough wooing. He was not very prepossessing, being of 'languid complexion, deformed person, and diminutive stature', with 'goggle eyes, an aquiline nose offensively large and a head disfigured by few and sparse hair', or so he is described by Andrea Mantegna's son in 1493.[39] But he was King of France and victorious.

The Duchess Queen survived, and when King Charles died seven years later she married his successor, her first love, the handsome Louis d'Orléans. Duke Louis had fought against France at St Aubin, been imprisoned after the battle and was released by the intercession of his wife, King Charles's younger sister. When he succeeded as King Louis XII, he promptly divorced his wife to marry Anne of Brittany, ostensibly for reasons of state but perhaps for love. Divorce was an accepted manoeuvre in medieval statecraft, always provided you were high in the Pope's favour.

The defeat at St Aubin had effectively finished Breton independence and the marriage removed the last of the French feudal dukedoms. The integrity of France was achieved. However, the battle had other consequences that were more immediate. Four hundred and forty men sailed from the Isle of Wight and local tradition has just one boy returning, Diccon Cheke, who had sailed as Edward's page and brought back the news of the 'overwhelming catastrophe'.

Theoretically this was more than a fifth of the island's fighting men.[40] But there is a remarkable lack of comment in the island's records for the time,[41] which would indicate that the majority of the men were not local, rather that they were non-indigenous professional soldiers. Some or most had probably been part of Edward's 'household troops three hundred in number', as they were designated in Spain, while others had just joined for pay and excitement. So that was the end of his company, some of which must have followed him in his adventures over the previous five years.

This was the final act for Edward but there was a little tidying up. There is an odd entry in the King's accounts for 30 April 1489: 'Item to a Scot with a beard that duelled [dwelled] with Sir Edward Wodeville, – l xvi.s. iiii.d.'[42] This is nine months after Edward had been killed, and the bearded Scot has been paid for being in his household. What had the Scot done in the household and where had he been? Did the Scot escape the massacre and return to claim expenses of 66 shillings and four pence? Being recorded in the Close Rolls suggests the Scot had been paid to watch Edward.

The other entries on the page complete a list of payments made on behalf of the King by Sir Thomas Lovel. They amount to some £120 and are all of an intelligence flavour: 'sent by a Brutain to Anthony Spynelle beyond the sea; to Wodelvose, that duelled with the King of the Romans; expenses to a Dane; to one that came from the king of Portingale'. It is clear that Henry wanted to know what Edward was doing once he had sailed to Brittany and was outside his control.

The next year, on the morning after the feast of St George, the herald reported that 'at the mass of requiem there were offered the swords, helms and crests of the Earl of Northumberland and of Sir Edward Woodville'. Separately the Inquisitions Post Mortem dealt with five of his manors, three in the Isle of Wight and two in Hampshire.

One loose end can be tidied up about the men who had been taken prisoner in Spain. They were sent to Fez in Morocco, but one of them, Petrus, escaped after three years. He and his gaoler's daughter fell in love and then escaped to Spain where they married. On 30 June 1490 King Ferdinand issued *cartas comendaticias* for 'Petrus Alamanç of Bruges who came to Spain with Lord Scales, to fight in the Granada war, and having fallen prisoner was liberated through his friendship with his master's daughter, whom he took to Castile, converted to Christianity, and married'. The letter tells of the 'remarkable Count of Scales' who 'motivated by zeal of faith and charity … came to us, bringing with him numbers of men, horses and arms, prepared for war, so that he could fight bravely against the Moors: amongst which men was Petrus

Alamanç, a native of the said city of Bruges. ... In this war the courage of the Count and his men was great. ... But Fortune, enemy of all favourable events, permitted the same Petrus ... to be captured by the Moors.' (See Appendix D for the full text of the letter.)

So Edward was not yet forgotten in Spain, or indeed Brittany. Such evidence as there is shows he was driven by faith and honour. He was a knight errant with his own supporting company of professional soldiers. The company would need pay. It would be surprising if there were not contracts between Edward and his troops, also between Edward and Duke Francis. In effect, he was probably an early military enterpriser, one of the type that became so important in the wars of the sixteenth century.

When Duke Francis sent his ambassadors to Edward they gave him 'funds in silver'. This may well have been a down payment of wages, which would be fair, as soldiers needed paying and rulers had money and needed fighting men. Freelance mercenaries have been around for a long time, but in the late fifteenth century the contractual arrangements for hiring soldiers were becoming more structured, soldiers were becoming more professional, while new tactics and better cannon were changing the art of war. Castles were currently of little use and engineers had not yet developed the fortifications that would resist heavy artillery.

The Spanish campaign showed that Edward managed an efficient company of archers and foot soldiers. He commanded himself, as a tactical infantry officer, which was unconventional. It was new and very different to the traditionally knightly officer leading a wing of lances or a company of dismounted men-at-arms, or merely giving an order to the mass of infantry.

But he was also the last of the knights errant. The code of chivalry had run its course. The Middle Ages were over – humanism and printing saw to that. This was the start of the modern era and Edward saw its dawn. However, his real importance is political. It was his contribution to putting Henry Tudor on the throne of England that was critical; without the credibility that he and his soldiers brought to the Tudor cause, history might well be different.

The man who called himself 'Sir Edward Wydevile kynghte' is an extraordinary paradox: the last knight errant riding from battle to battle across Europe, a quintessentially medieval figure, and yet one who finds himself accidentally ushering in the post-medieval states of England, Spain and France.

EPILOGUE

T he Woodvilles rose like meteors in the second half of the fifteenth
     century, but vanished by the start of the sixteenth. None of those five
     brothers left a son to carry on the name. Three died violent deaths,
although that was quite usual in those times. But their name lives on in the
records and – particularly – in King Richard's propaganda.

Richard was the third and last earl, who died in 1491. He appeared at
various functions and is not recorded as married, although a 'Lady Rivers'
appeared at court in the late 1480s. By Woodville standards he was a non-
entity and is buried in the abbey church of St James's at Northampton.

Edward's niece was Queen Elizabeth of York, whose gentleness was well
noted. Sir Thomas More wrote an elegy for her and the Spanish envoy reported
that she was 'a very noble woman and much beloved'. She was tall for her time,
with her mother's fair complexion and long golden hair, and was probably the
inspiration for the Queen in English packs of playing cards. She remembered
her uncle Anthony, and 20 years after his execution gave money 'to a man of
Poynfreyt' (Pumfret or Pontefract) because Anthony had lodged in his house
'at the time of his death'.

A late fifteenth-century painting of the *Kiss of Judas* has recently been found
in the church at Grafton. Is its presence there a coincidence or was there a link
to the betrayal of Anthony after his convivial dinner with Gloucester? [1]

Elizabeth of York, who died at the age of 38, was the mother of Henry VIII
and grandmother of Elizabeth I. Both were monarchs of strong character and
considerable intellect, scholars, linguists and musicians who were masters of
statecraft and unencumbered by too many moral scruples. One of her daughters, Margaret, married King James IV of Scotland, from whom the present
royal family is descended. Edward's other sisters also had children but they,
like Elizabeth, became a part of their husbands' families.

The Dowager Queen, Edward's sister, had a remarkable life and spent her
last years, out of trouble, in Bermondsey Abbey, dying in 1492. One of his
other sisters, Catherine, appears in the margins of Edward's life and embarked

on her third marriage after Jasper Tudor died in 1495. She then married Sir Richard Wingfield, ten years her junior and the 11th of 12 sons from a distinguished Suffolk family, who was later elected to the Garter. (Perhaps he was the younger brother of the 'Edward Wyngfield' knighted in Spain.) She brought with her an annual jointure of £1,000 and the use of Kimbolton Castle. However, she died two years later and so did not enjoy her husband's youth for long.

Thomas Gray, Marquis of Dorset, inherited Grafton. After his death, his son sold the place to his first cousin, Edward's great-nephew, King Henry VIII, who added 'Regis' to the name. It was at Grafton that the papal legate had his last interview with Henry before the King made the Church in England independent of Rome.

Fame is fickle and when Tudor historians wrote their chronicles there were no Woodvilles to patronize them or ensure that their family was lauded. All plaudits were for the King, who was not much interested in other people's contributions to the winning of his crown. Polydore Vergil ignores Edward where he might well, or should, have mentioned him. This was either because no one told him about Edward and his contribution or because he was erased from memory as irrelevant.

Henry and his historians did have a tendency to forget when it suited. They certainly forgot that the majority of the successful army was Scottish and French. That would not look good, with France and Scotland being England's traditional enemies. Equally, if Edward was seen to have flouted the crown's authority then he would not be a natural candidate for remembering. 'What Tudor historians valued from the usurpation story was the critique of Richard III. What they did not want, because it was irrelevant, was material that was favourable to the Wydevilles.' [2]

The bill that King Richard had laid before parliament in 1484 had called the Woodvilles 'insolent, vicious and of inordinate avarice'. It is hardly surprising that the popular movement to rehabilitate King Richard has seized on this and spent much time and effort posthumously blackening the family. The Woodvilles were the victims of Richard's 'virulent and puritanical propaganda campaign' and so we only read of their supposed shortcomings. But Edward had shown no interest in his brother's will and left an annuity of £50; this does not sound like a man of 'inordinate avarice'.

As far as we know, the only child of the Woodville brothers was Anthony's illegitimate daughter, Margaret, who married Sir Robert Poyntz, Anthony's friend and lieutenant. They lived at Iron Acton in Gloucestershire in a manor house that still survives but was largely rebuilt by their son. Robert had risen against King Richard at the time of Buckingham's rebellion. He then joined Henry Tudor and Edward in Brittany and was rewarded with a knighthood soon after Bosworth. King Henry certainly regarded Robert and Margaret Poyntz as friends, for he stayed with them when he came west, rather than four miles down the road with his uncle Jasper at Thornbury.

In 1501 Sir Robert was appointed guardian to Princess Catherine of Castile and Aragon, Ferdinand and Isabella's daughter, when she arrived in England to marry Prince Arthur, the eldest son of Henry VII and Elizabeth. Her dowry included six elephants and one of them walked the ten miles from Iron Acton to Bristol with a little castle ('Castile') on its back. The others stayed in London, hence 'The Elephant and Castle'.

Perhaps this appointment partially stemmed from Sir Robert's relationship with Edward Woodville, the particular friend of Ferdinand and Isabella. Edward was the one they called their 'faithful servant' and 'the remarkable Count of Scales', 'motivated by zeal of faith and charity'. So who better to be guardian to their daughter than his friend who was married to his niece?

Robert and Margaret Poyntz had four children. The eldest was Anthony, a naval commander; the next was John, a noted courtier and translator of Latin texts and probably one of the figures in the drawing of Henry's court by Holbein; the third was Francis, a diplomat. They also had a daughter, Anne, who married Sir John Walsh and lived at Little Sodbury Manor where she was possibly the 'Anne Walsh' who employed William Tyndale between 1521 and 1523, when he started work on his great translation of the Bible; his translation of the New Testament was mainly from Erasmus's edition of the Greek text, while his Old Testament was direct from the Hebrew, the first since St Jerome's Vulgate 1,000 years before.[3]

There was a Thomas Poyntz who ran the 'English house' in Antwerp and lost both his wife and his business trying to save Tyndale from death by the imperial fires; he was a cousin. As history knows, Thomas was unsuccessful and Tyndale was burned at Vilvoorde in October 1536. His last words were, 'Lord ope the King of Englands eyes.'

In the Lord Mayor's chapel in Bristol, originally St Mark's, there is the Poyntz family chapel with wonderful fan vaulting and a Spanish tiled floor, the largest such tiled area of the period outside Spain. In the chapel are escutcheons with Robert and Margaret's combined coats of arms: Rivers and Scales on the bottom half with the silver scallops on the left. On the upper half, the Poyntz arms incorporates the stars and stripes of their forebears, the Ameryks.[4]

Edward and his family contributed a huge amount to the colour and politics of their day, but it is difficult to judge the value of that. Anthony was a particularly civilized and intelligent man whose patronage of Caxton was crucial to the development of printing in England. They contributed to literature, architecture and, indeed, the art of war, but most of the evidence is lost in the fog of history. But the energy and ambition of the family are well documented.

We can do little more than speculate about Edward. However, what is beyond doubt is the importance of Edward's role in putting Henry Tudor on the throne of England and his contribution to the excitement of the time. Woodville blood still flows in the royal veins and a lot of other veins as well.[5]

APPENDIX A

ACCOUNTS FOR THE PROPOSED EXPEDITION OF 1483

Records (*Financial Memoranda of the Reign of Edward V*, Camden Society, 1987) show that in early 1483 Edward Woodville had responsibility for assembling a seaborne expeditionary force. The probable assembly point was Porchester where Edward was 'Captain'. However, it is not clear from the records who would actually command, or where the expedition would go. Dr Horrox has suggested the objective was Brittany.

The recorded costs were:

	£	s	d
Wages and victuals for 2,000 men for two months including a 3d per week per man supplement	2,066	13	4
Their captains	193	6	8
Two new carracks (plus captains)	856	13	4
2,000 new jackets	100	0	0
Pilots for the fleet	20	0	0
New ordinance (extra to that in the Tower)	226	7	7
Total	**£3,269**	**14**	**3** (sic)

NB. It shows the cost of paying and feeding the private soldiers of the expeditionary force was 8d per day per man.

As part of the operation, Lord Dorset had arranged for 1,000 men to watch and guard the West Country coast until 'Michaelmasse' (29 September) at a cost of 1,200 marks (£800), i.e. about 2d per day per man.

Men were sent to Calais and paid 6d per day, with the 'peti-captains' paid 12d per day. Their pay was made up to 12 June. The cost of shipping the additional 300 men was £15 and their jackets cost £20.

The accounts also dealt with pay to 'therls of Northumberland for the wagis of sondiours kepying … Berwick' until 10 May: £175.

The cost of producing 'fresh accounts' for the royal household (£230) and the funeral expenses of 'the right noble and famous prince King Edward IIII late our sovereign Lord who god hath taken to his mercy': £1,886.

All this expenditure had drained the coffers and there was not enough cash to pay the funeral expenses so silver plate had to be sold to cover the costs.

Dr Horrox estimates that the records were written between 16 May and 9 June. The dates for most of the events are not recorded but some certainly go back well into April and probably March. To commission an expeditionary force of 2,000 men would need royal authority and so King Edward must have been arranging this before he fell ill on 31 March. Also the accounts record that Lord Rivers was paid his butler's fee from Sandwich (£33-5s-8d), so that was certainly before his arrest on 29 April.

At the time the navy had 15 ships but not all were available — some were on convoy duty and others patrolling the coast of Scotland. Mancini thought there were 20 ships in Edward Woodville's fleet, which would be about right for the 2,000 men of the original expeditionary force, but that seems too many for this operation. It is more likely to have been cut back by the Council to a squadron with perhaps 400–500 soldiers, probably in four to six ships. A squadron of this size was sent to Scotland with a similar role in May 1480.

The two Tower ships are in the records: *The Falcon* was originally a Spanish ship that King Edward bought for £450 in 1475; her weight is not recorded but may have been in the 100-ton range. (*The Kateryn Plesaunce* was 100 tons, built in 1518 and cost £324.) The building of *The Trinity* had been authorized by Henry VI nearly 40 years before. The captain of *The Trinity* in 1470 was John Porter and in 1478 William Comersal (or Combersale). The latter became 'Clerk of the Ships' – the controller of naval organization – in 1488. *The Trinity* was 350 tons and there is an indication of the men and munitions for fighting ships in a 1513 state paper. Further confirmation of a sort is in the company of the 200 or so soldiers who arrived in Brittany with Edward; if the tonnages are correct then the distribution would have been around 150 on *The Trinity* and 60 on *The Falcon*, using the 1513 scale.

These warships were painted bright red with various other colours for decoration and their sides were lined with *pavasses* (wooden shields). On the sterns there were effigies of saints, with shields bearing the King's arms within a collar of gold and the arms of St George, within the garter.[1] Both vessels were still in royal service in 1503.

At the time merchant ships were chartered for one shilling per ton per month.[2]

A typical merchant ship, such as Cabot's *The Matthew* of Bristol, was solid and built to bob along rather than slice through the waves. She would have a crew of about 50 and would be around 85ft long, 30ft wide, with about a 100-ton displacement with the same burden, i.e. able to carry that many tons (a ton is a barrel of wine). There were four sails on three masts; the mainsail which weighed half a ton or more, took ten men to raise, as there were no winches. The ship was steered by a heavy rudder, moved by a massive tiller, 12–15ft long.

A replica of *The Matthew* was recently built and a journalist wrote of sailing her down the Channel in a Force 5 with the sea running at angles behind him, every wave slamming the rudder and making half a ton of tiller hammer into his ribs. He declared it very hard work.

The Genoese carracks that Edward chartered would have been substantially larger than English merchant ships such as *The Matthew*. There was 'the great carvel of Portingale' in Lord Howard's naval expedition of 1481 which carried 160 sailors and 240 soldiers and *La Calanta*, which Anthony had commanded for the invasion of 1471 and which carried 200 soldiers.

APPENDIX B

EDWARD WOODVILLE'S RECEIPT FOR £10,201, DATED 14 MAY 1483

'This indenture made the xiiij day of may the furst yere of the kyng oure sover-ayne lord Edward the V, kyng of England and of Fraunce and lord of Irlond etc betwixt Sir Edward Wydevile kynghte, unckle unto oure seid soverayne lord and grete capetayne of his navy onthat one partye and [blank] patron of the grete carake then lying at Hamton Watre on that othir partye. Witnessethe that the seid Sir Edward hathe receyved and taken out of the seid carake xMCCI li of golde in Englisshe kune on this condicion, that if it kan be proved not forfeted unto the kyng oure seid soverayne lord that then the seid Sir Edward and his frendes in England shalle content and repaye unto the seid patron the valure of the seid money in Englisshe merchaundise within iij monthes next after he shalbe so requyred,and if that kan be proved by the lawe of Englond the seid money to be forfeture, than the seid Sir Edward to be answerying to the kyng oure seid soverayne lord and not to the seid patron. In wittnesse wherof to thise present indentures as well the seid Sir Edward as the seid patron have putte theire seales & signe manuelle the day and yere aboveseid.'

Published by the Camden Society, Fourth Series 34, 1987. Folio 4 (p 216), *Financial Memoranda of Reign of Edward V*, ed Rosemary Horrox.

ACCOUNT ENTRY OF QUEEN ISABELLA FOR 15 JULY 1486

'By a roll of Her Highness, signed and entered, dated 15 July 1486, 88,791 maravedis, that she spent in the said year, in this manner:

One hundred and two yards of holland cloth, 90 yards for four mattresses and twelve for eight pillow covers, that cost 110 maravedis per yard, and 14½ quarter-hundredweight[1] of wool, to stuff them, at 385 maravedis per quarter-hundredweight, and to Alonso, the harness-maker, to pay for the carding of the wool, for the making-up, and the thread, 806 maravedis, which gives a total of 16,883 and a half maravedis.

Thirty-one yards of holland cloth, for two sheets, that cost 150 maravedis per yard, 60 yards of black and white ribbons to put on them, at 25 maravedis, and an ounce of twist to sew them, 110 maravedis, which are in total 6,250 maravedis.

Nine yards of scarlet cloth, for a bed-cloth, that cost 1,200 maravedis per yard, and for trimming it and making it up 124 maravedis, which are in total 10,924 maravedis.

One and two-thirds yards of smooth green and brown brocade, to make the valance of a bed-canopy, cost, at fifteen doblas per yard, 15 doblas, which adds up, at 365 maravedis each, to 9.125 maravedis, and another yard and two-third of white damask, to line the said brocade, that cost 700 maravedis per yard, which are a total of 10,291 and a half maravedis.

To Alvaro de Carrion, ribbon-maker, for eight and three-quarters ounces of gold thread at 375 maravedis each, and for a further 19 and four-eighths ounces of twist at 110 maravedis, which are 6,551 maravedis, and for the making-up of some fringe trimmings from the said gold, and silk, and from another eleven and one-eighth ounces of gold, that was given to Her Highness's camber, 1,315 maravedis, which are in total 7,866 maravedis.

For a rectangular armorial hanging, embroidered with red and white, five yards of scarlet cloth, that cost 900 maravedis per yard, and another five yards of white london cloth at 450 maravedis, and four buckrams to line it, at 186 maravedis, and for making the said armorial hanging 730 maravedis, and for trimming the cloth 100 maravedis, which is in total 8,324 maravedis.

A thick silk cord, with silver endpieces, to sew a scarlet mattress-carrying bag, for which the silk cost 318 maravedis, and the silver ends 300 maravedis, which are iin total 618 maravedis.

Two canvas-covered chests, 1800 maravedis.

All of which was delivered to Martin Cuello, to present to the Count of Scale, the Englishman.'

Cuenta de Gonzalo de Baeza, tesorero de Isabel la Católica (The Accounts of Gonzalo de Baeza, Treasurer of Isabel la Católica), ed Antonio de la Torre and E.A. de la Torre, trans David Hook (Madrid: CSIC, 1955), vol. i, p 125.

APPENDIX D

KING FERDINAND'S LETTER OF COMMENDATION FOR PETRUS ALAMANÇ

Ferdinand issued letters of commendation on behalf of Petrus Alamanç of Bruges, who came to Spain with Lord Scales (Sir Edward Woodville) to fight in the Granada war, and having fallen prisoner was liberated through his friendship with his master's daughter, whom he took to Castile, converted Christianity, and married.

'... there having been heard thought nearly the whole world the resonance of the war which, against the kingdom of Granada, enemy of the name of Jesus Christ, we are waging, motivated by zeal of faith and charity the remarkable Count of Scales, when these years had already passed, came to us, bringing with him numbers of men, horses and arms, prepared for war, so that he could fight bravely against the Moors: amongst which men was Petrus Alamanç, a native of the said city of Bruges, assembled with his brother and two relatives. Thus, with troops of armed men, with the opportunity of time given to us we ordered them to be moved against the kingdom itself of Granada, where we performed great and noble deeds for we subjugated some cities, towns and settlements which were a great impediment to our reducing the city of Granada and other cities of its kingdom to the Christian religion and to our rule. In this war the courage of the Count and his men was great, for they conducted themselves in an energetic and manly fashion. But Fortune, enemy of all favourable events, permitted the same Petrus Alamanç, his brother and his relatives, to be captured by the Moors, in fighting with them. In which captivity he remained for three years, and would have remained, as there remained and remain his said brother and relatives in the city of Fez, were it not that he had brought the daughter of his master to the faith of Christ and into union with him, whom he brought to these our realms of Castile, and made to

181

be adorned with holy Baptism, and took her as his wife. Whereon, that all this should be noted by you, at the humble supplication of the said Petrus Alamanç, we have ordered these our letters to give testimony of the truth.

Juan de Colona

30 June 1490, Córboda'

Documentos sobre Relaciones Internacionales de los Reyes Católicos, volumen III 1488–1491 (Barcelona: Antonio de La Torre, 1951), trans David Hook, document 59, p 323.

KING HENRY'S LETTER TO KING CHARLES OF 20 MAY 1488

'Windsor, Tuesday the 20th May 1488.

Most High, Most Excellent, and Most Powerful Prince, Most Dear and Most Beloved Cousin, we believe you remember well that by one of our equerries named Michelet, who lately saw you, we have written about the rumour, prevalent and certified, that no one of our subjects had been in Brittany; and that was the truth, for we had forbidden, under the pain of death, anybody to go there.

However, we have just been informed that the Breton ambassadors, who came lately from there with the intention of procuring our help and assistance, seeing that they could not obtain their wishes nor have any aid, have gone to the Isle of Wight to Sir Edward Woodville, Knight, calling himself Lord of Scales, who had his residence there and who has had for some time the custody of the Isle of Wight, and have by their subtle ways and intrigue so much exhorted and seduced him, that to our very great displeasure he went away with them to Brittany and managed to take with him up to some 300 men, most of whom he extracted from places of asylum where they had been for several years on account of their crimes and misdemeanours; most of these men went without armour and the apparel of war. [Clearly a bunch of ill-armed miscreants.]

These people gathered in that Island, which is entirely surrounded by the sea, so secretly and hastily, that we did not know of it until after their departure. True, it is that the said Sir Edward Woodville has asked us many times for a permission to go and we not only have never given him permission, but we have expressly forbidden him to go there so positively that he knew he would incur our indignation, and we would never have believed he would dare to infringe our order.

There was also a young knight; brother of the Earl of Arundel [Edward's sister, Margaret was married to Arundel] who made ready to go after the said Sir Edward; but as soon as we knew it, we seized his ships and his company and caused him to be arrested, and because, Most High Most Excellent, Most Powerful Prince, Most Dear and Most Beloved Cousin, we are certain that these things will come to your knowledge, and we know not in which way you would accept or interpret them, for concerning such matters many tales are often reported, we apprise you willing of the truth, earnestly praying you that concerning these things you would not entertain any suspicion or imagination that there is any fault on our part, for we certify to you upon our honour that all has been done without our knowledge and assent and against our prohibition and interdiction and we are as much displeased as of anything that has ever happened since we have been in this kingdom.

For we would by no means allow anything to be done to your prejudice or displeasure and believe for certain that before long we shall know by the result that Edward and his people have been badly counselled in making such a foolish attempt.

And so that you be fully aware of these things and our intentions upon this point, we send to you our Garter King of Arms, by whom you will be able to know the exact truth, praying you to believe him and to put faith in what he will say to you, and to inform us by him of your good news and if there is something you desire to be done by us, we shall accomplish it most willingly, as the good Son of God helping, Most High, Most Excellent, Most Powerful Prince, Most Dear and Most Beloved Cousin, and may He have you in His Holy Protection and grant you the full accomplishment of your good desires.

Written in our Castle of Windsor the 27th day of May,

Your good cousin

Henry'

There was a further superscription, 'to the Most High Most Excellent, and Most Powerful Prince, our Most Dear and Most Beloved Cousin, King Charles of France'.

Letter from King Henry to King Charles, written in French and published in *Correspondence de Charles VIII et de ses consellors avec Louis de la Trémoille*, pp 213, 238.

CHRONOLOGY, 1453–88

1453	August	Henry VI goes insane
	October	Birth of Henry VI's son, Edward of Lancaster
1454	April	Duke of York appointed Lord Protector of England
	Christmas	Henry VI regains sanity
1455	February	York ceases to be Protector
	May	First battle of St Albans won by York
	November	York reappointed Protector
1456	February	End of York's second protectorate
1458		Probable year of Edward Woodville's birth
1459	September	Battle of Blore Heath
	October	Rout of Ludford: York and the Earls of March, Salisbury and Warwick flee from England
	November	Parliament outlaws Yorkists
1460	June	Yorkist leaders land in Kent
	July	Yorkist victory at Northampton
	October	Parliament recognizes York as heir to the throne
	December	York defeated and killed at Wakefield
1461	February	Yorkist victory at Mortimer Cross
		Lancastrian victory at second battle of St Albans
	March	Edward IV proclaimed king in London
		Yorkist victory at Towton
1464	May	Edward IV marries Elizabeth Woodville in secret
		Defeat of Lancastrian army at Hexham

1465	July	Capture of Henry VI in Lancashire
1467	June	Anthony Woodville fights the Bastard of Burgundy
1468	July	Charles of Burgundy marries Margaret of York
		Lancastrian plots
1469	July	Clarence marries Warwick's daughter, Isabel Neville
		Yorkist defeat at Edgecote
	August	Edward IV confined at Middleham
		1st Earl Rivers executed
	September	Edward IV regains his freedom
1470	March	Rising in Lincolnshire defeated by Edward IV at Losecote Field
	April	Warwick and Clarence flee to France
	July	Margaret of Anjou and Warwick are reconciled
	September	Warwick invades the West Country
		Edward IV flees to Burgundy
		Birth of Edward (later Edward V)
		Execution of Worcester
1471	March	Edward IV lands in Yorkshire
	April	Yorkist victory at Barnet – death of Warwick
	May	Yorkist victory at Tewkesbury
		The Bastard of Fauconberg besieges London
		Murder of Henry VI
1472		Richard of Gloucester marries Anne Neville
1475	July	Edward IV invades France
	August	Edward IV makes peace with Louis XI at Picquigny
		Anthony Woodville in Italy
1477		Death of Charles of Burgundy
		William Caxton establishes a printing press in England
1478	February	Execution of Clarence
1482	July and August	Invasion of Scotland

1483	April	Death of Edward IV
		Richard of Gloucester's coup
	June	Gloucester proclaimed King
		Coronation of Richard III
		Execution of Anthony Woodville
	July?	Murder of Edward V and Duke of York (the princes in the Tower)
	August	Death of Louis XI of France
	October	Buckingham's rebellion
1485	7 August	Henry Tudor lands at Milford Haven
	22 August	Defeat and death of Richard III at Bosworth
	October	Coronation of Henry VII
1486	January	Henry VII marries Elizabeth of York
		Edward Woodville in Spain and Portugal
1487	June	Defeat of Lambert Simnel at Stoke
1488	February	Bartholomew Columbus meets Henry VII
1488	April	Edward Woodville invested with the Garter
1488	May	Edward Woodville sails to Brittany
1488	28 July	Battle of St Aubin

NOTES

Introduction

1. W.H. Prescott, *The Art of War in Spain: The Conquest of Granada 1481–1492*, ed A.D. McJoynt (Greenhill, 1995).
2. For a serious review of the chivalric ethic see Richard Barber, *The Knight and Chivalry* (Boydell Press, 1995); Christina Hardyment's *Malory: The Life and Times of King Arthur's Chronicler* (Collins, 2005) is an engaging biography of the greatest exponent of the chivalric ideal.
3. According to D. Hay, translator of some of Polydore Vergil, 'if Vergil offends it is mainly in suppression of the truth'. He also observes that 'the main participants are still valued popularly as Vergil valued them' and so it is hardly surprising that those whom he did not value have been rather neglected.

Chapter 1. A Spanish Venture

1. Professor David Hook has kindly translated the relevant parts of Bernáldez, Pulgar, de Valera and other contemporary records; he has also provided invaluable advice. Otherwise the main sources for this chapter are *The History of the Reign of Ferdinand and Isabella the Catholic* by W.H. Prescott; *The Chronicle of the Conquest of Granada* by Washington Irving; *Moorish Spain* by Richard Fletcher provides an excellent commentary on the culture and history. The quotations used have been taken either from Professor Hook's translations or from Prescott, pp 337–407. The Bernáldez is taken from *Memorias del reinado de los Reyes Católicos*, ed M. Gómez-Moreno and J. de Mata Carrizo (Madrid, 1962), chapters LXXIX and LXXX; the Pulgar is from *Crónica de los señores reyes católicos Don Fernando y Doña Isabel de Castilla y de Aragon*, chapters LVI, LVIII, XCV; Diego de Valera, *Crónica de los Reyes Católicos*, pp 200–20, and the *Itinerario de los Reyes Católicos* for 1486.
2. See W.H. Prescott, *The History of the Reign of Ferdinand and Isabella the Catholic* (London: Gibbings & Co, 1894), vol. i, p 396.
3. Matthew Parris, *Chronica Majora*, ed H.R. Luard (Rolls Series, 1872–74) vol. ii, pp 560–3), reported that King John of England chose this time to send an embassy to the emir asking for help against his barons; in return he offered homage and conversion to the law of Mohammed. The emir was certainly unable

to help and, moreover, disapproved of the offer.

4. Ferdinand III of Castile captured Cordoba and Seville; James I of Aragon took Valencia. Gibraltar (Jebil-el-Tarik) fell in 1462 after 718 years of Arab occupation. The Spaniards had held it for 22 years in the fourteenth century and then for some 240 years the next time round. The British have now held it for 300 years.

5. The letter from de Valera noted that the merchants on the ships were well known in the city. Apparently the ships had a quick turn-round and sailed back up the coast, presumably to find their cargoes for the home run. John Edwards, *The Spain of the Catholic Monarchs 1474–1500* (Blackwell, 2001), pp 126–7.

6. Medieval command arrangements are not clear. The 800 men sent to Calais in 1483 included 25 'peti-captains', i.e. 1–32 men. The traditional arrangements dated from Edward I: archers were grouped into companies of 100 under a 'centenar' and then in sections of 20 under a 'vintenar' (the 'vingtaine' of 20 corresponded with the basic unit of the shire array). Now there are 'captains' (centenire) and peti-captains; the latter were paid 12 pence daily, twice the archer's rate. The rank of 'petty officer' is still used in the Royal Navy for a non-commissioned officer.

7. A cloth yard was 36ins (91cm) long. Archers practised every day and could fire six aimed arrows a minute, or ten unaimed; arrows could kill at 300 yards and penetrate 1in (2.54cm) of oak at 200 yards. A number of war bows were recovered from *The Mary Rose* which were between 6ft and 7ft (182–212cm) long, 1.33ins to 1.46ins (34–37mm) wide and 1.2ins (31mm) deep. It has been calculated they had a draw weight of between 135lbs and 160lbs (61–73kg) and would fire an 3.5oz arrow about 300 yards and a 4.5oz arrow at least 240 yards (220 metres). Few modern men can draw a 135lbs bow even half way.

8. Dominic Mancini, *The Usurpation of Richard III*, ed and trans C.A.J. Armstrong (Oxford, 1936), p 121.

9. Codex 443 of the Colecção Pombalina, Biblioteca Nacional. Lisbon.

10. One of the foot soldiers sent to garrison Alhama was Garcia de Montalvo, the author of *Amadis de Gaula*, a hugely popular novel of the sixteenth century.

11. Bernáldez, *Memorias del reinado de los Reyes Católicos*, vol. LXXIX, p 167.

12. British regiments have their own regimental bugle call so soldiers can identify their unit; this call is then followed by a call of particular instruction. There are several contemporary drawings of soldiers with trumpets. In Edward's next campaign, it is recorded that trumpet calls were used to instruct the cavalry.

13. There is no Spanish reference to their surcoat being quartered by the cross of St George. However, Edward Woodville's soldiers were wearing the cross in Brittany two years later, which is the first recorded use of it as uniform; it is also shown in the contemporary *Beauchamp Pageant*, ed Dillon and St John Hope (London: British Museum, 1914). Archers often wore 'uniform', viz the 'Flodden window' at Middleton (by Manchester) which shows the 17 kneeling archers

all dressed in blue courtmantles. Washington Irving, *Chronicle of the Conquest of Granada* (London, 1902), p 155, tells us that the English soldiers shouted 'St George for England', but it is not clear how he knew this.

14. Edward was probably wearing a morion, i.e. an open-faced helmet.

15. Alonso de Palencia, *Cronica de Enrique IV* (Madrid, 1975), p 163.

16. In von Eyb's biography (1507) of Wilwot von Schaumberg (1446–1510) there is the first (known) recorded understanding of the difference between a knight and an infantry officer; Wilwot was both a knight and leader of *lansquenets*, German infantry. See Fritz Redlich, *The German Military Enterpriser and His Work Force* (Wiesbaden, 1964), p 15, note 25.

17. The exchange was 375 maravedis to one gold ducat; the ducat was worth about 4s-3d in sterling, so 88,791 maravedis is 235 ducats which would convert to about £47-7s-0d. P. Spufford, *Handbook of Medieval Exchange* (Royal Historical Society, 1986), pp 157–8, covers the period 1480–97. Based on sources for 1480, 1480–86 and 1497, 1 Venetian ducat = 375 maravedis.

18. Joanot Martorell and M.J. de Galba, *Tirant Lo Blanc*, trans D.H. Rosenthal (London: Macmillan, 1984), pp 234–5.

19. Lombards are heavy cannon about 12ft (3.65m) long that fire a stone or marble ball of around 14ins (35.5cm) in diameter and weighing 175lbs (80kg).

20. Bernáldez, *Historia*, vol. LXXIX, p 168.

21. There is a description of Isabella with 'auburn hair and clear blue eyes' quoted by Washington Irving in his *Christopher Columbus* (p 52) from Garibay's *History of España* 11/xvii/1; portraits of her show a strong square jaw.

22. W.C. Metcalf, *A Book of Knights* (London, 1885), p 12.

23. It seems to have been the Queen who drove the campaign forward with single-mindedness and determination. She stopped the King being distracted. In 1484 he wanted to capture Roussillon from the French but she would not allow it. Later the nobles persuaded the King to finish campaigning early but the Queen disapproved and shamed them all into returning to the original plan. The King and Queen with their complementary skills made a remarkable team, she dealing with logistics while he led the armies. The Queen, stationing herself close to the scene of operations, received hourly intelligence of the war. She sent supplies to the troops and had tents, known as 'the Queen's hospitals', ready for the sick and wounded, and provided them with attendants and medicines.

24. The army was reported to be 10,000–12,000 cavalry and 20,000–40,000 foot, certainly an exaggeration. There was also 'a body of Germans skilled in the service of ordnance and the art of battering walls'.

25. C. Oman, *The Art of War in the Sixteenth Century* (London: Methuen, 1927), p 51.

26. *Punto de blanco* or 'point-blank range', the distance of the archer from the target where he needed no elevation to hit the white spot at its centre, i.e. he pointed straight at it. The expression was adapted to gunnery and meant the cannon was horizontal with a short range. The heavy cannon were attached to their carriages

and incapable of either vertical or horizontal movement. Aim was by line along the top of the barrel. Smaller cannon were more manoeuvrable and a good one could put a 12lb ball through the hull of a ship at up to 300 yards.

27. Las Casas and Fernando Columbus agree that Christopher met the King and Queen in Cordoba. The monarchs arrived there on 28 April; Ferdinand left on 14 May, Isabella was there until 9 June (*Itinerario de los Reyes Católicos, 1474– 1516*).

28. Ferdinand and Isabella arrived back in Cordoba on 29 June and stayed there until 17 July when they moved to Linares (*Itinerario de los Reyes Católicos, 1474–1516*).

29. Codex 443 of the Colecçao Pombalina in the Biblioteca Nacional, Lisbon, quoted in Elaine Sanceau, *The Perfect Prince: A Biography of King Dom João* (Porto, 1959).

30. Loja was a critical victory in the build up to the end of the Reconquista and the event seems to have stuck in the collective imagination of Spain. Unfortunately no contemporary ballad about the siege and capture has survived. However, there is a late, literary, chronicle-based composition: no. 1076 from 'Coleccion de Romances Castellanos' (published in Madrid in 1851) and newly translated by David Hook:

> '... took the foremost position
> and with rage in his spirit
> boldly daring the difficult
> did so much with his sword
> that he opened a way
> through the thick of the Moors
> without the densest squadron
> being able to prevent it
> striking to all sides
> agile as a loose leopard,
> followed by many
> who saw so marvellous a deed;
> to the city he then
> laid the closest of sieges.'

Chapter 2. Passion

1. Grafton is on the road between Stony Stratford and Northampton, overlooking the valley of the Tove. The Woodville family had lived there since the reign of King John (1199–1216).

2. Hastings's price was marriage between her eldest son, Thomas, and any future daughter of either Hastings or his younger brother. If no daughter was born within five years then Elizabeth would have to pay 500 marks (£333) to Hastings.

3. R. Fabyan, *New Chronicle of England and France*, ed H. Ellis (London, 1811), p 654.

4. His grandson, Henry VIII, was to do the same thing several times.

5. Jean de Waurin, *Anciennes Chroniques d'Engleterre*, ed Mlle Dupont (Paris, 1858–

63), vol. ii, p 326.

6. *Calendar of Patent Rolls, Henry VI, 1422–1441*, p 53; *Rotuli Parliamentorum*, ed J. Strachey et al, vol. iv, p 498.

7. Sir Richard was selected as the English Champion to 'deliver' Pedro Vasque de Saavedra, a Spanish jousting star who had come to London to 'run a course with a sharp spear for his sovereign lady's sake'. Sir Richard came from the same mould as the most celebrated tournament fighter of all time, William the Marshal, Earl of Pembroke (1147–1219). The Marshal started as a penniless knight and made his living from the ransoms of those he vanquished in the lists, and elsewhere. His top score – in partnership with a Sir Roger de Gaugi – was 103 in one season (the tally was kept by a kitchen clerk called Wigain). He was tutor and mentor to three kings, married the heiress to the Earl of Pembroke and was confirmed in that earldom. He became the leading English statesman of his time and is the archetypal hero of chivalry.

8. Rivers or Ryvers. The origin of the name is uncertain: there was a parish of 'Ryver' by Dover Castle, but more likely is a link – real or imagined – to the early Earls of Devon. Rivers was their family name in the twelfth and thirteenth centuries and their arms included the Griffin Sergeant which appears on the Woodville arms. *Medieval Pageant: Writhe's Garter Book* (Roxburghe, 1993), p 7.

9. She was rumoured to have had lovers and gossip was rife, particularly when the simple but saintly King, on being told of the birth of his heir, remarked that it must have been through the agency of the Holy Ghost.

10. John Talbot, Earl of Shrewsbury (1390–1453), was one of Henry V's great captains, the 'English Hector', of whom Hall reported, 'the French to frighten their young children cry "the Talbot commeth"'.

11. *Calendar of Patent Rolls, 1452–1461*, p 36. (Hatclyf was a career civil servant who was the 'King's Secretary'. He was paid 2 shillings per day on Edward's French expedition of 1475.)

12. The battle of Blore Heath in September 1459 was followed in October by a Yorkist disaster at Ludford Bridge and the flight of the leaders.

13. Richard Neville became the Earl of Warwick through his wife Anne, daughter of the great Harry Beauchamp, Earl of Warwick, and hero of the French wars. The new Warwick was a man of energy, charm and pride. He took over the Captaincy of Calais from Rivers who insisted the garrison be paid. With no cash Warwick made his own arrangements by capturing five Lubeck ships with cargoes worth £10,000 and driving a further 26 ships ashore. There were bitter complaints from the owners and Rivers was appointed as the King's investigator. He found Warwick guilty. The *English Chronicle* is a contemporary record of the events.

14. Paston letter dated 28 January 1460, in *Paston Letters 1422–1509*, ed J. Gardner, vol. 3, p 204.

15. The French put Lord Scales in the same class as Salisbury and Talbot (Jacques Duclos, *Chroniques et Mémoires*, ed Buchon (Paris, 1865), vol. iii, p 308). He was

also recognized as 'one of the strongest and bravest champions' and actually features as such in *Tirant Lo Blanc*, a novel written in Catalan by Joanot Martorell who visited England in 1438 and wrote around 1460.

16. *An English Chronicle of the Reigns of Richard II, Henry IV, Henry V and Henry VI*, ed J.S. Davies (London: Camden Society, 1856), p 96.

17. Lord Scales's wealth in 1436 was assessed at £376 a year. See H.L. Gray, 'Incomes from Land in England in 1436', *English Historical Review*, vol. 49 (1934), p 617.

18. Northampton in July 1460, Wakefield – where Duke Richard of York was killed – in December 1460, Mortimer's Cross and St Albans in February 1461. The latter was a Lancastrian success which gave the Queen and her seven-year-old son the chance to decide what form of death should be inflicted on the prisoners and then watch the proceedings.

19. The population of England and Wales was then, perhaps, around 2.5 million; now there are probably around 40 million people descended from indigenous stock. A.W.G.Sykes has calculated that if you are mainly of English or Welsh stock then the odds are on you having an ancestor who fought at Towton. *The Battle of Towton* (Stroud: Sutton, 1994) by A.W. Boardman deals with the prelude, battle and aftermath in detail.

20. Waurin, *Anciennes Chroniques*, vol. ii, p 326. King Edward reiterated to Commines, *Memoirs 1461–1483* (London, 1855), vol. iii, p 5, that this was his policy.

21. Edward issued a proclamation in English in March 1461 which started with a recital of 'the evils' he intended to rectify. He lamented the loss of the overseas territories, i.e. France, the decline in trade, oppression of his subjects, the general state of lawlessness and corruption of justice which had all arisen 'through the negligence, ambition, greed ... of such as have ruled'. He referred to 'our adversary, he that calleth himself King Henry VI' and went on savagely to condemn such recent Lancastrian activities as terrorizing parts of the country, plundering the churches, preying on defenceless women and killing people 'in such detestable wise and cruelness as hath not be heard done among [even] the Saracins' – a good example of an early political manifesto. The proclamation was designed to be read in full and to sway public opinion. Previously proclamations had been short statements in Latin which were translated into English locally but this one was issued in full, in the vernacular, complete with supporting arguments. For further detail on the royal propaganda of Edward see Alison Allan, 'Royal Propaganda of Edward IV', *BIHR*, vol. lxix (1986), pp 146–55.

22. *Calendar of State Papers and Manuscripts Existing in the Archives and Collections of Milan, I, 1385–1618*, ed A.B. Hinds (London: HMSO, 1913), p 102.

23. *Calendar of Patent Rolls, Edward IV*, pp 81, 169–70.

24. Sir John Grey's mother was Lady Ferrers of Groby, a peeress in her own right. Though his father, Sir Edward Grey, had gained livery of his wife's title, he had died in December 1457. Lady Ferrers remarried (May 1462) a younger son of the Earl of Essex and wanted all the money.

25. Waurin, *Anciennes Chroniques*, vol. ii, p 326.
26. G. Smith (ed), *The Coronation of Elizabeth Wydeville: Queen Consort of Edward IV on 26th May, 1465* (London, 1935).
27. There were 14 or 15 siblings; Elizabeth was the first and probably born in 1437. Anthony was born in 1442, John in 1445, Richard about 1450. Walter Paston was at Oxford with Lionel, whom he regarded as a contemporary, which would make Lionel born in 1455. However, Professor Lander suggests that Lionel was born in 1451 (*Crown and Nobility 1450–1509* (London, 1976), p 116) but a papal dispensation refers to him being 29 in 1481, i.e. born in 1452 (*Calender of Entries in the Papal Registers, 1471–1484* (London: HMSO, 1955), pp 744, 806). Catherine was born in 1457, and there was a younger sister who is said to have married Sir John Bromley. The creation of Knights of the Bath for the wedding is a good indicator; the Duke of Buckingham was born in 1455, and Humphrey his younger brother was probably born in 1457; both were knighted at the wedding. Ten years later the Earl of Shrewsbury was knighted at the age of seven. If Edward Woodville was too young to be knighted at the wedding in May 1465 then he might have been born around 1458 or 1459, a date which also ties in with his subsequent career.
28. The Master of 'Henxmen' was required 'to show the schools of urbanity and nurture of England, to learn them to ride cleanly and surely; to draw them also to jousts; to learn them [to] wear their harness [armour]; to have all courtesy in words, deeds, and degrees; diligently to keep them in rules of goings and sittings. Moreover, to teach them sundry languages and other learning virtuous, to [play the] harp, to pipe, sing, dance, with other honest temperate behaving; and to keep daily and weekly with these children due convenites [lessons] with corrections in their chambers according to such gentlemen.' (Being of noble birth henchmen were not beaten in public.) Such were the instructions in the 'Ordinances and Regulations for the Government of the Royal Household'. Sir John Fortescue, the political thinker of the day, wrote: 'I look on it [the King's palace] as an academy for the young nobility of the Kingdom to inure and employ themselves in robust and manly exercises, probity and a generous humanity.'

Chapter 3. Politics

1. Anthony was one of the commanders at the siege of Alnwick; the castle fell on 6 January 1463. Warwick's younger bother, John Neville, Lord Montague, was in overall charge and Lord Worcester was there as constable.
2. *Excerpta Historica*, ed Samuel Bentley (London, 1831), p 178.
3. The herald was 'Nucélles Pursuivant', who was rewarded by the Bastard with a 'rich gown furred sable' and a black velvet doublet with gold clasps. The Bastard had taken 2,000 men crusading to redeem the pledge his father had made at the Feast of the Pheasant in 1454; he sailed in May 1464 and helped raise the siege of Ceuta, a Portuguese town on the North African coast. This was a great period for

bastards, who were regarded as more handsome and personable than legitimate children. The four Valois Dukes of Burgundy produced 68, who formed a sort of 'bastardocracy' in the ducal administration.

4. *Paston Letters*, vol. ii, p 303.
5. *Excerpta Historica*, p 206.
6. Alwite or white was the term used for uncovered plate armour. Its origins are in the term 'blanca' or bleaching, i.e. to whiten the metal, usually by treating with an acid or coating with tin. (Incidentally, it is probably the origin of the name of the 'White Company' of Sir John Hawkwood.)
7. A 'made' charger was always difficult to find. Most of the surviving fifteenth-century letters about tournaments refer to borrowing horses. From the report above it sounds as if it was the Bastard who had a problem with his charger, as he must have ridden or driven his horse into Anthony's saddle and that probably means it was his horse that had swerved out on the first run.
8. In a challange issued by Tirant Lo Blanc, he specifies 'axes four-and-a-half feet long without concealed advantage, swords with forty inch blades, and daggers two feet long'. This was written in 1460 (*Tirant Lo Blanc*, p 109). The heads of poleaxes in the Wallace Collection weigh around 5–6lbs (2.330–2.950kg).
9. Hans Talhoffer's *Fechtbuch* of 1467 has 23 plates showing various movements for axe fighting and over 200 drawings showing other close-quarter fighting techniques. Talhoffer was one of many fencing masters; Paul Kal, a rival, lists 17 masters-of-arms belonging to the 'Society of Liechtenauer', named after a celebrated tutor and the top rank for the profession.
10. *Excerpta Historica*, p 202.
11. *Ibid.*, pp 208–9.
12. Comprehensive accounts of the marriage and subsequent festivities are recorded by Olivier de la Marche (*Mémoires*, ed H. Beaune and J. d'Arbaumont (Paris: Société de l'Histoire de France, 1883–88), vol. ii, pp 123–200). Sir John Paston also wrote glowingly to his mother about the splendour of the arrangements. Richard Barber provides a helpful view of the whole in *The Knight and Chivalry*, pp 186–9.
13. G.D. Painter, *William Caxton* (Chatto & Windus, 1976), p 45. The engraving is in a copy of *Recuyell of the Histories of Troy* that was once owned by Queen Elizabeth (Woodville). The initials of Margaret and Duke Charles are on the canopy of the bed with the motto *Bein en auiengne* ('may good come of it'; it did not!); a lap dog is held by one of five ladies in waiting; there is a pet monkey and courtiers in their winkle-picker shoes.
14. *Excerpta Historica*, pp 240–5.
15. 4,000 marks is around £2,600 – comfortable but not generous. King Edward had not put the estate at the level of earlier queens: both Margaret of Anjou and Katherine (Valois) had been awarded 10,000 marks (£6,600) a year.
16. Margaret married the heir to the Earl of Arundel; Anne married the heir to the

Earl of Essex; Eleanor married the heir to the Earl of Kent; Catherine the Duke of Buckingham and Mary the eldest son of Lord Herbert.

17. Young men coupling with older women seems not to have been out of the ordinary in the fifteenth century. In *Tirant Lo Blanc*, the page, a minor hero, has an affair with the empress, who is – she observes – 'old enough to be your grandmother'. The page retorts, 'My lady, this is no time for idle chatter. Lead me to your bed where we shall find both solace and delight.'

18. *The Great Chronicle of London*, ed A.H. Thomas and I.D. Thornley (1938), p 208.

19. G.H. Orpen, 'Statute Rolls of the Parliament of Ireland, 1-2 Edward IV', *English Hitorical Review*, 30 (1915), pp 342–3.

20. The Council consisted of the great noblemen and principal bishops together with some powerful peers, clerics and Council officials. Up to 60 strong, there were never more than 20 at a meeting and usually far fewer. Between 1461 and 1485 the Council met, on average, more than once a week.

21. There are two obvious Woodville tombs in Grafton church, one just a solid medieval stone box stripped of its carvings; it is supposed to be Sir Richard's grandfather, also a Sir Richard. The other is still rich in detail; on the top is a deeply engraved picture of a knight in full plate armour, sword and dagger, long pointed feet, open helmet and a face with a long drooping moustache. The lettering round the edge states this was 'John Wydeiul' but sadly the marble is rather battered and covered in graffiti, so the rest is illegible. However, he is probably an earlier Woodville, perhaps the Sir John who lengthened the church and added the tower.

22. *Calendar of State Papers of Milan*, 177/133 (23 October 1469).

23. *The Chronicle of John Hardying*, ed H. Ellis (1812).

24. Sir John Fortescue (1394?–1476?), chief justice under Henry VI and loyal Lancastrian. One of his principal works was *De Natura Legis Naturae*, which distinguished absolute from constitutional monarchy. He also wrote *De Laudibus Legum Angliae* for the young prince, from which this excerpt is taken. Translated and edited by S.B. Chrimes, *Henry VII* (London: Eyre Methuen 1972).

25. J. Warkworth, *Chronicle of the First 13 Years of the Reign of King Edward IV*, ed J.O. Halliwell (London: Camden Society, 1839). The captain of *The Trinity*, John Porter, certainly helped as he was rewarded with a royal annuity of £20. J.S. Davies, *History of Southampton* (London, 1883), reports that Anthony and his officers were given a celebratory dinner by the town.

26. Painter, *William Caxton*, p 113. The quotation is from the prologue of 'De Amicitia'.

27. 'Hearne's Fragment', in J.A. Giles (ed), *Chronicles of the White Rose of York* (1834), p 28.

28. A ship dated at 1467–68 has been found preserved in the mud of the Usk at Newport. She is clinker built with heavy oak planks, around 25 metres long and had, amongst other things, stone cannonballs aboard.

29. Edward III fighting the Spaniards (24 June 1340). See Sir John Froissart, *Chronicles of England, France and Spain* (London: Routledge, 1874), vol. i, p 198.

30. Actually it was *Bishop's* Lynn; it did not become *King's* Lynn until the Reformation.

31. 'Easterling' was a general term used to describe people who came from the east, i.e. the Baltic, the Hanseatic League and Scandinavia. (Holinshed: 'used by the English of traders or others from the coasts of the Baltic ... because they lie east in respect of us'.)

32. The London chronicler was scandalized by Henry's appearances in the same old blue coat, months apart in 1470–71, and his square-toed (farmer's) boots. M.R. James (ed), *John Blackman's Memoire of Henry VI* (Cambridge: Cambridge University Press, 1919), p 36.

33. Thomas Fuller, *Worthies of England* (1662), p 155.

34. Duke Charles was descended from Philippa, one of John of Gaunt's daughters, who had married King João I of Portugal. One of their daughters, Isabella, married Philip of Burgundy, so Charles was a Lancaster cousin; however, he was married to King Edward's sister, Margaret (of York).

35. Painter, *William Caxton*, p 42.

36. Commines, *Memoirs 1461–1483*, pp 115–16.

37. *Historie of the Arrival of Edward IV*, ed J. Bruce (London: Camden Society, 1838).

38. Casualties were estimated at 1,500, with over 10,000 arrows used. C.L. Scofield, *The Life and Reign of Edward IV* (London: Longman, 1923), vol. i, p 581.

39. An archer's pay was 6 pence per day and there is a record of one complete 'harness including ostrich feathers' costing £6-16s-8d (1,640 pence), i.e. nine months' pay. Warwick's probably cost much more.

40. A typical dagger of the period has a thin tapering double-edged blade around 12in (30cm) long.

41. G.E. Cokayne, *The Complete Peerage* (London: St Catherine's Press, 1910).

42. During the dodge and chase round Gloucestershire, divisions of both armies camped in the Iron Age fort at Little Sodbury. Queen Margaret spent the night of 29 April in the manor house there and King Edward was there on the nights of 1 and 2 May.

43. Oman, *The Art of War in the Middle Ages*, p 412.

44. A recurring theme in medieval romances is of a knight going on a crusade, or joining either the Templars or the Hospitallers, because they felt the need to atone for a sin of some kind or they were hopelessly enamoured of an unobtainable lady. There were also vows made publicly in response to an idea, for instance Duke Philip of Burgundy at the Feast of the Pheasant in 1454 to go crusading. Alternatively it could be, and this probably was, a vow made as part of a bargain with God, such as that which Charles the Bold made when there was a night attack on his lodgings. He swore he would walk 30 or 50 miles to give thanks at a particular shrine if his life was saved. It was, he did (R. Vaughan, *Charles the Bold* (Longman, 1973), p 161).

45. On one occasion they had reached the walls of Tangier itself and were set to make a surprise attack; the scaling ladders were up but so many wanted the honour of climbing first and the argument became so loud and prolonged that the Moors were alerted – with disastrous results.

46. Tangier remained Portuguese until Catherine of Braganza brought it to England as part of her dower when she married Charles II. The English abandoned it in 1683 and corsairs (pirates) took possession.

47. *Archaeologia*, vol. xxvi, p 280.

48. Record of Bluemantle Pursuivant in C.I. Kingsford, *English Historical Literature in the Fifteenth Century* (Oxford, 1913), p 382.

49. The visitor was Louis de Gruthuyse, the Burgundian governor of Holland. In September 1472 King Edward repaid him for his help in the hard times by making him Earl of Winchester and giving a lavish party when he came over on a diplomatic mission. The events were recorded by Bluemantle Pursuivant (*ibid.*, pp 386–7).

Chapter 4. Princes and Peers

1. The works of M. Hicks, R. Horrocks and D.E. Lowe have been very helpful for this chapter, while Kirk's monumental *History of Charles the Bold*, Vaughan's biography and Philippe de Commine's *Memoirs* have been particularly useful, together with *The Practice of English Diplomacy in France 1461–71* by Edward Meek, for the European dimension. *James III* by N. Macdougall has provided much on the Scottish issues.

2. 'Dub' comes from *adouber* which originally meant to equip a man with martial arms. The knight-to-be would dress in a chamois leather undercoat, a chain-mail shirt and his plate armour, which would probably be a new gleaming suit made for the occasion.

3. Royal revenues came from land ownership, customs duties, land trusteeship and confiscation, as well as more imaginative ways such as 'first benevolence', paid by the rich in lieu of military service. Parliament only raised money for war.

4. *Calendar of Patent Rolls, Edward IV*, vol. ii, p 339.

5. For instance, the Earl of Pembroke was 14 when he took part in the great expedition of 1475; in 1417 the son of Sir John Cornwall, at 13, swam across the Seine with his father to make a bridgehead at Pont d'Arche; when Henry V made his call up in 1415, men-at-arms had to be 'at least 14 years of age'.

6. D.E. Lowe, 'Patronage and Politics: Edward IV, the Wydevills and the Council of the Prince of Wales 1471–83', *Board of Celtic Studies*, 29 (1981), p 568.

7. Louis de Bretelles (or Bretaylle) crops up several times in this history. He was sent by King Edward to Spain in the summer of 1462 to provide intelligence on its rapidly changing politics. Previously he had performed 'valiant deeds' in France under the great Talbot in the campaign of 1452–53. He was used for a number of diplomatic missions. He fought, after Anthony, in the tournament

with the Bastard and his Burgundians – against Jean de Chassa – on foot on the Saturday and mounted on the Sunday.

8.   H. Cust, *Gentlemen Errant, Being the Journeys and Adventures of Four Noblemen during the Fifteenth and Sixteenth Centuries* (London: John Murray, 1909), pp 86–7.

9.   A plum job for many of us, responsible for the national supply of wine which included licensing imports and collecting duty payable on the cargoes.

10. *Calendar of Patent Rolls, Edward IV, 1467–77*, p 417.

11. Thomas More, *History of King Richard III*, ed R. Sylvester (London, 1963), p 15.

12. A marriage treaty was signed on 26 October 1474 for Prince James, the Scots heir and Princess Cecilia. Her dowry was 20,000 marks, to be paid in instalments over 17 years.

13. *Calendar of State Papers of Milan*, p 193.

14. King Edward's objective in taking his army to France is unclear and different views obtain: C.D. Ross believed there was an aggressive war plan, while J.R. Lander believed it was an essentially defensive expedition. It was probably opportunist to start with and then became driven by domestic momentum.

15. Clarence and Gloucester each took 1,000 archers and 120 lances, Norfolk and Suffolk each 40 lances and 350 archers, Northumberland 60 lances and 250 archers. The wages for the expedition for the second quarter (three months) were £32,015-13s-10d.

16. The muster roll in *Edward IV's French Expedition of 1475*, ed F.P. Barnard (College of Arms; Oxford: Clarendon Press, 1925). In this period a 'lance' was the smallest cavalry unit and consisted of five men: the man-at-arms, a squire, a page and two mounted archers. The 'lances' in this expedition may not have had their complement of mounted archers.

17. Olivier de la Marche (*Mémoires*, vol. ii, p 266) says that Louis de Bretelles was 'in the service of Lord Scales'.

18. *Medieval Pageant: Writhe's Garter Book*.

19. J. du Clercq, *Mémoires sur le Règne de Philippe le Bon, Duc de Bourgogne*, ed de Rieffenberg (1835–36), vol. iv, p 7.

20. Sir Robert Neville to Lord Wenlock, in J.F. Kirk, *History of Charles the Bold* (London: John Murray, 1863), p 169.

21. Jean de Troyes, *The Scandalous Chronicle* (London, 1856). It is disappointingly short of scandal.

22. Commines reported how King Louis was hugely entertained by a recent arrival from the Burgundian court who mimicked Duke Charles flying into a rage at the mention of King Edward. The Duke stamps, shouts a string of expletives and finishes up saying that Edward's name is Blaybourne, as his father was only an archer. It was the Milanese ambassador who reported the Garter incident.

23. *Calender of State Papers of Milan*, pp 217, 219, 296.

24. Francis Bacon made the observation about Henry VII's expedition of 1492, but Henry was only following in his late father-in-law's footsteps.

25. Commines, *Memoirs 1461–1483*, p 179.
26. *Ibid.*, p 279.
27. *Biographie Universelle* (Paris, 1854), vol. xxv.
28. C. Ady, *History of Milan under the Sforza* (Methuen, 1907), pp 261–4.
29. In the late fifteenth century Milan stretched from the border of Padua to the border of Piedmont and the Trevisan March.
30. Boccaccio developed the writing of the short story (*novella*) to a fine art in the fourteenth century and the following two centuries were the golden age of the Italian novella which, in turn, gave many a plot to the Elizabethan dramatists.
31. Pope Sixtus IV (1471–84) had been a Franciscan monk. He is described by James Lees-Milne, *St Peter's* (London: Hamish Hamilton, 1967), pp 128–9, as astute yet simple, an ecclesiastical scholar of renown, a patron of learning and art but inordinately profligate of money. He built the Sistine Chapel, founded St Luke's association of painters and re-established the Vatican Library.
32. *Paston Letters*, no. 369. *Calendar of State Papers of Milan*, p 324. *Venetian Papers*, p 136. *Vatican Regesta*, vol. DCLXV, Sixtus IV, 221. Lords 'Scroop and Hurmonde' were with him.
33. P. Spufford, *Handbook of Medieval Exchange*, pp 316, 320–1.
34. San Michelle in Isola, the Scula di San Giovanni Evangelista and a number of palaces were under construction, the façade of San Zaccaria had just been completed, as had a major rebuild of the Doge's Palace. In the sixteenth century the arsenal is recorded as building up to 100 ships a year.
35. J. Wullschlager, 'Arts Review', *Financial Times*, 19 May 2006.
36. Mauro Lucco, *Antonello da Messina, L'Opera Completa* (Silvana, 2006). Antonello worked in Venice 1475–76.
37. C.R. Clough, *The Duchy of Urbino in the Renaissance* (Varorium Reprints, 1981), p 211.
38. J.F. Kirk, *History of Charles the Bold*, vol. iii, pp 361, 423.
39. Loose translation of what the Milanese ambassador reported: 'Si ne he riso dicendo, per paura si ne ha andato.' Anthony left on 9 July and Charles's defeat at Morat took place on 22 July 1476. Both armies were about 35,000 strong.
40. Vaughan, *Charles the Bold*, pp 204–17.
41. W.H. Black, *Illustrations of Ancient State and Chivalry* (London, 1840), vol. iii, pp 25–40.
42. Anthony had married Elizabeth Scales in 1460; six years later she made a will giving Anthony outright possession of the bulk on the Scales estates with the remainder going to feofees (trustees); nothing was left to any of her remote blood cousins. There were 15 manors in Norfolk, one in Cambridge and the advowsons of two priories and several parish churches. Anthony inherited when she died on 2 September 1473. Writs to the escheators of Norfolk, Suffolk, Essex and Hertfordshire were issued on 12 October 1473.
43. Francis Blomfield, *History of Norfolk* (Linn, 1796), vol. i, p 26.

44. Maximilian (1459–1519) was then 17 years old. There is a fine woodcut by Albrecht Dürer of him as Emperor, drawn in 1518. His contemporaries did not rate him highly. Machiavelli later wrote, 'He is very fickle, he takes council from nobody and yet believes everybody. He desires what he cannot have and leaves what he can readily obtain.'

45. Painter, *William Caxton*, pp 86–9.

46. The manuscript of the works of Christine de Pisan (1363–1431), which he probably used, is now in the Harleian collection (BM no. 4431). The one in the collection was Anthony's and he evidently received it from his mother. He later gave it to a Burgundian friend, the Seigneur de la Gruthuyse. Christine de Pisan was the daughter of an Italian astronomer who married a Frenchman and 'took to letters' after his death; she later removed to a convent.

47. Rivers delivered the manuscript to Caxton on 2 February 1479, printing started the next day and the 78 leaves were finished on 24 March.

48. Written from Middleton, probably on 28 May 1482. PRO no. 38 in augmentation 486, reproduced by Gardener in *Richard III* (London: Longman, 1878), annex B, p 340.

49. *Weever's Funeral Monuments* (London, 1767), p 269. It also notes that the chapel was close to St Stephen's but somewhat smaller.

50. A particularly close relationship is apparent from Anthony's will. We know Edward was with Anthony in Brittany and the fact that Edward knew the King of Portugal also points to him having been there with Anthony in 1471, so it seems reasonable to conclude that he was squire and companion to his brother.

Chapter 5. The Graduate

1. E.W. Brayley, *The Graphic and Historical Illustrator* (London: Chidley, 1834), p 27.

2. *Tirant Lo Blanc*, p 115 (with some minor changes to the translation).

3. Wardrobe accounts of Edward IV.

4. Scofield, *The Life and Reign of Edward IV*, vol. ii, p 284.

5. Painter, *William Caxton*, p 113.

6. Lotte Hellinga, *Caxton in Focus* (London: British Library, 1982), p 89.

7. Lowe, 'Patronage and Politics'. John Giles was looked after. On 30 July 1484 he was awarded £20 a year from the customs of Exeter and Dartmouth.

8. *Three Books of Polydore Vergil's English History*, ed H. Ellis (London: Camden Society, 1884), p 227.

9. 'Grant for life to Edward Wydevill, knight, of the custody of the king's castle and town of Porchester and forest and warren there and the supervision and governance of the king's town of Portsmouth and his place there, with power to appoint under him a porter, an artiller and a watchman within the castle, receiving 12d. daily of his own fee, 3d. daily for the wages of the porter and 1d. daily for the wages of the groom under him to keep the warren, 6d. daily for the wages of the artiller and 3d. daily for the wages of the watchman and

the accustomed fees for the supervision and governance, from the issues of the castle, forest and warren and the fee-farm of the town, so far as their extent suffices, and the residue from the issues of the county of Southampton with all other accustomed profits, in the same manner as John, late earl of Shrewsbury, or any one else had the same; in lieu of a like grant to the king's kinsman Anthony Wydevill, earl Ryvers, lord of Scales and Nucelles, by letters patented dated 9 November, 17 (rectius 19 November, 7) Edward IV, Surrendered.'

10. Grafton's chronicle records Edward as one of only four (named) officers in the 'Middleward' of 5,800 men, under the command of Duke Richard himself.

11. Coventry Leet Book, p 505.

12. N. Macdougall, *James III: A Political Study* (Edinburgh, 1982), p 188.

13. The arrangement operated from 4 July until 12 October and consisted of riders stationed at 20-mile intervals; a letter could cover 200 miles in two days. This is the first recorded example of the courier system being used in England. See Scofield, *The Life and Reign of Edward IV*, vol. ii, p 344.

14. The conspirators had met to grumble about their king. One of them told the fable about the parliament of mice who met to decide what to do about the cat. They decided to 'bell the cat'. Lord Angus volunteered to 'bell the cat' and so acquired his nickname. The fable is told in *Piers Plowman* but appeared before that in the early thirteenth century.

15. Metcalf, *A Book of Knights*. A Knight Banneret is a field commander, a military rank which carried the right to a square banner with arms. It was awarded for distinguished battlefield service. The King or most senior nobleman in the field cut off the two points of the knight's pennon, thus creating a banner (the 1475 expedition had just 12 knight bannerets). The active-service day rate of pay for a banneret was 4 shillings which was the same as a baron; a knight was 2 shillings; men at arms and scurriers were 1 shilling and archers were 6 pence. At the other end of the scale a duke was 13/4 and an earl 6/8. (One pound had 20 shillings (20s) and 1s had 12 pence (12d). One mark was 13s-4d.)

16. C.D. Ross, *Edward IV* (Yale, 1974), pp 289–90.

17. Pope Sixtus IV, *Calendar of State Papers at Venice*, p 145.

18. E.W. Ives, 'Andrew Dymmock and the Papers of Anthony, Earl Rivers 1482–83', *BIHR*, 41 (1968), pp 216–29.

19. Commines, *Memoirs 1461–1483*, p 240.

20. *Ibid.*, p 242.

21. Thomas Rotherham, John Morton, William Hastings, Thomas Montgomery, John Howard, John Cheyeny, Thomas St Leger, Thomas Grey (Dorset). Commines knew about the payments, as he was involved in the offers of pensions and had paid Hastings when he had worked for the Duke of Burgundy. See Commines, *Memoirs 1461–1483*, p 167.

22. More, *History of King Richard III*, p 11. Precise records of sexual activity are rare but, as an indication, the Duke of Clarence's household passed through Lichfield

in 1466 and a single lady of the town, Cecelia, enjoyed 14 men in 24 hours and earned herself £3. A. Goodman, *The Wars of the Roses: The Soldiers' Experience* (Tempus, 2005).

23. 'The Nut-Brown Maid', a long fifteenth-century poem in praise of woman's fidelity.

24. Nicolas von Poppelau, a visitor to England in 1484.

25. Tradition has Elizabeth of York as the model for the Queen in the classic pack of English playing cards. This seems perfectly possible, as playing cards were imported until the late fifteenth century when production started in England. Elizabeth was then queen. By all accounts she was tall, beautiful and had her mother's long golden hair.

26. Fifteenth-century prayer published in B. Green and V. Gollancz (eds), *God of a Hundred Names* (London: Gollancz, 1962), p 24.

27. *Richard III*, Act 1, Scene 1.

Chapter 6. The Great Coup

1. The main sources for this chapter are *The Usurption of Richard III* by Dominic Mancini, *The Crowland Chronicle* and *The History of Richard III* by Thomas More. Mancini was in the service of the Archbishop of Vienne and visited England between late 1482 and July 1483 when he wrote an objective report for his patron, who seems to have had a particular thirst for intelligence. The details in More's account are believed to originate from someone who was directly involved in the events, perhaps Bishop Morton. Both of these works have been widely used and quoted.

2. The hall still exists and measures 101ft by 36ft (30.8 metres by 10.9 metres) and 55ft (16.8 metres) high to the apex of the roof. It is a magnificent 'false' hammerbeam construction decorated with fine tracery and there is evidence that it was once partly gilded. It was built by Thomas Jordan, the King's chief mason, and his chief carpenter Edmund Gravely.

3. King Edward blamed Hastings, partially, for allowing the treaty to happen. As Captain of Calais, Hastings was close to Burgundy and had intelligence responsibilities for the area.

4. R. Horrox, *Financial Memoranda of the Reign of Edward V* (London: Camden Society, 1987). It covers some folios of Exchequer notes in the Longleat Library and amongst them are the financial records of the defence measures taken immediately after King Edward's death. They show there was real anticipation of war with France and preparations had (probably) started before Edward died. See Appendix A.

5. *Richard III*, Act 2, Scene 1.

6. Henry Tudor is rated as shrewd but he inherited the Yorkist system of sound finance and, even at the end of his reign, he had only managed to increase his annual revenues to £105,000. However, English royal revenues were dwarfed

by those of France at 5.4 million livres in 1482, i.e. around £600,000; in 1484 French military expenditure was about £100,000. See D. Potter, *A History of France, 1460–1560* (London: Macmillan, 1995), p 144.

7. Commines, *Memoirs 1461–1483*, iii, vii. Seven of the battles are identifiable but two are unknown.

8. A king's title had three parts: hereditary, acclamation or election, and coronation. Edward V was king from 10 April and was recognized as such everywhere.

9. Ives, 'Andrew Dymmock and the Papers of Anthony, Earl Rivers 1482–83'.

10. Full details are in *Letters and Papers Illustrative of the Reigns of Richard III and Henry VII*, ed Gardener, p 6.

11. *The Mariners Mirror*, vol. x, p 216.

12. M. Oppenheim, *A History of the Administration of the Royal Navy and of Merchant Shipping in Relation to the Navy* (London: Bodley, 1896), vol. 1, pp 49, 56. (The armaments and companies for ships of those sizes are in a 1513 state paper.)

13. Scofield, *The Life and Reign of Edward IV*, vol. ii, p 414.

14. The restitution programme agreed later between Duke Richard and Lord Cordes refers to French ships held at Sandwich and Plymouth, also to 'damages' and 'as for other prizes and takings'. It would be surprising if Edward was not responsible for some or all of this.

15. Horrox, *Richard III*, pp 108–9.

16. M.A. Hicks, *Richard III: The Man Behind the Myth* (Collins and Brown, 1991), p 103.

17. Mancini, *The Usurption of Richard III*, pp 90–1.

18. Ives, 'Andrew Dymmock and the Papers of Anthony, Earl Rivers 1482–83'.

19. A troop of 2,000 would cost around £1,500 for 30 days plus rations, a large and seemingly needless expense. Another example is Duke Charles of Burgundy's bodyguard which was 309 strong when he was campaigning in 1474. See E.A. Tabri, *Political Culture in the Early Northern Renaissance* (Edwin Mellen, 2004), p 41.

20. 'uch ein grosses hertz'; Nicolas von Poppelau in the journal of his visit to King Richard in May 1484.

21. The dinner was recorded in detail by Mancini, More and in *The Crowland Chronicle*; the quotations are from More, pp 18–21, and Mancini, pp 91, 93.

22. British Library, Harleian Manuscript, vol. iii. Richard was obviously ignorant of Dorset's whereabouts.

23. Horrox, *Financial Memoranda of the Reign of Edward V*, p 216. The full text is in Appendix B.

24. 'Grants from the Crown during the reign of Edward V', xv, 3, 15, 17, 51. 'Whightmede Parc' is in the Forest of Dean and very much in the Woodville sphere of influence; the pay was 4 pence daily. William 'Slatter' had been granted it in 1481, *Calendar of Patent Rolls, Edward IV*, p 234. The new grant of Whitmede was to John Cotington and is undated but together in a batch with one dated 26

May 1483; the grant is in the *Calendar of Patent Rolls* for 26 January 1484, p 457.

25. Hicks, *Richard III*, p 102.

26. J.A.F. Thomson, 'Bishop Lionel Woodville and Richard III', *BIHR*, vol. lxix (1986).

27. More, *History of King Richard III*, p 52.

28. *Richard III*, Act 3, Scene 5.

29. More, *History of King Richard III*, p 49.

30. *Ibid.*, p 42.

31. For instance, the petition laid before the parliament of 1484 to justify Richard's title to the throne refers to the Woodvilles as 'insolent, vicious and of inordinate avarice'. Michael Hicks in *Richard III* explores Richard's case against the Woodvilles and finds it wanting (pp 158–86).

32. *Excerpta Historica*, pp 240–5.

33. Rous quotes the first two verses in his *Historia Regum Angliae* (Oxford, 1745 edition, p 214) and the three others are in Ritson (*Ancient Songs*, II). There seems to be no doubt about the ascription to Rivers. Caxton also mentions that Anthony composed ballads.

34. Blomefield, *History of Norfolk* (Middleton), p 25.

35. C. Ross (*Edward IV*) regards Richard as 'the first English King to use character-assassination as an instrument of policy'. M. Hicks (*Richard III*, p 99) noted that King Richard effectively charged the late king, his brother, with the sort of misgovernment that had led to depositions in the past and he saddles the Woodvilles with the responsibility. Ross also wrote of a 'virulent and puritanical propaganda campaign by which Richard sought to discredit the Woodvilles'.

36. H. Ellis (ed), *Original Letters Illustrative of English History* (London, 1825), letter v, p 9.

37. Commines, *Memoirs 1461–1483*, p 270. However, there is no other evidence to confirm this theory.

38. The promise of marriage given in exchange for the promise of the other party was binding in English law and marriage before witnesses was standard. Church weddings did not become obligatory until the Council of Trent in 1564.

39. M.A. Hicks deals with the matter in detail in *Anne Neville: Queen to Richard III* (Tempus, 2007), pp 133–4, 145.

40. Vitellis A XVI, quoted in Ross, *Richard III*.

41. The origin of the custom is from the Norman conquests when Marmion, a powerful baron, challenged anyone to dispute King William I's right to the throne. Marmion's successors held the right for 300 years. It then passed to the Dymmocks who had married a Marmion daughter and inherited Scrivleby in Lincolnshire. See William Hutton, *The Battle of Bosworth Field* (Stroud: Sutton, 1999).

42. The officers of *The Trinity* and *The Falcon* would be in the mould of Chaucer's sea captain: '... But he was a good enough fellow. He had tapped many barrels of fine

Bordeaux wine, when the merchant was not looking, and had no scruples about it. A ship's cargo was not sacrosanct. The sea was the element in which he felt at home. He had acquired all the skills of observation and navigation; he had learnt how to calculate the tides and currents, and knew from long acquaintance the hidden perils of the deep. No one from Hull to Carthage knew more about natural harbours and anchorages; he could fix the position of the moon and stars without the aid of an astrolabe. He knew all the havens, from Gotland to Cape Finistere, and every creek in Brittany and Spain. He told me of his voyages as far north as Iceland' (*The Canterbury Tales*, trans Peter Ackroyd (London: Penguin 2009)).

Chapter 7. Exile in Brittany

1. One of the best sources for the period is Polydore Vergil who was writing around 30 years later and knew some of the people who had been in Brittany. He was the King's official historian but he makes little of Edward Woodville, who was then long dead; however, other sources rate Edward highly. Additionally *François II, Duc de Bretagne, et l'Angleterre* by B.A. Pocquet du Haut-Jussé (Rennes, 1928), *The Making of the Tudor Dynasty* by R.A. Griffiths and R.S. Thomas and *Henry VII* by S.R. Chrimes have proved invaluable.
2. Her father was Charles VI of France (1368–1422) who was insane for much of his life, though he did father at least 12 children. France was in chaos for most of his reign.
3. Her father was John, Duke of Somerset, directly descended from John, Duke of Lancaster (John of Gaunt), third son of Edward III, but from his mistress Catherine Swynford. When Margaret's grandfather was legitimized there was a specific proviso that he and his heirs were forever barred from the royal succession. She inherited large estates and married Edmund Tudor, Earl of Richmond, by whom she had Henry. (Illegitimacy and kingship were not necessarily incompatible in the Middle Ages, e.g. William the Conqueror.)
4. *Three Books of Polydore Vergil's English History*, ed H. Ellis, p 158.
5. Henry was given 2,000 livres a year (about £400) plus a further 620 livres as pocket money; he was awarded a 10 per cent rise in October 1482. Jasper, Henry's guardian but not of the blood royal, was allowed 600 livres a year (£120) plus 40 for personal expenses.
6. Another Beaufort heir was Mary Lewis who had been safely married off to Anthony Woodville.
7. The deed was drawn up at Westminster on 3 June 1482 in the King's presence. In the same deed Lord Stanley promised not to ask for changes to Margaret's marriage settlement, i.e. Henry would inherit (see Griffiths and Thomas, *The Making of the Tudor Dynasty*, p 85). There is also the draft of a royal pardon for Henry in the *Calendar of Entries in the Papal Registers*, vol. 14, p 18, which shows there were discussions about him marrying Elizabeth of York.
8. Gardener (ed), *Letters and Papers Illustrative of the Reigns of Richard III and Henry VII*,

vol. i, pp 22–3.

9. A description of two 'Tower' ships in 1501, in Oppenheim, *Administration of the Royal Navy*, p 41.

10. Neither ship appears again in crown records for the reign of Richard III but they re-appear in Henry's reign (C.F. Richmond, 'English Naval Power in the Fifteenth Century', *History*, lii (1967), p 53). C.R. Ross in *Richard III*, p 195, concurs, as do R.S. Griffiths and R.S. Thomas in *The Making of the Tudor Dynasty*, p 86.

11. *Grants etc. from the Crown During the Reign of Edward the Fifth*, ed J.G. Nichols (London: Camden Society, 1854), p 51.

12. It might have been the French pension: £10,000 is roughly 50,000 crowns which was the annual payment due under the Treaty of Picquigny. If King Louis was unnerved by Edward's war preparations he may have decided to make peace by sending the suspended payment. If he did, then it could be in a ship on Southampton Water on 14 May 1483.

13. 'Retinue', according to the *Dictionary of Middle English*, is a 'band of retainers, attendants or followers of a king, lord, goddess etc; a train, suite; also an army'.

14. *Mémoires de la Société d'Historique de Bretagne*, vol. ix, chapter 8 ('Le Régne de Richard III'), p 431.

15. 'The Lord Skales is the scalop Schelles'. The silver scallop was the badge of the Rivers contingent recorded for the 1475 French expedition and presumably was used for the 1472 one to Brittany. It was presumably used by Edward in both Spain and Brittany, as he is regularly called Scales, i.e. the shell. In old French a shell is 'escale' and in old English 'scealu'.

16. In July Mancini reported a rumour that the princes were dead.

17. The generic term for a group of courtiers is a 'treachery'.

18. From the fifth son, Thomas of Woodstock, Duke of Gloucester. His mother was a Beaufort, Margaret's first cousin.

19. *Three Books of Polydore Vergil's English History*, p 196.

20. Pocquet du Haut-Jussé, *François II, Duc de Bretagne, et l'Angleterre*, p 419.

21. King Louis's reign is in two parts: in the first half he was preoccupied with survival, problems with Burgundy and aristocratic disaffection which came to a head in the War of Public Weal (1465) and the Treaty of Perronne (1468). In the early 1470s he was able to start pursuing an expansionist policy. At the start of his reign the kingdom was 425,000 km² and 460,000 km² at the end.

22. *The Crowland Chronicle*, p 491. Henry's title was weak but possible; if it was joined to Elizabeth of York's then the combination was much stronger.

23. *Calendar of Patent Rolls 1476–1485*, p 371.

24. Earlier dates suggested for Henry's voyage could have been reconnaissance or opportunity excursions, perhaps by *The Trinity* and *The Falcon*. Duke Francis authorized a loan of 10,000 gold crowns (£2,000) on 22 November 1483.

25. Henry's ship had trouble with the weather and dropped him at La Hogue in

Normandy. He went back by land, across France, and the ship sailed back to Brittany. Breton records are quite clear. There were five ships and 324 soldiers provided as an escort by Duke Francis for Henry who was – theoretically – joining a successful uprising, but the fleet was separated by storms. Pocquet du Haut-Jussé, *François II, Duc de Bretagne, et l'Angleterre*, vol. ix, p 419. Polydore Vergil recorded Duke Francis providing 15 vessels and a loan of 10,000 ecus d'or on 30 October. They sailed in November but were separated by storms and returned. A few Bretons were left behind in England and had to ransom themselves out of captivity.

26. Bishop Lionel went into sanctuary at Beaulieu Abbey, from where he continued to administer his diocese until his death the following year.

27. *Calendar of Patent Rolls, Richard III*, p 425.

28. The English exile community was 423 men who lived at Vannes in south-west Brittany. Commines noted they were a financial burden on Duke Francis who paid them 3,100 livres in June 1484, while the burgers gave them credit of 2,500 livres, which was guaranteed by the Duke. There were allowances to Dorset and his entourage of 400 per month while four others, one of whom was Edward, got 100 per month each. All in all the exiles were an expensive community to maintain.

29. Harleian MS 433, ed R. Horrox and P.W. Hammond, vol. iii, p 190.

30. Fabyan, *New Chronicle of England and France*, vol. viii, p 219.

31. Macdougall, *James III*, pp 208–10.

32. Vergil believes the intelligence came from other sources and Urswick was only used as the courier.

33. Edward Woodville, John Cheyne and Edward Poynings were each given 100 livres and the others five crowns (one livre) each. The total cost in the Exchequer accounts was 708 livres, i.e. 411 men. There had been 423 in June, Henry had taken 12: the figures add up.

34. On King Louis's death Charles inherited and his elder sister Anne (aged 22) became Regent. Anne was married to Pierre de Beaujeu, Duke de Bourbon, to whom King Louis had paid the highest pension in France, 20,000 livres a year.

35. Commines, *Memoirs 1461–1483*, vol. i, p 396.

36. There was no doubt in French minds about Richard's guilt. At the opening of the States-General on 15 January 1484 the Chancellor, Guillaume de Rochfort, delivered the inaugural address. It included special emphasis on French loyalty and devotion to the Crown which, he said, distinguished them from the English: 'Consider for instance, what happened in the country after King Edward's death; how his children were murdered with impunity and the Crown transferred to the assassin by the goodwill of the nation.' Bridges, *History of France*, vol. 1, p 66.

37. In 1473 Duke Richard made her hand over her own estates to him by 'coercion and compulsion'. Her son had been attainted but she had done nothing wrong or been accused of anything. There was snow and ice when Richard threatened to

send the old lady to Middleham and keep her there. 'She could not endure to be conveyed there without great jeopardy to her life.' See M. Hicks, *The Last Days of Elizabeth, Countess of Oxford*, p 91.

38. Pocquet du Haut-Jussé, *François II, Duc de Bretagne, et l'Angleterre*, vol. ix, p 433.

39. Sanceau, *The Perfect Prince*, p 206.

40. Ross, *Richard III*. Dr Hicks believes that Richard 'used his flair for public relations to make his case as convincing as possible' and so 'our history of April to June 1483 is very much Richard's creation' (*Richard III: The Man Behind the Myth*.)

41. Philibert de Chandée was an enthusiastic soldier who talked later of taking his retinue to Spain with Edward Woodville. He was created Earl of Bath on 6 January 1486 and awarded 100 marks a year. He was still in England in March 1487 but then returned to French service·

42. Scottish records (John Major and Pittscottie) have Alexander Bruce and John de Haddington as the commanders of the Scots contingent of 1,000 at Bosworth (Macdougall, *James III*, pp 215–16). Bernard Stewart (Lord d'Aubigny), the Franco-Scot commanding Charles VIII's Scots Guards, was particularly honoured when he visited England in 1508. The presence of the Scots companies also seems to be confirmed by the award by King Henry to Sir Alexander Bruce of Earlshall of £20 a year on 7 March 1486; Bruce joined Henry's household in 1485.

43. There are various views on the size and composition of Henry Tudor's army. The 4,000-man view is expressed in *The Making of the Tudor Dynasty* by R.A. Griffiths and R.S. Thomas (p 129) and in *Richard III* by C.D. Ross (p 201). However, C.S. Davies in 'The Wars of the Roses in the European Context' (*The Wars of the Roses*, ed A.J. Pollard, p 244) reckons there were no more than 2,000, including the 400–500 Englishmen, who sailed in seven ships. Vergil reports 2,000, and de Valera (a Spanish observer writing to Ferdinand in March 1486) reported 2,000 who had been paid for four months. To have two different contingents – each of 1,800 – joining up, as Molinet reports, seems too much of a coincidence, so I would discount that. On balance, the probability seems to me to be between 2,000 and 2,500, probably sailing in 15 ships. The French naval commander was Admiral Coulon.

44. Redlich, *The German Military Enterpriser*, vol. 1, p 107, and chapters 1 and 2.

45. Edward Hall (*Chronicle*) reports this remark being made in Richard's pre-battle speech.

Chapter 8. Blood and Roses

1. The main source for this chapter is Polydore Vergil. *The Battle of Bosworth* by Michael Bennett and *The Making of the Tudor Dynasty* by R.A. Griffiths and R.S. Thomas have been particularly helpful. Some of the detail of the battle (which may be a touch romantic) is taken from *The Battle of Bosworth Field* by William Hutton, first published in 1788.

2. 'So violent and motley was life that it bore the mixed smell of blood and roses': Johan Huizinga on the late Middle Ages.

3. Psalm XLIII. The translation is taken from the (Breeches) Bible of 1606.

4. To John ap Meredith of Eifionydd in Gwynedd.

5. The Scots were commanded by Sir Alexander Bruce of Earlshall and John de Haddington. See Macdougall, *James III*, pp 215–16.

6. The army landed on 8 August and marched the 176 miles from Dale to Bosworth in the following 12 days. Various Welsh gentry joined; one was Dafydd Saisylt, who became David Cecil and whose grandson was William Cecil, the great Lord Burghley.

7. George, Lord Strange, who was married to a niece of Edward Woodville.

8. King Richard travelled with his own bed, which he left behind at the White Boar, the inn in Leicester where he had spent the night. The bed had a false bottom in which he left £300 in gold. The cash was not discovered until 100 years later and the bed stayed in the inn for 200 years. See Gardener, *Richard III*, p 293.

9. Robert Lindsay of Piscottie, *The History and Chronicles of Scotland, from the Slaughter of King James I to the ane 1575*, ed A.J.G. Mackay (Edinburgh: Scottish Text Society, 1899–1911), vol. i, pp 197–9. It seems that Highlanders had a particular reputation. A fifteenth-century poem in the Bannatyne Manuscript is titled, 'How the first heilandman of God was made, of ane horse's turd in Argyll as is said.' It runs: 'Quoth God to the Helandman, where wilt thou now? / I will doun to the lowland, Lord, and there steill a cow.'

10. A gilt processional cross of fine workmanship was found at Bosworth in 1778.

11. A review of the evidence is in P. Foss, *The Field of Redemore: The Battle of Bosworth, 1485* (Kairos Press, 1998).

12. King Henry subsequently paid compensation to the farmers who lost their corn.

13. Goodman, *The Wars of the Roses: The Soldiers' Experience*, p 107.

14. The sequence of events is far from certain, as it happened in the helter-skelter of the battle and there are no eyewitness accounts. It was even muddled for those who were there, e.g. Sir James Blount sought, fought and killed John Babington, thinking his wife, who was a Babington niece, would inherit. But Sir James got the wrong John Babington, which was disappointing for the Blounts and bad luck for the wrong John.

15. Hutton, *The Battle of Bosworth Field*, p 89.

16. 'La malice des Francs-Archers (1448–1500)', *Revue des Questions Historiques*, LXI (1897), p 474.

17. *Richard III*, Act 5, Scene 4, written 100 years after the battle. Shakespeare would probably have known people who had talked to men who had fought there.

18. Lady Bessie was Princess Elizabeth of York, and the song probably dates from the early sixteenth century.

19. *Calendar of Patent Rolls, Henry VII, 1485–94*, 1485 and 1486.

20. *Calendar of Patent Rolls, Henry VII, 1485–94*, pp 112, 117.
21. W. Campbell (ed), *Materials for a History of the Reign of Henry VII* (Rolls Series, 1873–77), vol. ii, p 562.
22. Cloth of gold for the King was bought at £8 a yard and £2 a yard for the lords; purple velvet for the King was £2 a yard and Lord Oxford's was £1-10s; even the new confessor wore russet costing 12/6 a yard. It is difficult to put this into modern value but an archer was paid 6 pence a day; there were 240 pennies in a pound, so £2 or 480 pennies was nearly three months' wages for a skilled man.
23. Dated 6 December 1485, *Calendar of State Papers at Venice*, p 158.
24. Jasper died in 1495 and Catherine then married Sir Richard Wingfield of Suffolk, ten years her junior.
25. National Portrait Gallery.
26. The summary of the papal bull recognizing Henry states: 'His Holiness confirmeth ... by reason of his highest and undoubted title of succession as by his most noble [victory] and by election of the lords spiritual and temporal and other nobles of his realm and by the ordinance and authority of parliament made by the three estates of his land.' *Calendar of Entries in the Papal Registers*, proc. 5.
27. Ives, 'Andrew Dymmock and the Papers of Anthony, Earl Rivers 1482–83'.
28. E. Foss, *A Biographical Dictionary of the Judges of England* (London: Murray, 1870), vol. v, pp 46–8.
29. There is very little archive material for the period and it is impossible to determine whether the rather careful approach to policy was due to Henry's inexperience or to pragmatic civil servants; probably the latter, which meant middle-class professional administrators were exercising power.
30. After the death of a feudal tenant in chief (a direct tenant of the crown) a writ was issued to the local escheator who inquired into what lands were held and who should succeed. Campbell (ed), *Materials for a History of the Reign of Henry VII*, vol. i, p 85.

Chapter 9. Local Affairs

1. The near contemporary works of Polydore Vergil (Book xxiv), Bernard André (*Memorials of King Henry VII*, pp 49–52) and Jean de Molinet (*Chroniques*, chapter CLVIII) have been particularly useful, although Molinet, being Burgundian, is partisan while Vergil ignores Edward Woodville at Stoke, even though records confirm him as one of the five main commanders. Vergil names the other four and lists 67 of the captains. M. Bennett in *Lambert Simnel and the Battle of Stoke* gives a clear account which has been useful.
2. Sanceau, *The Perfect Prince*, p 294.
3. For a good telling of the story see Ann Wroe, *Perkin* (Cape, 2003).
4. The accuracy is well illustrated by a sixteenth-century example: 12 soldiers at a range of six yards all fired at a man and missed, which was fortunate as they were mutineers and their target was their officer. The longbow in trained hands would

remain infinitely superior to the hand-held gun until well into the nineteenth century. The first muzzle-loading percussion rifle was introduced in 1851 but it was not until 1874, when the Martini-Henry breech action was issued, that the British soldier could surpass his medieval forebears in range, rapidity of fire and accuracy.

5. *Accounts of Gonzalo de Baeza*, ed Torre and Torre (Madrid: CSIC, 1955), p 164. The value would be a little over £2 (37 maravedis equalled one gold ducat, which was worth about four shillings and three pence in London).

6. J. Leyland, *Collectanea* (London, 1787) ('The Herald's Report', vol. iv), p 205.

7. It has also been suggested that Edward Woodville wished to promote a Spanish marriage for his newly born nephew (R.B. Merriman, *American Antiquarian Society*, 1904) but no authority is given to substantiate the idea and it would be a little premature, as Prince Arthur was born on 20 September 1486, after Edward's return. Negotiations for Arthur's engagement started in 1488; he married Catherine of Castile and Aragon (born December 1485) in November 1501. He died five months later and she subsequently married his younger brother Henry, later Henry VIII.

8. PRO E 405/76, mem.2v.

9. Thornbury was their principal residence, which they started rebuilding. In 1510 dinner could be given to 'besides guests, 134 gentry, 188 yeomen and 197 garçons'. Young Buckingham seems to have taken after his father, with too much royal blood and arrogance; he lost his head in 1521.

10. Gwyn Williams, *Madoc: The Making of a Myth* (Methuen, 1979), p 35.

11. Campbell (ed), *Materials for a History of the Reign of Henry VII*, vol ii, pp 130, 202.

12. John Heron's accounts for 1492 and 1493 (all countersigned by the King) in the British Museum, reproduced in C. Falkus (ed), *Private Lives of the Tudor Monarchs* (London: Folio Society, 1974).

13. The son of King Edward's and King Richard's sister, Elizabeth, and her husband John de la Pole, Duke of Suffolk.

14. Polydore Vergil, *Anglica Historia*, ed D. Hay (London: Camden Society, 1950), p 17.

15. Redlich, *The German Military Enterpriser*, vol. 1, chapters 1 and 2, and p 107.

16. P.L. Hughes and J.F. Larkin (eds), *Tudor Royal Proclamations* (Yale, 1964), 5 and 6 June 1487.

17. Leyland, *Collectanea* ('The Herald's Report', vol. iv), p 210.

18. 'Deux mille chevaux' is certainly an exaggeration. So are Molinet's other numbers that add up to about 40,000 for Henry's army, about four times the correct number. So divide by four? If so, then perhaps Edward had 500 horsemen.

19. An arquebus is a portable long-barrelled gun, inaccurate except at close quarters.

20. Archers could shoot six aimed arrows a minute, or ten unaimed up to 300 yards.

21. The next Earl of Lincoln, his second brother, was beheaded, the third was kept prisoner in the Tower and the fourth escaped to France where he was called

the Duke of York and the 'White Rose'. King Francis I recognized him as King Richard IV of England but he was known as the 'Count of Suffolk'. He had a successful career as a military entrepreneur commanding a company of 'several thousand' called the Black Band. It finished at the battle of Pavia (1525) when he was killed and the Black Band annihilated fighting for France. The Band was recruited in Lower Germany but met their match when they fought the imperial mercenaries of Frundsberg, who had been recruited in Upper Germany.

22. From the 'Epitaph on the Army of Mercenaries' by A.E. Houseman.

23. Considerable mystery surrounds Lambert Simnel and it is uncertain which ten- or 11-year-old boy was the real Warwick. It is hard to understand why Lincoln and his Aunt Margaret should support an impostor when Lincoln himself was King Richard's designated heir. King Henry and his people presented a story that diminishes and ridicules his adversary and is believable. Whether it is true is another matter. The conundrum is explored in *Lambert Simnel and the Battle of Stoke* by M. Bennett. The Warwick in the Tower was slightly simple and was executed for no good reason, other than birth.

24. According to the *Middle English Dictionary* one meaning of *ape* is 'one who does tricks, a trickster'.

Chapter 10. Onwards to Glory

1. The principal sources for the chapter have been the *Chroniques* by Jean Molinet, chapter 192; Polydore Vergil's *Anglica Historia*, Book XXIV; Edward Hall's *Chronicle*, pp 439–41; Pocquet du Haut-Jussé, *François II, Duc de Bretagne, et l'Angleterre*; *Correspondence de Charles VIII avec Louis de la Trèmoille*; *L'expédition de Edouard Wydeville en Bretagne*; and Bridges, *History of France*, vol. 1.

2. *Revue Historique*, vol. xxv, quoted in Bridges, *History of France*, vol. 1, p 133.

3. Commines, *Memoirs 1461–1483*, vol. ii, p 122. He was second cousin of the late Louis XI and son of Duke Charles d'Orléans, taken prisoner at Agincourt, who spent 25 years in England waiting to be ransomed. Charles was an accomplished musician and poet who married his first cousin, Isabella. She was the widow of Richard II of England and Louis XI's aunt.

4. Alain, 16th Count d'Albret, 1440–1522, had been loyal to Louis XI. His son, Jean, married Catherine de Foix in 1486 and so ruled Navarre (Jean's great-grandson was Henry of Navarre who became King of France in 1589); his daughter married Cesare Borgia in 1500.

5. Bridges, *History of France*, vol. 1, p 151.

6. David Hume, *History of England* (New York: Virtue, 1859), vol. i, p 315.

7. Rev. E. Boucher James, *Letters Archaeological and Historical Relating to the Isle of Wight* (1896). The King was recorded visiting Southampton (close to Porchester) in both January and September 1487. See Davies, *History of Southampton*, p 475.

8. Oppenheim, *Administration of the Navy*, p 35.

9. Access was impossible without a patron. Bishop Russell told the Lords in 1483,

'the people must stand afar and not pass the limits; you speak with the prince which is like God on earth'. People without access had to use an intermediary to see someone powerful. Columbus, with his Spanish experiences, was well aware of that. He must have been confident of getting access, for his brother and Edward had easy access to the King.

10. Francis Bacon, *History of the Reign of King Henry the Seventh*, ed J. Weinberger (Cornell University Press, 1996), p 167.

11. A painted shield of Lord 'Wodwill' or 'Wodvill', encircled by the Garter, on a page of similar shields of Knights of the Garter dating from the reign of Henry VII, is on page 32 of the College of Heralds MS. M.7 (unpublished). The bulk of this manuscript was compiled by Sir Thomas Wriothesley (d. 1534 as Garter King of Arms), the son of John Wrythe (also Garter King of Arms), but this particular section of the MS may be earlier.

12. According to S.R. Chrimes, *Henry VII*, 'the Garter rather than anything that could be called a peerage was the ultimate mark of honour favoured by Henry VII'.

13. Leyland, *Collectanea* ('The Herald's Report', vol. iv), pp 185–257.

14. Bridges, *History of France*, vol. 1, p 159.

15. *Correspondence de Charles VIII et de ses consellors avec Louis de la Trémoille* (Paris, 1875), pp 121–2.

16. 'Cauldrons of hypocras,' a deeply aromatic and sexually stimulating drink made from ground Malaguetta (pepper) called *grains of paradise*, wine, sugar, ginger, mace and cinamon. It was said that Venus served it to lovers on their first visit to her tavern.

17. Campbell (ed), *Materials for a History of the Reign of Henry VII*, pp 322, 324.

18. Bacon, *History of the Reign of King Henry the Seventh*, p 67.

19. The numbers are (mainly) taken from de Beauchesne. As usual, they do not quite add up; perhaps some were exaggerated to show the international support.

20. The French artillery was built up by the brothers Bureau for King Louis XI. The brothers were succeeded by Jacques de Genouille who was constantly adding new technical improvements. See Oman, *The Art of War in the Sixteenth Century*, pp 30, 49.

21. *Correspondence de Charles VIII et de ses consellors avec Louis de la Trémoille*, pp 131–2.

22. *Calender of Letters, Dispatches and State Papers, England and Spain, Preserved at Simancas* (London: Longman, 1862), vol. i. Henry had just written (6 July) to congratulate Ferdinand and Isabella on their success against the Moors; their letters will have crossed. The Spanish ambassador in London was de Puebla and Johan de Sepalveda was a special envoy who journeyed between capitals.

23. Molinet, *Chroniques*, p 394.

24. *Hall's Chronicle*, p 141.

25. Pocquet du Haut-Jussé, *François II, Duc de Bretagne, et l'Angleterre*, provides a detailed description.

26. 'San-San-Son' sounds an excellent, onomatopoeic chant which would do splendidly on the battlefield (or indeed on the terraces) as does 'San-Lau-trois'; it is reported that around half the French army were Swiss mercenaries.

27. Molinet, *Chroniques*, p 396.

28. It is difficult to imagine the concentration, the adrenalin, the sweat and the scrambling. Hutton's *Bosworth* (1788) has a report of a nobleman in similar circumstances who had 'several [bodies] at his feet. He followed his blows as if determined his single sword should win the field ... he furiously engaged ... some of them surrounded him with a design to take him alive but he resolved not to yield but die sword in hand ... without one friend to support him he fought. Two courageous men resolved to rescue him. The enemy commander surrounded them with some of his soldiers who cut them to pieces ... he was again left to cope with a surrounding multitude and his powers gone ... himself as well as his sword was dyed in blood. One soldier tried to take him prisoner but collecting strength from anger, with one desperate blow, cut off his arm which fell to the ground.'

29. *Hall's Chronicle*, p 141.

30. Commines rated Galliota highly, both as a soldier and an honourable man. The Venetians had decided to appoint him their Captain General and he was due to take up the post after this campaign. Their ambassador to France had been instructed (4 January 1488) to visit the 'condottiere Jacopo Galeotto', inquire about his eyesight and offer him the job. *Calendar of State Papers at Venice*, p 169.

31. Molinet, *Chroniques*, p 396.

32. *Hall's Chronicle*, p 141.

33. *Correspondence de Charles VIII et de ses consellors avec Louis de la Trémoille*, pp 246–8.

34. The monument states 'Talbot Earl of Scales' which is a mistake. It could stem from 'Sir Edward Woodville called Lord Wideville' and 'George Talbot, Earl of Shrewsbury', both being installed as Knights of the Garter on 29 April 1488. Talbot was 10 years younger and a close Tudor supporter who was present at the signing of the Treaty of Etaples on 3 November 1492.

35. Jean de Beuil, *Le Jouvencel* (Paris: SHF, 1887), vol. ii, pp 20–1.

36. The embassy sailed on 22 December 1488 in two Spanish ships and returned on 25 July 1489. See Davies, *History of Southampton*, p 475.

37. *Calendar of State Papers at Venice* vol. i, p 177.

38. He wrote on 28 January 1489, *Calendar of State Papers at Venice*, vol. i, p 177.

39. J. Dennistoun, *Memoirs of the Dukes of Urbino 1440–1630*, ed E. Hutton (London: Lane, 1910), vol. i, pp 346–7.

40. The Isle of Wight Records Office has a census for 1559 (70 years later) which records the island's population as 8,767, of which 1,880 were rated as able for military service.

41. Rev. E. Boucher James, confirmed by the Records Office.

42. National Archives E 405/76 (215629), quoted in Campbell (ed), *Materials for a History of the Reign of Henry VII*, p 455.

Epilogue

1. The painting of the *Kiss of Judas* is dated *c.*1460 and is now in the Fitzwilliam Museum, Cambridge.
2. Hicks, *Richard III*, p 263.
3. Anne was married to Sir John Walsh and they lived at Little Sodbury Manor, Gloucestershire. It was during an argument in the great hall, which is still there, that William Tyndale famously put down a silly priest: 'If God spare my life, ere many years I will cause a boy that driveth the plough shall know more of the Scriptures than thou dost.' Tyndale is responsible for about 80 per cent of the wonderful English in the King James Bible and he was one of the seminal figures of the Reformation. Brian Buxton has published a paper on Thomas Poyntz (2005) showing he was of the Essex family, rather than of Gloucestershire. The conflict between Tyndale and Thomas More is well documented.
4. Richard Ameryk was a leading Bristol merchant, a Poyntz cousin and a backer of Cabot's voyage. There is an argument, but little evidence, to show that Cabot named America after Ameryk.
5. Among Elizabeth Woodville's grandchildren were Henry VIII and Margaret and Mary who married, respectively, King James IV of Scotland – from whom the present royal family is descended – and King Louis XII of France (his third wife and the same Louis d'Orléans who had fought at St Aubin). Amongst Margaret's great-granddaughters were Queens Mary and Elizabeth and great-great-granddaughters were Mary, Queen of Scots, and Lady Jane Grey.

Appendix A

1. Oppenheim, *Administration of the Royal Navy*, pp 48–58.
2. J.A. Williamson, *The Voyages of the Cabots and the English Discovery of North America under Henry VII and Henry VII*, ed N.M. Penzer (The Argonaut Press, 1929), p 91.

Appendix C

1. The *arroba* was about 25lbs; 'quarter-hundredweight' (28lbs) is probably the nearest pre-metric English dry-weight equivalent.

SELECT BIBLIOGRAPHY

Primary and early sources

André, Bernard, *Vita Henrici Septemi: Memorials of King Henry VII*, ed J. Gardner (London, 1858)

Bacon, Francis, *History of the Reign of King Henry the Seventh*, ed J. Weinberger (Cornell University Press, 1996)

Beauchamp Pageant, ed Dillon and St John Hope (London: British Museum, 1914)

Bernáldez, Andrés, *Memorias del reinado de los Reyes Católicos*, ed M. Gómez-Moreno and J. de Mata Carrizo (Madrid, 1962)

Black, W.H. (ed), *Illustrations of Ancient State and Chivalry* (London, 1840)

Blomfield, Francis (and Parkin), *History of Norfolk* (Linn, 1769)

Boucher James, Rev. E., *Letters Archaeological and Historical Relating to the Isle of Wight* (London: Frowde, 1896)

British Library Harleian Manuscript 433, ed R. Horrox and P. Hammond (Stroud: Sutton, 1980)

Buhler, C.F. (ed), *The Dictes and Sayings of the Philosophers* (Oxford: Early English Text Society, 1941)

Calendar of Entries in the Papal Registers 1471–1484 (London: HMSO, 1955)

Calendar of Patent Rolls (London: HMSO, 1900–14)

Calendar of State Papers and Manuscripts Existing in the Archives and Collections of Milan, I, 1385–1618, ed A.B. Hinds (London: HMSO, 1913)

Calendar of State Papers and Manuscripts Relating to English Affairs in the Archives and Collections of Venice and Other Libraries of Nothern Italy, vol. 1, ed Rawdon Brown (London, 1864).

Campbell, W. (ed), *Materials for a History of the Reign of Henry VII*, 2 vols. (Rolls Series, 1873–77)

Caxton, William, *The Prologues and Epilogues of William Caxton*, ed W. Crotch (Oxford: Early English Text Society, 1928)

Chaucer, Geoffrey, *The Canterbury Tales*, trans Peter Ackroyd (London: Penguin, 2009)

Commines, Philippe de, *Memoirs, 1461–1483*, ed and trans P.M. Kendall (London, 1855; Folio Society, 1973)

Correspondence de Charles VIII et de ses consellors avec Louis de la Trémoille (Paris, 1875)

Coventry Leet Book, ed M.D. Harris (London, 1907)

The Crowland Chronicle, Ingulph's Chronicle of the Abbey of Croyland with the Continuation by Peter of Blois and Anonymous Writers, trans H. Riley (London, 1908)

Crowland Chronicle Continuations 1459–1485, ed N. Pronay and J. Cox (London, 1986)

Davies, J.S. (ed), *An English Chronicle of the Reigns of Richard II, Henry IV, Henry V and Henry VI* (London: Camden Society, 1856)

Edward IV's French Expedition of 1475, ed F.P. Barnard (College of Arms; Oxford: Clarendon Press, 1925)

Ellis, H. (ed), *Original Letters Illustrative of English History* (London, 1825)

Essenwein, A. (ed), *Mittelalterliches Hausbuch. Bilderhandschrift des 15 Jahrhunderts* (Frankfurt, 1887)

Excerpta Historica, ed Samuel Bentley (London, 1831)

Fabyan, R., *New Chronicle of England and France*, ed H. Ellis (London, 1811)

Froissart, Sir John, *Chronicles of England, France and Spain* (London: Routledge, 1874)

Grafton's Chronicle, vol. ii (London, 1809)

The Great Chronicle of London, ed A.H. Thomas and I.D. Thornley (1938)

Hakluyt, Richard, *The Principal Voyages, Traffiques & Discoveries of the English Nation*, vol. vii (Glasgow University Press, 1894)

Hall, Edward, *Hall's Chronicle*, ed H. Ellis (London, 1809)

Hodgkin, Adrian, *The Archer's Craft* (London: Faber and Faber, 1951)

Holinshed's Chronicles of England, Scotland & Ireland, vol. iii (London, 1808)

Horrox, R. (ed), *Financial Memoranda of the Reign of Edward V* (London: Camden Society, 1987)

Hughes, P.L. and J.F. Larkin, *Tudor Royal Proclamations* (Yale, 1964)

Leyland, J., *Collectanea* (London, 1787) ('The Herald's Report', vol. iv)

Mancini, D., *The Usurpation of Richard III*, ed and trans C.A.J. Armstrong (Oxford, 1936)

Marche, Olivier de la, *Mémoires*, ed H. Beaune and J. d'Arbaumont, 4 vols. (Paris: Société de l'Histoire de France, 1883–88)

Martorell, Joanot and M.J. de Galba, *Tirant Lo Blanc*, trans D.H. Rosenthal (London: Macmillan, 1984)

Martyr, Peter, *De Orbe Novo*, trans Francis MacNutt, 2 vols. (New York: Putnam, 1912)

Medieval Pageant: Writhe's Garter Book: The Ceremony of Bath and the Earldom of Salisbury Roll (Roxburghe, 1993)

Mémoires de la Société d'Historique de Bretagne, vol. ix ('Le Régne de Richard III') (Paris, 1929)

Molinet, Jean de, *Chroniques*, ed J.-A. Bouchon (Paris, 1827)

More, Thomas, *History of King Richard III*, ed R. Sylvester (London, 1963)

Nichols, J.G. (ed), *Grants, etc. from the Crown During the Reign of Edward the Fifth* (London: Camden Society, 1854)

Orpen, G.H., 'Statute Rolls of the Parliament of Ireland, 1–2 Edward IV', *English Historical Review* 30 (1915)

Palencia, Alonso de, *Cronica de Enrique IV* (Madrid, 1975)

Paris, Matthew, *Chronica Majora*, ed H.R. Luard (Rolls Series, 1872–74)

Paston Letters 1422–1509, ed J. Gardner (London: Constable, 1895).

Rotuli Parliamentorum, ed John Strachey et al, 6 vols. (London, 1767–77)

Rous, John, *Historia Regum Angliae* (Oxford, 1745)

Talhoffer, H., *Fechtbuch aus dem Jahre 1467*, ed Gustav Hergsell (Prague, 1887)

Troyes, Jean de, *The Scandalous Chronicle* (London, 1856)

Vergil, Polydore, *Three Books of Polydore Vergil's English History*, ed H. Ellis (London: Camden Society, 1844)

___, *Anglica Historia of Polydore Vergil*, AD *1485–1537*, ed and trans D. Hay (London: Camden Society, 1950)

Warkworth, J., *Chronicle of the First 13 Years of the Reign of King Edward IV*, ed J.O. Halliwell (London: Camden Society, 1839)

Waurin, Jean de, *Anciennes Chroniques d'Engleterre*, vols. ii and iii, ed Mlle Dupont (Paris, 1858–63)

Secondary sources

Ackroyd, Peter, *The Life of Thomas More* (London: Chatto & Windus, 1998)

Ady, C., *History of Milan under the Sforza* (Methuen, 1907)

Allan, Alison, 'Royal Propaganda of Edward IV', *BIHR*, vol. lxix (1986)

Baldwin, D, *Elizabeth Woodville* (Stroud: Sutton, 2002)

Barber, Richard, *The Knight and Chivalry* (Boydell Press, 1995)

Beauchesne, Marquis de, *L'expédition d'Edouard Wydeville en Bretagne* (Vannes, 1911)

Bennett, M., *The Battle of Bosworth* (Stroud: Sutton, 1985)

___, *Lambert Simnel and the Battle of Stoke* (Stroud: Sutton, 1987)

Blair, C., *European Armour* (Batsford, 1958)

Boardman, A., *The Battle of Towton* (Stroud: Sutton, 1994)

Bridges, J.S.C., *History of France*, vol. 1 (Oxford, 1921)

Bruce, J. (ed), *Historie of the Arrival of Edward IV* (London: Camden Society, 1838)

Calmette, J., *The Golden Age of Burgundy* (London: Weidenfeld & Nicolson, 1962)

Caudall, J., *Wood Engraving* (London, 1895)

Chrimes, S.B., *Henry VII* (London: Eyre Methuen, 1972)

Cook, G., *Medieval Chantries and Chantry Chapels* (London, 1963)

Cust, Mrs H., *Gentlemen Errant, Being the Journeys and Adventures of Four Noblemen during the Fifteenth and Sixteenth Centuries* (London: John Murray, 1909)

Davies, J., 'The Decline of the Longbow in Elizabethan England', *Journal of the Society for Army Historical Research*, vol. 80, no. 32

Davies, J.S., *History of Southampton* (London: Gilbert, 1883)

Dennistoun, J., *Memoirs of the Dukes of Urbino 1440–1630*, ed E. Hutton (London: Lane, 1910)

Dockray, K., *Edward IV: A Source Book* (Stroud: Sutton, 1999)

Duclos, Jacques, *Chroniques et Mémoires*, ed Buchon (Paris, 1865)

Falkus, C. (ed), *The Private Lives of the Tudor Monarchs* (London: Folio Society, 1974)

Fellows, E.H., *The Knights of the Garter 1348–1939* (SPCK, 1939)

Fletcher, Richard, *Moorish Spain* (London: Weidenfeld & Nicolson, 1992)

Foss, P., *The Field of Redemore: The Battle of Bosworth, 1485* (Kairos Press, 1998)

Gardener, J. (ed), *Letters and Papers Illustrative of the Reigns of Richard III and Henry VII*, 2 vols. (Rolls Series, 1861–63)

____, *Richard III* (London: Longman, 1878)

Gardiner, Robert, *Cogs, Caravels and Galleons: The Sailing Ship 1000–1650* (Conway Maritime Press, 1994)

Gill, L., *Richard III and Buckingham's Rebellion* (Stroud: Sutton, 1999)

Gillingham, J., (ed), *Richard III: A Medieval Kingship* (Collins and Brown, 1994)

Goodman, A.G., *The Wars of the Roses: The Soldiers' Experience* (Tempus, 2005)

Gosse, P., *The History of Piracy* (London: Longman, 1932)

Griffin, N. (ed, trans), *Las Casas, Columbus*, vol. vii (UCLA, 1999)

Grummitt, D. (ed), *The English Experience in France 1450–1558* (Ashgate, 2002)

Haigh, P.A., *The Military Campaigns of the Wars of the Roses* (Stroud: Sutton, 1995)

Hallam, E., *Chronicles of the Wars of the Roses* (Bramley, 1996)

Hammond, P.W. and A.F. Sutton, *Richard III: The Road to Bosworth Field* (London: Constable, 1985)

Hardyment, Christina, *Malory: The Life and Times of King Arthur's Chronicler* (Collins, 2005)

Hicks, M.A., 'The Changing Role of the Wydevilles in Yorkist Politics to 1483', in C. Ross (ed), *Patronage, Pedigree and Power in Later Medieval England* (Stroud: Sutton, 1979)

____, *Richard III: The Man Behind the Myth* (Collins and Brown, 1991)

____, *Anne Neville: Queen to Richard III* (Tempus, 2007)

Hodnett, E., *English Woodcuts 1480–1535* (Oxford: Oxford University Press, 1935)

Horrox, R., *Richard III: A Study of Service* (Cambridge, 1989)

Hume, David, *History of England*, vol. i (New York: Virtue, 1859)

Hutton, William, *The Battle of Bosworth Field* (Stroud: Sutton, 1999)

Irving, Washington, *Chronicle of the Conquest of Granada* (London, 1902)

Ives E.W., 'Andrew Dymmock and the Papers of Anthony, Earl Rivers 1482–83', *BIHR*, 41 (1968), pp 216–29

Jacob, E., *The Fifteenth Century 1399–1485*, Oxford History of England (Oxford: Oxford University Press, 1961)

James, M.R. (ed), *John Blackman's Memoire of Henry VI* (Cambridge: Cambridge University Press, 1919)

Jones, M.K., *Bosworth 1485* (Tempus, 2002)

Keegan, J., *The Face of Battle* (Cape, 1976)

Keen, M., *Chivalry* (Yale, 1984)

Kendall, P.M., *Richard III* (Allen and Unwin, 1955)

___, *Warwick the Kingmaker* (Allen and Unwin, 1957)

___, *The Yorkist Age* (Allen and Unwin, 1962)

Kingsford, C.L., *English Historical Literature in the Fifteenth Century* (Oxford, 1913)

Kirk, J.F., *History of Charles the Bold* (London: John Murray, 1863)

Lamb, V.B., *The Betrayal of Richard III* (Coram, 1959)

Lander, J.R., *The Wars of the Roses* (Secker and Warburg, 1965)

___, *Crown and Nobility, 1450–1509* (London, 1976)

Lowe, D.E., 'Patronage and Politics: Edward IV, the Wydevills and the Council of the Prince of Wales 1471–83', *Board of Celtic Studies*, 29 (1981), pp 568–91

Macdonald, P., *Cabot and the Naming of Amercia* (Bristol, 1997)

Macdougall, N., *James III: A Political Study* (Edinburgh: MacDonald, 1982)

Macgibbon, D., *Elizabeth Woodville* (London, 1938)

Mackie, J.D., *The Early Tudors 1485–1558*, Oxford History of England (Oxford: Oxford University Press, 1952)

Merriman, R.B., *Edward Woodville, Knight-Errant* (American Antiquarian Society, 1903)

Metcalf, W.C., *A Book of Knights* (London, 1885)

Mitchell, R.J., *John Tiptoff* (London, 1938)

Okerlund, A., *Elizabeth Woodville* (Tempus, 2005)

Oman, C., *History of the Art of War in the Middle Ages* (London: Methuen, 1924)

___, *The Art of War in the Sixteenth Century* (London: Methuen, 1927)

Oppenheim, M., *A History of the Administration of the Royal Navy and of Merchant Shipping in Relation to the Navy*, vol. 1 (London: Bodley, 1896)

Painter, G.D., *William Caxton* (Chatto & Windus, 1976)

Pastor, Xavier, *The Ships of Christopher Columbus* (Conway, 1992)

Perry, M., *Sisters to the King* (London: Deutsch, 1998)

Pettoello, Decio (ed), *Italian Short Stories of the 14th and 15th Century* (London: Dent, 1932)

Pocquet du Haut Jussé, B.A., *François II, Duc de Bretagne, et l'Angleterre* (Rennes, 1928)

Pollard, A.J., *Richard III and the Princes in the Tower* (Stroud: Sutton, 1991)

Potter, D., *A History of France, 1460–1560* (London: Macmillan, 1995)

Prescott, W.H., *The History of the Reign of Ferdinand and Isabella the Catholic* (London: Gibbings & Co., 1894)

___, *The Art of War in Spain: The Conquest of Granada 1481–1492*, ed A.D. McJoynt (Greenhill, 1995)

Rapin de Thoyras, A., *History of England* (Paris, 1759)

Redlich, Fritz, *The German Military Enterpriser and His Work Force*, vol. i (Wiesbaden, 1964).

Ross, C.D., *Edward IV* (Yale, 1974)

___, *Richard III* (Yale, 1976)

Sanceau, Elaine, *The Perfect Prince: A Biography of King Dom João II* (Porto, 1959)

Scofield, C.L., *The Life and Reign of Edward IV* (London: Longman, 1923)

Seward, D., *The Wars of the Roses* (Constable, 1993)

Seymour, W., *Battles in Britain*, vol. 1 (Sidgwick and Jackson, 1975)

Skelton, Marston and Painter, *The Vinland Map and the Tartar Relation* (Yale University Press, 1995)

Smith, G. (ed), *The Coronation of Elizabeth Wydeville: Queen Consort of Edward IV on 26th May, 1465* (London, 1935)

Smith, R. and K. De Vries, *The Artillery of the Dukes of Burgundy, 1363–1477* (Boydell, 2005)

Spufford, P., *Handbook of Medieval Exchange* (Royal History Society, 1986)

St Aubyn, Giles, *The Year of Three Kings* (Collins, 1983)

Strickland, Miss, *Lives of the Queens of England*, vol. ii (London: Colburn, 1841)

Strickland, M. and R. Hardy, *The Great Warbow* (Stroud: Sutton, 2005)

Swanson, R.N., *Religous Devotion in Europe 1215–1515* (Cambridge, 1997)

Tabri, E.A., *Political Culture in the Early Northern Renaissance* (Edwin Mellen, 2004)

Talhoffer, H., *A Fifteenth-Century Manual of Sword-Fighting and Close-Quarter Combat*, trans M. Rector (Greenhill, 2004)

Taylor, E.G.R., *Tudor Geography 1485–1583* (Methuen, 1930)

Thomas, H., *Rivers of Gold* (Weidenfeld & Nicolson, 2003)

Thomson, J.A.F., 'Bishop Lionel Wydeville and Richard III', *BIHR*, vol. lxix (1986)

Touchman, B.W., *A Distant Mirror: The Calamitous 14th Century* (Macmillan, 1978)

Vaughan, R., *Charles the Bold* (Longman, 1973)

Warner, P., *British Battlefields: The North* (Oxford: Osprey, 1972)

Williams, Gwyn, *Madoc: The Making of a Myth* (Methuen, 1979)

Williamson, J.A., *The Voyages of the Cabots and the English Discovery of North America under Henry VII and Henry VIII*, ed N.M. Penzer (The Argonaut Press, 1929)

____ and R.A. Skelton, *The Cabot Voyages and Bristol Discovery under Henry VII* (Hakluyt Society, 1962)

Wroe, Ann, *Perkin* (Cape, 2003)

INDEX